ESCAPING THE
DELUSIONS OF CULTURE

ESCAPING THE DELUSIONS OF CULTURE

A Cultural, Familial, and African American Reality

STERLING T. ANDERSON

ESCAPING THE DELUSIONS OF CULTURE
A CULTURAL, FAMILIAL, AND
AFRICAN AMERICAN REALITY

iUniverse books may be ordered through booksellers or by contacting:

iUniverse
1663 Liberty Drive
Bloomington, IN 47403
www.iuniverse.com
844-349-9409

Because of the dynamic nature of the Internet, any web addresses or
links contained in this book may have changed since publication and
may no longer be valid. The views expressed in this work are solely those
of the author and do not necessarily reflect the views of the publisher,
and the publisher hereby disclaims any responsibility for them.

Any people depicted in stock imagery provided by Getty Images are
models, and such images are being used for illustrative purposes only.
Certain stock imagery © Getty Images.

ISBN: 978-1-5320-8616-8 (sc)
ISBN: 978-1-5320-8615-1 (e)

Library of Congress Control Number: 2019916704

Print information available on the last page.

iUniverse rev. date: 07/28/2023

Contents

Preface xvii

Acknowledgments xix

Chapter 1   Race Relations – A Predatory System 1

Political and Social Bondage.................................. 1

Religious Bondage.. 5

Chapter 2   Hidden from View 7

Traces 7

Swallowed Up.. 8

Manifest Destiny 9

Hidden from View 10

Questioning and Exposing 11

Food and Water Contamination.......................... 15

Chapter 3   My Family History 18

Evelina, Evelyn and Great Grandfather
Reed the Inventor... 19

Engine and Patent... 20

Crowder, Anderson and more............................. 24

Evelina Ramsey Crowder
(Great Grand Mother).. 25

After the Fire 26

Visiting Granddad Ramsey.................................. 26
Marriages and Family...................................... 28
Grandfather Ernest Anderson and
Wife Evelyn... 29
Evelyn and Ernest Anderson............................. 30

Chapter 4   Great Grandfather James Anderson...... 32
    Ernest and Evelyn 32
    Granddad Anderson Passes.............................. 34

Chapter 5   The Struggle for Equality 36
    Forward /Backward 36
    Four Hundred Years 38
    Justice and the Illegal Underground Budget 39

Chapter 6   African Americans Who We Are –
             A Secret, Not a Mystery 42
    So-called Africans Americans – Who Are We? 42
    Count Constantine de Volney.......................... 43
    Return of Black Land 45
    The Original Man 47
    Columbus and Indigenous Genocide.................. 48
    Discoveries of the Past – African Influence
    in the Americas 51
    Slavery in the Western Hemisphere &
    Black Origins... 56
    The Y Chromosome 58
    Black Indigenous North Americans................... 61

Native Americans and Slavery of African
Americans... 63
Seminoles and Black Seminoles......................... 67
1866 Treaties 68
Massacres of Indigenous Peoples........................ 71

Chapter 7   The Big Lie from Black to White........ 75

Europeans Claim to Israel................................. 77
Who are the Indigenous Hebrews?..................... 78
From the Beginning.. 79
The Black Connection – Dispelling the
Delusion of Biblical White Supremacy............... 81
The Curse 85
The North African Amazigh / "Berber" 87
The Ancient Story of the So-Called
African American... 89
Egyptians, Grand Canyon and American
Mounds 90

Chapter 8   Systems of Suppression 94

Unions, Politicians, and Prevailing Wage 94
Recent Advancements....................................... 96
Substance Abuse.. 98
The Religious Scheme......................................100
Repression through Highway Construction
and City Destruction;......................................103
Rampage against Black Cities:..........................107
Now You Have It, Now You Don't
(the Subprime Scandal) 110

A Common Response 112

The Scourge of Racism 112

The Kenosha Shootings 114

The Unite the Right Rally 115

Chapter 9   Killing the Leaders and
             Destroying Alkebulan Civilizations.....117

Killing the Leaders 117

The Hidden Hand of Colonialism....................126

The Real Africa before European Desolation ...130

Kilwa 133

Vaida..133

Permission to Destroy 136

Chapter 10   Delusions and the Moral Universe 138

Chapter 11   Bacon's Rebellion, Infant
             Mortality, Stoking the fire, Hope........142

Bacon's Rebellion of 1676 142

Infant Mortality 145

Stoking the Fire 146

Hope 148

Chapter 12   The Political Billionaire's System........149

Corrupt Politicians and Greedy Business
Owners..149

Austerity for the Poor Prosperity for
the Rich 151

Environmental Cuts Increase Corporate
Profits 152
Taxes 154
Protecting their Masters and the
Indiscriminate Killing of Palestinians 155

Chapter 13   Freedom and Beyond.........................158
Boundaries and the Freedom to Explore 158
Grandma Evelyn Anderson...............................160
Grandma – Beyond the Norms.........................161
The Tearoom 162

Chapter 14   Free Will? Albert Einstein, Unjust
             Laws and the UFOs/UAF
             Phenomenon.....................................164
Free Will?...164
Albert Einstein...166
Science's Influence in Countering Unjust
Laws and Tradition 167
UFOs /UAF (Unidentified Aerial
Phenomenon) 169

Chapter 15   Berta Caceres, the Generals and
             Modern Day Manifest Destiny...........173
Berta..173
The Generals 175
Modern Day Manifest Destiny 180

Chapter 16   The Call – Breaking through –
             The Eyes 181

    The Call 181
    Breaking Through 183
    The Eyes...184

Chapter 17   Holy Trinity D&B Corp, Music,
             Introvert or Extrovert?, The
             Family & Religion, Commitment......186

    Holy Trinity Drum and Bugle Corp.................186
    Holy Trinity Cadets
    (Father Carr is in front in Black) 192
    Music 192
    Introvert or Extrovert?......................................197
    Family & Religion...200
    Commitment..202

Chapter 18   Civilized Humans? 205

    The Universality of Love and Compassion 207
    The Cambridge Declaration on
    Consciousness..209
    The Love Transfer 211
    Acceptance 211

Chapter 19   Ma's Parents and Her Caretakers........214

    The Grandisons 216
    Grandfather Thomas Johnson 218
    The Depression..219

Chapter 20   Ongoing Injustice..............................221

   Ongoing Injustice 221
   Lawsuits against Police 225
   Police Brutality Bonds.....................................227
   Violence against Native Americans 228

Chapter 21   *Ma* 230

   Ma's Beauty 230
   Jordan Marsh 234

Chapter 22   Dad and the Early Years 238

   The Knight...238
   The Shoe Lasting Machine...............................240
   The Navy 241
   Haymarket Square..242

Chapter 23   Family Matters – Religion's Love
               Claim – Quick Fix and Phony
               Healers 245

   Family Matters...245
   Religion's Love Claim.......................................246
   Quick Fix and Phony Healers 247

Chapter 24   Stealing Souls 250

   Stealing Souls...250
   The Deeper Level 252
   The Critical Question..255

Chapter 25   Reprogramming/Awakening 257

Reprogramming 257
The Meditation Process 258
Overcoming Resistance 261
Patience 264
The Clearing 265
Meditation's Impact on Crime 266
What Meditation is and is Not..........267
The Control Factor...........................268

Chapter 26   Science and its Warnings 269

Science's Giants..............................269
The Scientific Method 270
Co-opted.......................................272
Analysis of Global Warming Deniers.................272
Environmental Warnings 273
Carl Sagan 1995.............................274

Chapter 27   Delusion vs. Reality........................275

Delusion vs. Reality 275
Mind Control Bernays's Style 277
Strategies of Bernays 279
Resist the Sales Pitch 280
Decision Time 282

Chapter 28   Profit vs. Spirit...............................284

Profit vs. Spirit...............................284
At the People's Expense 285

Chapter 29   Alternative Reality 286

    Religion or Spirituality 286
    Sinful by Nature? 290
    Non-Violent Cultures................................292
    Chewong Society.....................................292
    Ifaluk Society...293
    Hutterites Society 294
    Nubians Society......................................294

Chapter 30   "The Good Old Days" 297

    Tied Up..297
    Excitement and Fear 297
    Suffolk Street 298
    Clams 298
    Baseball Cards..299
    Swimming 300
    Transition 301
    Off Limits 302
    Blue Laws 303

Chapter 31   The Move 305

    From Lynn to Boston................................305
    The Closings...306

Chapter 32   A New Beginning 308

    A New Beginning....................................308
    Dudley Street..310
    Fight or Flight and the First Kiss 311

Chapter 33   The School Experience 314

The School Experience.....................................314
The Teachers...315
Physical Punishment a Roadblock to Growth...320
Teachers (continued) 321
High School 322
Decision despite Uncertainty 325
Post Office to University.................................328
Teaching at South Boston High and
Desegregation 330
The Student...331
Social Work and Desegregation 333

Chapter 34   Dad Was Always Growing 335

Dad was Always Growing...............................335
A Special Energy...340
Availability 341
At His Bedside 342

Chapter 35   Forward in the Face of Roadblocks....343

Complainers and Haters..................................343
HBUCs 345
Daniel Payne...347

Chapter 36   Encouragement – Spiritual Quest.......348

Encouragement..348
Spiritual Quest..351

Chapter 37   The Meeting, Life Together,
             and Musicians......................................356

    The Meeting..356
    Life Together...360
    Musicians...366

Conclusion 373
Endnotes 375

Preface

From an early age I started my journey seeking answers. At the time I was unaware this was what I was doing. I also didn't know what I was trying to find. This unknown drive pushed me to explore outside the boundaries of what society had presented me. I was an explorer then, and I still am today. I was determined not to accept the status quo without question. Religious, political, and historical orthodoxy were on the chopping block.

My first exploration outside the boundaries of accepted tradition was my acceptance in 1959 of the fiercely controversial teachings of the Honorable Elijah Muhammad, the leader of the Nation of Islam. I was twelve years old at the time. Muhammad's teaching rejected the history of Black people as portrayed in public school history books and by academics of that time. They depicted Blacks as unintelligent and inferior to Whites. Muhammad taught a message that honored Black people. For me, it was irresistible.

In my late teens I began to practice and study the physical and meditative science of Yoga, an East Indian tradition.

At thirty years of age I married a wonderful woman. A year or two after our marriage, I converted to Christianity, which was the faith my wife embraced.

In addition to conversion, I became passionate about politics from a Conservative Christian perspective. We raised our five children in the Christian faith. Yoga the teachings from the Nation and Christianity all have been influencing factor in my life.

Today, I no longer practice religion in a traditional sense; instead, I acknowledge the divine through meditation and gratitude.

When I started this book, my aim was to chronicle my family's history. I quickly realized my family's story was a microcosm of the African American experience that is inextricably linked to America's history. Today, more than 150 years after Blacks were given the right to vote in 1870, civil rights issues like equality and the struggle against voter suppression continue. Even after the Civil Rights Act of 1964 was established, egregious injustices like the relentless murders and abuse of unarmed Black men, and other people of color, by law enforcement and vigilantes continued. The issues that affect Black communities do not stay in Black communities. Eventually the contagions in Black communities will spread into communities throughout America. This is a reality ignored by policies makers and others until they are forced to face it.

The various topics in this book will no doubt challenge the reader, but my main goal is to inform the reader, and hopefully inspire an appetite to question and examine personal assumptions, ideas and beliefs that may have been accepted without question; beliefs that for many may have been passed down through generations.

Acknowledgments

First and foremost, I want to thank the Creator/Spirit who has continuously given me inspiration, desire, and energy over the years to complete the work. This strength was undoubtedly a source far beyond my own.

Thank you to my wife, Vernice Anderson for her genealogical research and editing that made it possible for the book to be published. She patiently, and at times impatiently traveled with me until I completed this project. I love you.

Thank you to my daughter, Oshea Popescu for her editing and photograph contributions. Her husband, Sebastian's computer expertise played a crucial part in the completion of this work.

Thank you to my sisters, Evelyn Browne and Paulette Anderson, who were major sources of knowledge relating to our immediate family history.

Thank you to my Aunt Arlene, one of six of my father's (Sterling E. Anderson's) sisters, who provided much of the family history regarding my Grandmother, Evelyn Anderson. Aunt Arlene, also provided information about Evelina Crowder, my great-grandmother. Pamala Mimms-Cox, thank you for contributing family pictures.

Thanks to my cousin Deborah Cooke for providing information about Arthur W. Reed, my great-grandfather.

Thank you to my cousin Jacqueline Arkord, who contributed information regarding great-grandfather, Albert Prince Ramsey.

Further thanks to Cyril Chapman for providing the names of musicians with whom we performed with over the years.

Personal thanks to others who encouraged me as I worked to complete the book, including my sons Uriel and Sterling Anderson Jr., my brother in law Henry Browne, daughter Bethany Jackson and her husband A.J., my friend Elijah Haywood and Anthony Bryant and countless others. Thank you for your encouragement.

Chapter One

Race Relations -
A Predatory System

Political and Social Bondage

In America, race has always been an uncomfortable subject. America has never fully come to grips with the racial quandary it has created for itself. Consider the ceaseless tension that seems to exist and in some cases downright hostility between the races. Also consider the unresolved financial disparity between White and Black. "In 2011 the median White household had $111,146 in wealth compared to $7,113 for the median Black household and $8,348 for Latino's; U.S. Census Bureau Survey of Income and Program Participation."[1] White households wealth are approximately 16 times higher than that of Blacks. I believe these disparities reflect systematic discrimination/racism at all societal levels. Politicians and other power brokers have maintained a permanent underclass, with color and or class to this day being the dividing line.

In 1965, the Supreme Court passed the Voting Rights Act; designed to prevent racial discrimination in voting. It focused on fifteen states where racial prejudice stood as an obstacle preventing Blacks from voting. In June 2013, the Supreme Court repealed Section 4 (a) of the Voting Rights Act. This section established a formula that identified states where voting rights were suppressed and provided remedies to address the problems. With the repeal of section 4 (a), many politicians returned to policies geared to suppressing the Black vote. North Carolina, where I live, is one of those states where voting rights were suppressed. In 2019, the Supreme Court of North Carolina ruled politicians were systematically gerrymandering electoral districts. This is nothing new in electoral politics. Parties continue to carve up districts in order to win elections. The extreme nature of North Carolina's gerrymandering caused the court to demand the districts be redrawn to reflect political fairness. In 2021, in response to President Trump's defeat, an intense effort has been made by many states to reduce voting accessibility in districts of color.

In the documentary *13th*, 2016, filmmaker, Ava DuVernay brings to light that long before the repeal of the Voting Rights Act there were other methods used to suppress Black empowerment. The Thirteenth Amendment eliminated slavery but left open the door for continued bondage of Black Americans. It states: "Neither slavery nor involuntary servitude except as a punishment for crime…shall exist within the United States." This gave legal justification for the continued enslavement of African Americans. It however did so in a less conspicuous framework—prison.

The Black Codes, laws passed by Southern states after the Civil War in 1865 and 1866, restricted African American freedoms and compelled Black people to work in a labor economy with low wages. The Black Codes were also part of a larger pattern of southern Whites trying to suppress the new freedom of emancipated African American slaves. "Over the period 1689 to 1865, Virginia enacted more than 130 slave statutes; among which were seven major slave codes, some containing more than fifty provisions."[2] One such statute, "required Black people to sign yearly labor contracts; if they refused, they risked being arrested, fined and forced into unpaid labor."[3]

In the Antebellum South (pre–Civil War) Southern Black Codes contained more regulations for free Blacks than for slaves. Chattel slaves lived under the complete control of their owners."[4] "Free Blacks presented a challenge to the boundaries of White-dominated society."[5] These codes created the legal structure that allowed abuse, physical violence, and a system of bondage to continue.

Penal servitude (the leasing out of prisoners to private enterprise) either within prison walls or in outside workshops, factories, and fields was established in the North almost fifty years before the instituting of the Black Codes and the passage of the Thirteenth Amendment. This was originally known as the "Yankee Invention." First used at Auburn Prison in New York

State in the 1820s. The system spread widely and quickly throughout the North, the Midwest, and later the West. It was developed to serve the same function that slavery had served in the South. Blacks earned wages from $0.93 to $4.73 per day.[6] An example of modern day entrenched racist imprisonment of Blacks can be seen in Vermont. According to 2021 data, there is a 94.16% White population which totals to 587,883 people and a 1.36% Black population of 8,502.[7] Of the 8,502 Black people, 1737 are imprisoned or incarcerated, totaling 20% of the Black population. This, in comparison to only 238 Whites incarcerated or imprisoned, which is only .0004% of 587,883. In general, Blacks are incarcerated nearly 5 times the rate of Whites. In other states like Vermont, the disparity is greater.[8] Prisons have become the modern day free labor replacement for the historical slave plantations.

The Thirteenth Amendment continues to affect African Americans living in the twenty-first century. Like the example above, such disparities illustrate how politicians use the political and criminal justice system to continue to deprive African Americans of their human rights. In this particular case, they are incarcerating people of color at an increased rate in order to maintain the system of corporate slave labor as illustrated by Michelle Alexander in her 2019 book, *The New Jim Crow: Mass Incarceration in the Age of Colorblindness.*

Religious Bondage

The correlation between racial disparities and politics is hard to refute. How religion plays into the mix may not be as obvious. Religion and religious ideology has undergirded the system of politics throughout history. It has been used to justify actions of some leaders. Some have used America's cultural religion of Christianity, as a rallying cry to abolish the caste system of slavery and racism. Many others in the religious community have used it to do just the opposite. For centuries, the Bible has been used by malicious opponents of freedom to justify the vicious treatment of Black Americans, such as: Ephesians 6:5 "Servants, be obedient to them that are your masters according to the flesh, with fear and trembling." or Genesis 9:25-27: "Cursed be Canaan (the son of Ham) a servants shall he be unto his brethren..." (His brethren were not White. We will explore this later in the book) Ham has long been perceived to be Black a belief drawn from the Old Testament which both Christian, and Jews honor. The Old Testament Hebrew Lexicon defines the meaning of Ham to be, "hot or "sunburnt." Because of the perception of Ham being Black, Noah's other sons Shem and Japheth would have also been Black. Gen. 9: 25-27 has long been used by the religious as a rational for the slavery and degradation of people of color.

Simon of Cyrene is another symbol of Black subservience. Simon, is depicted as the Black man carrying the cross of the "white" Jesus, Matthew

27:32 and Luke 23:26. The depiction of Old and New Testament characters as Caucasian, including the heavenly host of angels, has dominated our cultures and is a way of maintaining the myth of white supremacy.

Religion has long been a cover used to dominate marginalized groups. Today, those who do not fall into the standard sexual orientation are oppressed by those who use religion as their basis for mistreatment and violence. Religion has also been a tool to subjugate women so that males can maintain their predatory system of dominance, power, and control. It is my hope that a death blow has been delivered to this system of domination as a result of the ongoing exposure of men in positions of power who have been caught engaging in sexual violence.

A February 8, 2018, New York Times article, *"After Weinstein: 71 Men Accused of Sexual Misconduct and Their Fall from Power"* is a clear indication that "times are a changing." No more will those in position of power so easily hide their acts of sexual misbehavior. Clearly, a major shift has transpired. On February 24, 2020 Harvey Weinstein was found guilty of rape and sentenced to 23 years in prison.[9] A clear message of repudiation has been sent when an influential film producer is held accountable for his actions.

Chapter Two

Hidden from View

Traces

I never knew my grandparents on my mother's side or my grandfather on my father's side; they died before I was born. My father's mother, Evelyn Anderson was the only grandparent I knew.

Some believe that the spiritual presences of our loved ones remain with us though we are unaware. Others believe the soul is destined for heaven or hell. Some hold that reincarnation is the vehicle through which people continue to evolve. There are those who believe that death is the end of any form of existence. One thing is sure: those who go before us leave traces of themselves in their offspring. You may look like, sound like, and display mannerisms akin to your parents. You may even pick up traits and likenesses of a close or distant relative. There are definitely remnants of my father's father in his offspring. Relatives have spoken of my father's father my grandfather Ernest's mild mannerisms and temperance. Five of his nine children displayed his characteristics while the other four displayed their mother's, my grandmother Evelyn's (Nana) tendencies. The latter were more outgoing and verbally assertive. Some believe that this is our hereafter, a reflection of ourselves in others.

Swallowed Up

There are many views regarding our mortality. Some have rigid belief structures and believe that they alone have the answers to life and death. Dominant cultures historically have imposed their will and views of reality on others. Usually these views are inflicted through intimidation and violence until they seem like a natural and normal part of the victim's cultural landscape. This has been the case for the indigenous peoples of the Americas and for African Americans cut off from cultural connections. It could be a death sentence for African Americans to display anything other than what was given to them by the slave master.

This ancestral cultural disconnect among African Americans has left us feeling like we have no home or culture to call our own, and no religion other than the one forced on us while in slavery.

For African descendants in America and indigenous cultures of America, physical reality had a spiritual connection. Land was sacred. For most today, this perception has been lost. The worldview of connectedness is in complete contrast to the materialistic worldview held by those in positions of power today.

They value land only as a means of financial profit and see those living on it as things to be dominated, destroyed or managed for gain. This worldview has infected the entire planet.

Indigenous cultures have known for millennia that there is more to reality than just the physical. There exists a connection between the physical and the spiritual. The struggle of indigenous cultures is not only to hold on to their land but also to maintain the spiritual connection with their land. Awareness of this connection has for the most part been lost in the modern age – but there *is* hope. Climate change has forced modern culture to examine behaviors that are destroying the planet. It is unfortunate that this knowledge is coming at such a high cost.

The swallowing up of true spirituality that holds all life as sacred and replacing it with a religious imitation of spirituality is sending the world into a death spiral. But true spirituality, which once seemed lost, is slowly being revived. Resistance against the destruction of the environment and the gradual understanding that all things are connected is a positive sign.

Manifest Destiny

Manifest Destiny, the religious idea that all land was ordained for European Christian domination, was the rationalization used to energize and accelerate the expansion and conquest of North and South

America as well as other nations of color. Unrestrained materialism with religious undertones was and still is a potent combination rationalizing land theft. Today the semblance of the religious mandate of Manifest Destiny is now exemplified in the term full-spectrum dominance; a military term referring to the total dominance of the battlefield.[1] This domination today extends to the earth's resources. This is the goal of capitalism in the twenty-first century—to gobble up everything in order to maintain itself. The Standing Rock Sioux Tribe, in North Dakota, the Lenca in Honduras, and other indigenous groups throughout the Americas are all desperately fighting for survival. This battle for survival is universal among indigenous people; in their fight against state and corporate interests that want to develop indigenous lands for themselves.

Hidden from View

Societies routinely distort and hide truth from their populations. For the most part, what we *believe* is true, has little to do with truth. Those in power fashion and manipulate truth to suit themselves and to maintain their power.

In America and around the world we are gradually seeing some of these deceptions exposed. Wars and military incursions are routinely initiated in the name of national security, when in reality they are often schemes to acquire resources. The foundations of many modern nations are rooted in this type of deception. The corruption of "Big Business" which knowingly destroys our environment for profit is continually being exposed. Ongoing revelations of sexual misconduct by those in positions of power, allegations that have been kept suppressed for decades, are now in the open for the world to see. The list of criminality is long. In these times, things that have been hidden are being brought into the light.

If it is true that truth will set us free, then we need to open our minds to perceive the truth and then accept it. For most, this acceptance is a gradual process. We begin to have an intuitive sense that some things we've been taught are flawed. Gradually, often after years of resisting obvious contradictions, we may begin to question fundamental beliefs. This is where research begins, after which, one embraces truth or rejects it and remains in darkness.

Questioning and Exposing

The 2008 financial real estate crash and the events that followed prompted many Americans to ask fundamental questions. Why did the federal government give millions to those who through their own manipulation of real estate values caused the economy to crash? Why did the government protect them from the reality of the "free market" which allowed others to fail? Being "too big to fail" is a poor excuse for allowing criminals to go unpunished. This major upheaval in the real estate market forced some to question long-held assumptions. I was one of those who began to question.

After the lies about the Iraq War were exposed (the non-existence of weapons of mass destruction, WMDs) investigative reporters and whistleblowers seemed to display a greater sense of urgency to reveal the truth that is often hidden under the façades of truth, the fronts which government puts up often in the name of national security. In reality, it seems, they are schemes designed to enrich the ruling class, as well as a few societal elites, at the expense of many. Claire McCaskill, Democrat Senator from Missouri, "In the last decade(s) we've seen billions in taxpayers' money spent on services and projects that did little – sometimes nothing – to further our military mission."[2] Wars are hidden under a façade of truth in order to motivate the masses to support and ultimately put their lives on the line to ensure that the corrupt elite stay in power and increase their overall power.

The military service enlistees may get an honorable discharge or a medal of some sort and maybe even some federal benefits, but the rate of suicide and homelessness among veterans is a glaring problem and impossible not to notice. These problems among veterans is a gulf that needs to be closed. Returning veterans never got a share of the $39.5 billion in federal money awarded to Halliburton, a company operated by Dick Cheney just before he became Vice President. Contractors reaped $138 billion from the Iraq war. Those who reaped the most were Halliburton, KRB, once known as Kellogg Brown and Root a subsidiary of Halliburton, Agility Logistics and Kuwait Petroleum.[3ibid] This money was acquired fraudulently, having been allocated under false pretenses (the existence of WMDs). Yet in this great bonanza giveaway of billions of dollars those who put their lives on the line got nothing.

Another facade that attempts to hide truth says, "no one is above the law." "If you work hard and play by the rules you will get ahead." We all should know that these platitudes do not apply to all. If you are rich, powerful or well - connected you may be able to by-pass the laws that others are held accountable to. With wages not keeping pace with the cost of living and people needing to work multiple jobs to barely get by, to say "if you work hard and play by the rules you will get a heard" is no longer true for vast portions of the populations; and what "rules" are we talking about? The rules that give billions of dollars in subsidies and tax breaks to millionaires and the corporate elite who are already making huge profits while at the same time their employees are under paid. The federal government maintains a $7.25 minimum wage which is part of a system that deprives Americans a living wage and only benefit plutocracies (societies ruled and controlled by people with great wealth).

Socialism is fine when the money goes to billionaire friends of politicians under the illusion of a free market system. Whenever the socially conscious ask for funds to assist the general population, the billionaire class and politicians that serve them rise up from their troughs and cry "socialism" as they did when President Lyndon Johnson worked to pass Medicare for seniors in 1965. When Senator Bernie Sanders ran for the 2020 presidential nomination, the cry of socialism was again heard. Sanders's call for Medicare for all, free college tuition and the rolling back of student loans raised the ire of politicians and the rich. It seems, in our societal class structure, "socialism" is okay when it benefits the elites and the ruling class under the pretense of a free market, but of course "socialism" is rejected for the non-elite class. I believe it is clear there are two sets of rules: one for the majority of hard working Americans another for the wealthy and those connected to American politicians.

The truth about our constructed sense of reality, which is created by politicians and others with power and influence, is gradually being revealed for what it really is; a mirage. Layer by layer the truth is being exposed. Since October 2006, WikiLeaks editor-in-chief, Julian Assange has documented revelations of government secrecy and misdeeds; information citizens have a right to know. Assange was escorted from the Ecuadorian embassy in April of 2019 where he had been in asylum for six years evading prosecution from America. The U. S. government was angry that its secrets and dirty laundry were being exposed.[4]

Edward Snowden, a National Security Agency whistleblower disclosed that the NSA was spying on Americans through their phones and emails.[5] In 2016 the NSA collected 151 million records of metadata—the time, date, location, duration, telephone numbers, and email addresses of American's communications, though it had warrants from the secret, Foreign Intelligence Surveillance Court (FISC) to spy on only forty-two terrorist suspects.[6]

In April 2016, the Panama Papers were exposed by a mysterious whistle blower going by the name John Doe. He exposed more than eleven million files from the law firm Mossack Fonseca.[7] A year later the Paradise Papers made their debut. Both revealed millions of documents detailing the deception, money laundering, and other illegal dealings committed by wealthy individuals, companies, and other entities in an attempt to avoid paying their legal share of taxes.[8]

Reporters and Black Lives Matter activists have uncovered corruption in police departments and other facets of the criminal justice systems all over the country. These departments have invested time and money covering up murders of unarmed African Americans. Widespread use of cell phone video recordings are making crimes committed by police much more difficult to hide.

Food and Water Contamination

The adulteration of our food and water is another concern. "The Environmental Protection Agency (EPA) lacks adequate scientific information on the toxicity of many chemicals found in the environment – as well as on tens of thousands of chemicals used commercially in the United States. A Government Accountability Office (GAO) report criticizes the EPA for failing to routinely assess the risks of the roughly 80,000 Industrial chemicals that are already in use in the US."[9] For further information see Rebecca Harrington, *The EPA Only Restricts These 9 Chemicals out of Thousands*, businessinside.com, 2/2016.

Artificial sweeteners may be associated with long-term weight gain, obesity, diabetes, heart and blood pressure problems and other health issues.[10] The commonly used artificial sweetener aspartame is among the fraction of substances that have been examined by the Food and Drug administration (FDA) and was rejected for use in the food supply. It has been surrounded by controversy.[11] Aspartame was approved in 1974. Why did the FDA approve aspartame after rejecting it twice? This is an interesting piece of research. The story reveals how those with power and influence get what they want; in this case Donald Rumsfeld. He got approval of aspartame despite its effect on the American people. For additional information, Google the "Aspartame Story." Given the abundance of artificial substances in our foods and water, readers *beware.*

Most of the issues above have become known through independent investigation. It is our responsibility to question and search for the truth, it will not be handed to us on a silver platter. The mainstream media are often not giving us the whole story. Much of their information comes from government sources. These sources reveal only what is in their best interest. Media outlets are owned by corporations that are in business to make money. Their agenda often clashes with the interest of the American people. They knowingly and sometimes unknowingly are a part of the agenda of hiding the truth under the façade/illusion of truth.

Chapter Three

My Family History

My DNA results according to Ancestry.com are as follows: Nigerian 20%, Cameroon 13%, Ivory Coast and Ghana 12%, Norway 9%, Mali 9%, Ireland 8%, England 7%, Scotland 6%, Benin/Togo 5%, Wales 3%, Spain 2%, Sweden 2%, Indigenous Native American 1%, Senegal 1%.[1]

John Ramsey(1716 -1776) of Glasgow, Lanarkshire Scotland moved to South Carolina in 1734.[2, 3] where he lived with his wife, Jane Hervey (1720 -1810).[4] They had a son, Alexander Edgar Ramsey Sr., (1747-1826) who married Mary Egger (1755-1841).[5,6] Their son Alexander Edgar Ramsey Jr., (1799-1871) married Sarah Hartgrove (1804 -1894).[7,8] The couple had a son Alexander A. Ramsey, (1836-1907) who married Martha.[9] Alexander also had a son by Evelina, a slave.[10] Evelina's son Albert P. Ramsey (b.1806-) married Eugenia Southwell.[11,12] They had a daughter Evelina (b.1880) in Beaufort S.C.[13]

She was the mother of Evelina Crowder who would become Evelyn Anderson, my grandmother.[14]

Evelina, Evelyn and Great Grandfather Reed the Inventor

Evelyn was born on October 20, 1899, and raised in Lynn Massachusetts. She died on February 13, 1984.[15] She was the daughter of Evelina Ramsey Crowder and Arthur W. Reed.[16,17] Ramsey was Evelyn's mother's maiden name. Everett Crowder was Evelyn's stepfather.[18] Evelyn's biological father was Arthur W. Reed. He was born in Boston, Massachusetts on August 26, 1882.[19] While attending college in Boston he met Evelina Ramsey. He graduated from the University of Amherst College and Massachusetts School of Technology.[20]

He moved to Detroit, Michigan after completing his studies in 1900. In Detroit he founded the Atlas Power Corporation one of the largest Black industrial organizations in the United States.[21] He also established the Atlas Power Publishing Company.[22] He was known for his inventions. On March 28, 1950 he received a patent for his Internal −Combustion Engine Fuel System and Cooling Means.[23] He also invented the Atlas power brakes for automobiles, trucks and trains, Atlas Power mobile refrigeration, non-skid heavy duty motor vehicle equipment, the Reed Ball - Marine boats, Atlas Power window hoist, a convertible top hoist opener and closer, Atlas Power dump truck lift and other inventions.[24]

Engine and Patent

March 28, 1950

A. W. REED
INTERNAL-COMBUSTION ENGINE FUEL
SYSTEM AND COOLING MEANS
Filed Oct. 2, 1943

2,501,739

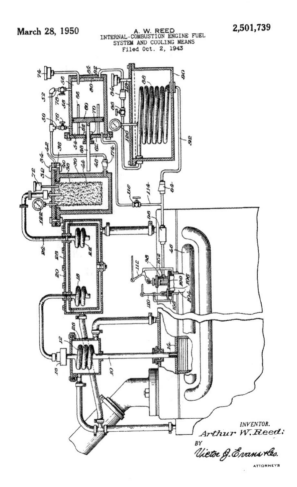

INVENTOR.
Arthur W. Reed:

BY

Victor J. Evans & Co.

ATTORNEYS

25

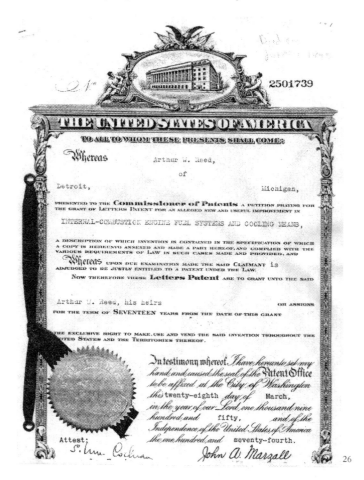

My Great- Grandfather Arthur Reed was honored in
the *Detroit Diurnal* on July 2, 1945 a week before his
death. The front page read A.W. Reed Day, Leader of
the Common Man.

LEADER OF THE COMMON MAN

For over two years to install into the mind the law of coo along the lines of i but ce scrupul laters down heads Colore C. A. mande may should continu my

Reed was th dation of economics other words, meat and based on the industri of the Negro mind, w they to offset in a that would cupercede t trine of preparing to earth. Since the majc their sermons pertai death and the hereafte much brighter must r tures be than their s

THE LATE ARTHUR W. REED

Arthur W. Reed, 62, inventor, engineer, and president of the Atlas Power Industrial Co-operation with office at 260 E. Vernor Highway, Detroit, whose funeral services was held Thursday afternoon, July 12, 1945, at Mason's Funeral Home. Rev. Wm. McHenry officiated. Internment was at Roseland Memorial Park Cemetery.

Arthur W. Reed was the inventor of the Automatic Brakes for autos, trains, trucks, and other heavy power vehicles, he also invented the Atlas Power Refrigeration System for cargo trucks and trains, also Non-skid Motor Vehicle Equipment. Inventor of the Reed "Ball" Marine Boat, also Atlas Power Window Hoist, Power Auto Jacks, Atlas Power Windshield Wiper, Door Opener and Closer, Convertible Top Hoist and Closer, Power Dump Truck Lifts.

Arthur W. Reed was born in Boston, Mass., August 26, 1882. Operated machine shop in Boston in 1899. Educated in public schools of Boston, graduated of Amherst College and Massachusetts School of Tech.

Arthur W. Reed suffered a cerrebral hemmorage June 24 while addressing 200 Atlas Power members of the Atlas Power Building assembly room which lingered until July 4, when he fell into a semi-coma and remained in that coma until he died at 5 a. m. July 9, 1945.

Arthur W. Reed is survived by a daughter and six grandchildren, George F. Sipkes, engineering assistant, formerly of Boston, Mr. William Water, his close financial aid since 1900, and many close friends, business associates, and thousand of acquaintances.

27

Reed Wrote:

> For over two years I tried to install into
> the Negro's mind the law of cooperation
> along the lines of industry; but certain
> unscrupulous   ministers   demanded
> of the Y.M.C.A that my lectures be

discontinued. If my doctrine was the foundation of economics or, in other words meat and bread based on the industrialization of the Negro mind, what had they to offset in a sermon that would supersede the doctrine of preparing to live on earth. Since the majority of their sermons pertain to death and the hereafter, how much brighter must my lectures be than their sermons?[28]

Now I understand from where my father and his mother Evelyn got their entrepreneurial and independent spirits, as well as their mistrust of religion. My sister Evelyn was told by Nana that her father invented products for the Ford Car Manufacturing Company.[29] The relationship between Atlas Corporation and the Ford Company is not clear but it makes sense that Ford would be interested in Reed's inventions.

On June 24, 1945 Mr. Reed suffered a stroke while addressing his Atlas Power organization and died on July 7, 1945 five years before receiving a patent for his Internal- Combustion Engine Fuel System and Cooling Means.[30] My sister Evelyn explained the following as told to her by Nana: Mr. Reed tried to contact Evelyn (Nana) but was prevented from doing so by Nana's her parents. When Nana was old enough, she traveled to Detroit to find him, but was unsuccessful. According to Nana, there was an orchestrated effort to prevent her from finding her father for fear that she would share in any inheritance. Nana said she left Chicago with a feeling of dread.[31]

Crowder, Anderson and more

Evelina Ramsey Crowder married Everett Crowder on May 11, 1903.[32]

Evelyn (Nana) my grandmother was four years old at that time and became the stepdaughter of Everett Crowder. At that time Evelina, Everett, and daughter Evelyn lived on Elm Street in Lynn, Massachusetts.[33]

The family moved from Elm Street to 6 Cherry Street in Swampscott, Massachusetts.[34] Albert P. Ramsey had bought the house as a gift for his daughter Evelina.[35]

Evelina Ramsey Crowder
(Great Grand Mother)[36]

Swampscott was and still is an affluent White community located next to the blue collar working-class community of Lynn. Swampscott separated from Lynn in 1852. In those days when people of African heritage moved into a Caucasian community, they were often scorned. The Crowder's were no exception. Nana said being called "nigger", among other colorful names was normal.[37] Being so young and not always realizing the intent of words helped protect her from some of the pain the insults were meant to inflict.

One day on the way home from school, Nana saw smoke in the distance. It was coming from the direction of her home. She feared that her house might be on fire. To her horror, it was.[38] This happened two years after the move from Lynn to Swampscott, where they lived from 1908 to 1910.[39]

We heard the family suspected the fire was an act of arson although it was never proven. As far as I know, there was no investigation. A lack of investigation was to be expected for injustices perpetrated against Black people at that time. I'd like to think that mindset has changed; but too often crimes against Black people are discovered after they have been hidden, ignored or individuals committing the crimes are exonerated by authorities.

After the Fire

After the fire in Swampscott, the family moved to Charles Street in Lynn.[40] Fifteen years later in 1925, Great-Grandmother Evelina Ramsey Crowder bought a house on Villa Place in Lynn.[41] What an accomplishment!

Visiting Granddad Ramsey

In the interim between Charles Street and the Villa Place purchase, Evelina sent Evelyn, her sisters Mable, May, Daisy and her brother John south by train to visit their grandfather Albert Prince Ramsey in Beaufort, South Carolina.[42] At that time in the early 1900s, living in the South was extremely oppressive. This precipitated the migration of millions of Black Americans to Northern States where the treatment of Blacks was precarious. Despite the perceived dangers for Black Americans in the South, Evelina may have been more concerned about her children's safety in the North, particularly after the suspected torching of her family's house in Swampscott.

My sister Evelyn saw the deed of our great-grandfather, Albert Prince Ramsey, while on a trip to Beaufort, South Carolina. Grandfather Ramsey owned his own land, which had been in the family for at least a generation. It had been passed down to him from his father Alexander Ramsey. I was told by my second cousin Jacqueline Arkord that Albert P. Ramsey was a veterinarian.[43] My great- grandfather a long-time farmer, landowner, and veterinarian (at least in practice if not by education), may have been shielded from overt racial hostility due to his standing in the community.

According to Evelyn (Nana), the large tract of land owned by her grandfather isolated them from Whites. They would rarely see them until it became necessary to go into town to shop. This may have given Evelina less trepidation when sending her children to visit her father. The truth is, no place in America was safe for Blacks at that time. Some places may have been less dangerous, but none were absolutely safe!

I, a Black man in 2023, more than a hundred years later, do not take my safety for granted. I am often on my guard. It is not wise for Blacks in America to be naïve to think they are perfectly safe anywhere.

My great-grandfather Albert Prince Ramsey despite his probable standing in his community it did not protect him from disaster. According to my cousin Jacqueline, Great-Granddad Ramsey's house was burned to the ground by racist. These haters have been trained by their racist and self-serving leaders.[44] Today, these leaders continue to manipulate the ignorant masses into doing their bidding by encouraging the white supremacist mindset.

I thought it was unusual that two of my relatives had their houses torched. I learned from my sister Evelyn that my mother's father, Thomas Johnson, had crosses burned on his lawn in Lynn, Massachusetts. He fought off the threat and eventually sold his house.[45] This story was told to my Sister Evelyn by my mother, Frances Anderson who witnessed it. My research made it clear that the destruction of Black people and their property was not unusual, but common practice not only in the South but across America.

Marriages and Family

In 1927, two years after Great Grandmother Evelina bought her house on Villa Place, her daughter Evelyn married Ernest Anderson and her other daughter Mable married Fredrick Meekins. Sisters May and Daisy had short-lived marriages. May and Daisy continued to live at Villa Place into the 1950s. Pauline, Evelyn's youngest sister also lived there with her children.

The following are the names of my Grandmother Evelyn's sisters and their families: Mable Crowder married Fredrick Meekins. They had five children: Herbert, Edward, Robert, Ronald, and Mable. Pauline Crowder married James Arkord Jr. They had four children: Jacqueline, Mable, Victoria, and James. Daisy, Mae, and John had no children.

Grandfather Ernest Anderson and Wife Evelyn

Nana told my sister Evelyn the following: Her husband Ernest, our grandfather, was born on an Indian reservation in Connecticut. Ernest's father James was Indian and his mother was African American.[46] James changed his indigenous surname, thinking it would be easier to make it in White society. "As bad as it was for Negros, Whites treated Indians even worse" Ernest told his wife, Evelyn.[47] Genealogy research indicates I have a 1% percent of Native American DNA.[48] How can this be if Nana's husband's father was Indian? One way to explain this apparent contradiction is that Granddad and his father were African Americans raised by Indians.

Famed genealogist professor Henry Lewis Gates reports most Black Americans who claim Indian heritage have none or an insignificant amount of Native American DNA;[49] why then claim Indian heritage? Black Americans who were fair with hair that is straighter than that of their brothers and sisters would much rather have been associated with Native American heritage. Indians were seen as possessing a history of nobility. They were seen as courageous fighters against European invasion. This was clearly preferred over the depiction of Blacks as portrayed by Whites. It was up lifting to believe that one's fair skin and straight hair was because of Native America roots. The truth was an indignity many were not willing to accept; a violation by a slave holder or some other Caucasian.

I was told Nana's husband was fair, though the picture below clearly shows a man with dark brown skin and Black features. Subsequent investigation into this inconsistency confirms what the picture reveals.

Evelyn and Ernest Anderson[50]

Complexion continues to be of concern among many African Americans and can affect a person's acceptance in some circles. The slave system bred into Blacks and Whites the consciousness of racial color-coding. The lighter you were, the more acceptable you were to the slave master and other Whites. For some Blacks, passing for White was seen as an opportunity for a better life despite the great risk of being exposed for who you really were. The pretense for some served as an escape from rejection by some Blacks who labeled you "too light." There was a popular phrase often uttered among Blacks in the 1960s, "If you're Black, step back. If your brown, stick around. If you're white, you're all right." Although said in jest, we all knew this was often how life went. The greatest racial prejudice was—and I believe still is directed toward those believed to be "too dark"

Chapter Four

Great Grandfather James Anderson

Ernest and Evelyn

A genealogy search performed by my wife, Vernice Anderson found that my great-grandfather on my father's side, James Anderson, was born in Vermont in September of 1850.[1] He married Augusta Cooper Loomis.[2] Vermont may seem an unlikely place for Blacks to retreat but Vermont was the first state to abolish slavery in 1777.[3] Vermont became part of the United States in 1791.[4] Laws can never immediately transform ideas and customs, but they can be a step in the right direction.

My grandmother reported that the tribe of James Anderson, her father- in- law, was extinct.[5] Many smaller tribes in Connecticut (an Algonquian word meaning "long river," referring to the Connecticut River) banded together in an attempt to survive European extermination. The tribes that exist today include the Eastern and Mashantucket Pequot Nation, the Mohegan, and the Schaghticoke.[6] If there is any trace of my great-grandfather's tribe, it would probably be among one of these populations.

According to genealogy records Ernest Anderson, son of James was born in August of 1896 in East Granby, Hartford County, Connecticut.[7] Ernest made his way to Lynn, Massachusetts. He worked as a waiter in the dining cars for the railroad. I was told this was where he met Evelyn (Nana). They married in 1918 and had nine children.[8] Arlene Anderson Carter (my aunt) described her father as devoted and hardworking.[9]

Sometime during their marriage, pneumonia threatened Ernest's life. Doctors had given up on his recovery. Evelyn asked if she could take him home and care for him there. She got their permission. Using natural remedies, Nana did what doctors could not. She nursed Ernest back to health.[10]

Ernest and Evelyn took up residence in a three-family house at Villa Place in Lynn. They lived a couple of houses down from Evelyn's mother, Evelina Ramsey-Crowder. Evelina had bought her house more than a decade after the Swampscott fire. Evelyn and Ernest lived at Villa Place for a number of years and began to raise their family. After a fire in one of the apartments in the three family house, they temporally moved in with Evelyn's mother Evelina until they found their own apartment in Lynn.[11]

The following are the children of Evelyn and Ernest Anderson and their children's children (in chronological order): Information provided by Crowder Family Reunion Bulletin 8/11/2012 compiled by Pamela Mimms

- Fredrick Anderson married Pearl. Children: Fredrick Jr., Steven, and Judy Anderson
- Sterling Anderson married Frances Johnson both deceased. Children: Sterling, Evelyn and Paulette
- Pearl Anderson married Edmund Carlton Brown. Children: Carlton and Deborah
- Shirley Anderson
- Arlene Anderson married Vernon Carter. Children: Bernadette and Vernita
- Avon Anderson married Fredrick Arnold. Children: Linda, Carolyn and Fredrick
- Audrey Anderson married John Veal. Children: Karen, John and Kenneth
- Barbara Anderson married Andrew Mimms. Children: Andrew Jr., Reginald, Donald, and Pam
- Jeanette Anderson married Tommy Tibbs. Children: Stephanie, Thomas, Leroy, Charlene, Kenneth, Eddie, and James
- Warren Anderson married Mary. Children: Brenda and Yvette

Granddad Anderson Passes

Ernest Anderson was born on August 26, 1896 and died on August 7, 1944.[12,13] The passing of Ernest happened while his children were in middle and high school. His death was caused by an infection he acquired after a dental extraction. it devastated the family.[14]

My grandmother now faced the awesome task of raising nine children alone. Between Ernest and Evelyn, my grandmother was the primary disciplinarian. If anyone was capable of doing the job of raising nine children alone, it was my grandmother. She was strong-willed and not afraid to discipline and administer punishment when she felt it was needed. She had high moral standards, attended church faithfully with her children and expected them to reflect what they were taught.

Her strength did not make her immune to the sorrow of being alone and raising nine children. Aunt Barbara once told me she would sometimes hear her mother sobbing.

Chapter Five

The Struggle
for Equality

Forward /Backward

"African American and Black" are terms used by Blacks
in the quest for identity. These terms became acceptable
in the 1960s. Before the 1960s, the terms "African and
Black" were seen by most as a put down. "Negro and
colored" were the accepted terms for people of African
descent and indigenous peoples of North America. The
rejection of Blackness and anything related to Africa was
the result of centuries of slavery and white supremacy
that degraded people of color.

Young people of the 1960s were instrumental in
the transformational shift from "Negro" and "colored"
to the terms "African American" and "Black." As
early as the 1930s, decades before the terminology
transitioned, Elijah Muhammad (leader of the Nation
of Islam and once mentor of Malcolm X and Louis
Farrakhan) described Negros as "so-called Negros"
and used the term 'Black people." Jesse Jackson, shortly
after Elijah Muhammad's death in February 1975 said

of Muhammad, "During our colored and Negro days, he was Black." Muhammad pioneered an interest in Black history, emphasized Black pride, and practiced Black entrepreneurship and self-reliance.[1] Before Elijah Muhammad, Jamaican born Marcus Garvey by 1919 claimed a following of 2,000,000. He preached an independent Black Economy within the frame work of white Capitalism. His group started businesses in the Black community. He organized the first American Black nationalist movement.[1a] It appears that the Nation of Islam was inspired by the Garvey movement because it proclaimed the same message of Black independence. The Major difference between them is that Garvey's movement did not have a religious foundation.

In the 1960s, linguist and anthropologist Dr. Keith E. Baird was an early advocate and articulate spokesman for the classification "African American." This term invoked cultural heritage when referring to people of African descent in the United States. Baird, a scholar and writer of a multitude of articles and books regarding the African American experience had professional affiliations at numerous academic institutions and was skilled in more than fourteen languages. He had received numerous honors.[2]

Blacks who changed their slave names to names that are representative of their assumed continent of origin, understand the connection between identity and self-actualization. The slave name was symbolic of ownership, not freedom. After the chains were removed the psychological and social bondage still remained.

African names represent a disowning of American/ European slave identity. Changing one's name provides a greater sense of freedom, pride and connection beyond America. Changing one's name also showed a desire, in spirit to connect to one's own people. In most cases it does not connect us to our lineage; yet its symbolism is powerful.

Four Hundred Years

After four hundred years, and by some estimates more, Black people are still engaged in the struggle for civil rights. The descendants of slaves both from Africa and indigenous Blacks and other indigenous peoples of North America were never originally meant to be accepted as equals in America. Our color, our altered names, and the lies told about our American and indigenous history, for some, are present reminders of the delusion that Blacks do not deserve our current freedom or respect.

White supremacists have become more emboldened since the election of Donald Trump. Their spewing of hate has become more open likening to the days of Jim Crow. Trump appears to sympathize with their point of view or a least his willingness to give that impression to capture that segment of the vote.

The 1863 the Emancipation Proclamation was signed by President Lincoln. Some slaves became free. In 1865, the thirteenth Amendment of the Constitution abolished slavery and involuntary servitude, except as punishment for a crime. In July 1868 African Americans born on U.S. soil were made citizens by The Fourteenth Amendment. Murders, lynching's and the destruction of Black communities continued across America despite citizenship. Racial intimidation by the KKK and other white supremacist groups was rampant. The murder of Blacks by law enforcement and vigilantes continues today as an example of the lingering racism of the past.

In 2013, the Supreme Court lifted the Department of Justice's monitoring of those states that had a history of voting rights violations against African Americans. Since the lifting of supervision, those states have reinstituted laws that harshly restrict voting rights for Black Americans.

Justice and the Illegal Underground Budget

Individuals and groups have lobbied for decades without success for reparations for slavery and for the ongoing mistreatment of Black Americans. An endorsement of reparations would be extremely costly, but money is not the problem. The government allocates billions to the military industrial complex. In 2020 the U.S. estimated military expenditure was $778 billion. It surpassed the defense budgets of all other Western nations including China's 2020, $252 billion, and Russia's spending of approximately $61.7 billion.[3]

According to Whitlock and Woodward, the Pentagon buried evidence of $125 billion in bureaucratic waste. The Pentagon's own internal review found $125 billion in unaccounted funds. It has estimated that billions more, if not trillions are spent on illegal projects hidden from the public.[4]

Donald Rumsfeld, Secretary of Defense from 1975 to 1977, under President Gerald Ford and from 2001 to 2006 under President George Bush, stated: "The financial systems of the Department of Defense are so snarled up we can't account for some $2.6 trillion in transactions that exist, if that's believable." On July 16, 2001 in front of the House Appropriations Committee Mr. Rumsfeld stated on CBS, January 29, 2002: "According to some estimates we cannot track $ 2.3 trillion in transactions—that's $8000 for every man, woman and child in America."[5]

The Office of the Inspector General (OIG) in a July 26, 2016 report, indicated that for fiscal year 2015, a $6.5-trillion - discrepancy was found in the Department of Defense accounting system. From the years 1998 to 2015, researchers found $21 trillion in unsupported adjustments for both the Department of Defense and the Department of Housing and Urban Development.[6]

Where is all this money going?

Money has never been the problem for providing reparations to Black Americans. The endorsement would put a spotlight on the inherent injustice and moral bankruptcy of those who have always ruled

America. It would expose the enormity of the injustices inflicted on indigenous and African Americans historically. Reparations would be a catalyst for the truth and reconciliation America so badly needs. Both truth and reconciliation are unlikely. America has too many secrets she wants to keep hidden. If by some chance, reparations happens, it will most certainly be a political move. By no means will there be adequate compensation; just enough to say the government did something, or helped the powers that be stay in power.

One of the traditional falsehoods spread by those who establish and maintain the underclass in America, is that Blacks are not equal or worthy of equality. Dehumanizing people of color has helped to maintain systems of slave wages, poor education, inferior social services, inadequate housing etc. Of the White majority who have been taught that Blacks are unworthy, some will mistreat and rationalize the mistreatment of people of color using the overt and covert messaging they have internalized.

There will be a time of reckoning. Rev. Martin Luther King Jr. quoted Theodore Parker, American Universalist minister, abolitionist and reformer. "The moral ark of the universe is long, but it bends toward justice."

Chapter Six

African Americans Who We Are - A Secret, Not a Mystery

So-called Africans Americans - Who Are We?

Tacoma Johnson, Pastor of "A People of God Church" in High Point, North Carolina cuts through the deception. He draws from primary sources of research material to dispel lies. He uses maps constructed during the time of the slave trade, biblical text, and more in his YouTube presentation, "Who Are We?" He sheds light on questions by dispelling falsehoods regarding Black Americans.

History as recorded by the Caucasians elite is full of lies regarding the identity and history of Black people; their tentacles extend in all directions; from continent to continent. Gamal Abdel Nasser, the late president of Egypt said: "The Europeans, claiming to be Jews are nothing more than Hebrew speaking Gentiles. You will never be able to live here in peace because you left Black and came back White. We cannot accept you!"[1] For centuries, white supremacist leaders have used their whitewashed versions of their holy books as tools in a scheme to gain and maintain dominance over people of color.

The Old Testament is describing the experiences of people of color in Africa and the "Middle East." The Egyptians were and are people of color. In Egypt today, Blacks are underrepresented which might lead one to assume the historically inaccurate assertion that ancient Egyptians were very fair or even white skinned. Black Nubians are the indigenous inhabitants of Egypt.

Gamal Sorour, businessman and prominent activist, died in October 2017 while in custody of the Egyptian police. He was among twenty-five Nubians arrested for staging a peaceful protest demanding the return of Nubians to their ancestral lands. They were evicted in the 1960s to make way for Lake Nasser located behind the High Dam on the Nile.[1a]

Count Constantine de Volney

De Volney was a French noblemen and historian who lived in Egypt for months in 1782. During his journey he recorded the following:

> All the Egyptians have a bloated face, puffed-up eyes, flat nose, and thick

lip – in a word, the true face of a mulatto. I was tempted to attribute it to the climate, but when I visited the Sphinx; its appearance gave me the key to the riddle. On seeing that head, typically Negro in all its features, I remembered the remarkable passage where the Greek historian Herodotus says; "As for me I judge the Colchians to be a colony of the Egyptians because, like them they are Black with wooly hair...

This race of Black men, today our slave and the object of scorn, is the very race of to which we owe our art, sciences, and even the use of speech! Just imagine. Finally, that it is in the mist of people who call themselves the greatest friends of liberty and humanity that have approved the most barbarous slavery, and questioned whether Black men have the same kind of intelligence as Whites!

In other words, the ancient Egyptians were true Negroes of the same stock as all the autochthonous peoples of Africa and from the data one see how the race after some centuries of mixing with the blood of Romans and Greeks, must have lost the full blackness of its original color but retained the impress of its original mold.[2]

Today the decedents of the Colchians are considered Black Russians living in the area of Batumi in Georgia on the southwestern coast of the Black Sea. The theory is that the Colchians whose existence was discovered in the early twentieth century are descendants of the legendary army of the Egyptian Pharaoh Sesotris dating back to the eighth century BC.[3]

Return of Black Land

Author Paul Barton explains:

Blacks owned about one million square miles of land in the Louisiana Territories and the South Eastern/Florida region, as well as California. In all these areas of the U.S., there were Black African-American nations before Columbus, who were targeted for enslavement due to the Papal Edict. It gave the Christian nations of Europe the go-ahead to make slaves of all descendants of Ham found in the newly discovered lands.... In 1991, the U.S. returned about 68,000 square acres of land to the Black Washitaw Nation of North America /Louisiana, one of the prehistoric Black nations of the United States. This group of Blacks is the evidence of the Black ownership of land and the Black presence before European colonization of North America.[4]

In Dr. R.A. Umar Shabazz Bey's, *We Are the Washitaw*, the author outlines the tremendous hardship, persecution and violent attacks that powerful vested interests waged against them to prevent them from retrieving and developing their land. The Washitaw have survived because of the leadership and research of the deceased Verdiacee Tiara Washitaw-Turner Goston El-Bey author of *Return of the Ancient Ones the true history uncovered of the Washitaw de Dugdahmoundyah Empire. We Are the Washitaw* was compiled under her direction:

The return of land to the Washitaw was a court case; United States v. Turner, (1850). It dismissed the petition of the claimants (the United States) efforts to reverse the 1848 verdict that awarded the Louisiana land to the Turner/Washitaw. "On June 19, 1848 the Turner heirs won the court case that affirmed them as the lawful owners with good title, securing the land rights of the Empirical Nation forever."[5]

The Original Man

It is pretty much an established fact that all modern humans have their origins in Africa. Geneticist David Reich of Harvard University researched 300 genomes from 142 populations. "The take home message is that modern humans today outside of Africa are descended from a single founding population almost completely."[6]

In Shum Laka rock shelter in Cameroon DNA findings of four children buried 3000 and 8000 thousand years ago were found. Some of the oldest DNA was recovered from the African tropics. Two thirds of the DNA found was distantly related to present day West Africans and about one-third of their DNA from ancestors most closely related to the hunter-gathers of Western Central Africa. Results suggest that lineages leading to today's Central African Hunter-gatherers, Southern African Hunters-Gatherers, and all other modern humans diverged in close succession about 250,000-200.000 years ago.[7]

Skulls almost identical to modern man have been found in Jebel Irhoud Morocco and other parts of Africa. No longer does it appear that people evolved in a single location in East Africa. These skulls have been dated by high-tech methods to be 300,000 and 350,000 years old. It puts into question the 200,000 year time frame of man's evolution.[8]

I mentioned in my preface that at a young age I joined the Nation of Islam. At that time in the late 1950s and decades before, Elijah Muhammad celebrated

Black people and taught that the Black man was the original man of planet earth (a reality that has finally been accepted). This type of talk was not accepted by white supremacists who greatly influenced the thinking of the people. In decades past large proportions of the brain washed Black community simply echoed what "master" said.

Columbus and Indigenous Genocide

During the time of the exploration, invasion, and decimation of the North American populations, explorers, artists, and historians described the inhabitants as those of African heritage. This information is virtually unknown to the public.

The American Webster Dictionary (1828) defines American as "a native of America originally applied to the aboriginals, or copper-colored race found here by the Europeans; but now applied to the descendants of Europeans born in America."[9]

When I use the term "Black" in this section and throughout this book, I am referring to all shades of aboriginal peoples who inhabited North America and those brought over on slave ships unless otherwise specified.

Columbus's first journey to the "New World" was on the ship Santa Maria piloted by an experienced Spanish navigator by the name of Pedro Alonso Nino of African descent. He was known as El Negro (the

Black). Before working with Columbus Pedro and his brothers Juan and Francisco were known for their navigational skills. Juan was the navigator of the Nina. The brothers were thought to be integral parts of Columbus's voyages.[10] When Columbus and his crew arrived in the "New World" their primary intention was to acquire gold and dominate the inhabitants. The indigenous Arawak people greeted the strangers in peace and overwhelming hospitality. Columbus Stated:

> "They are the best people in the world and beyond all mildness"... a people with such kind hearts and so ready to give the Christians all that they possess, and when the Christians arrive, they run at once to give them everything."[11]

Peter Martyr, the king's recorder wrote, "They seem to live in that golden world of which old writers speak so much, wherein men lived simply and innocently without enforcement of laws, without quarreling, judges and libellees, content only to satisfy nature, without further vexation for knowledge or things to come."[12]

Benjamin Franklin and other Europeans who came in contact with indigenous people echoed the same sentiments of Columbus. Why then the horror of slavery torture and every other horrible abuse and eventually the extermination of indigenous people? These people posed no threat or harm to the Europeans; or did they? Greed is not the answer for the sadistic treatment imposed upon the Arawak and other indigenous people, the cause for these actions of evil are much deeper than greed. What "civilization" has sought to destroy is the image of uprightness that indigenous people represented. This is what "civilization" has always done when it comes face to face with *true* righteousness. "Civilization" at large seems much more comfortable pretending to be righteous. The only way they (the people and their leaders) can continue their pretense of "civilization" is to destroy the real righteous ones as historically, "civilizations" have always done when ever prophets and individuals bring a righteous message. "Civilization" says we come to bring "God" to the indigenous "savage", yet the gods they bring have not been able to bring peace to the "civilized"; a peace that many of the indigenous people enjoyed long before the introduction of the European versions of God.[13]

★★★★★★★★★★★★★★★★★★★★★★★★★★★★★★★

This is a partial list of the tribes in North America with a significant degree of African ancestry; the Shinnecock in Eastern Long Island New York State, – the Iroquois in New York State, – the Pequot in Connecticut, – the Narragansett in Rhode Island, – the Choctaw in Alabama, Florida, Mississippi, – the Creek, Cherokee and Seminole historically from the Southeast Georgia, Alabama, Florida, South Carolina, North Carolina, Kentucky, Virginia, and Tennessee, and the Wampanoag in Southern Massachusetts, Rhode Island, Martha's Vineyard and Nantucket.[14] All have a significant degree of African ancestry.

In 1835 the Cherokee, Choctaw, Chickasaw, Seminole and Creek were forced to move along The Trail of Tears. The forced migration numbered in the range of 100,000. These and other tribes were forcibly moved by the Federal Government thousands of miles from their native lands to west of the Mississippi. Over 15,000 died of starvation and disease in this genocidal act of forced relocation.[15]

The stealing, enslavement and slaughter in lands belonging to indigenous people were sanctioned in 1455 by the Papal Edict of Pope Nicholas V. This edict gave the crown of Portugal and other European nations permission to seize "new" lands and enslave its occupants in the name of "God." This edict was preceded by others as early as 1095 by Pope Urban the second.[16]

Discoveries of the Past - African Influence in the Americas

African artifacts and linguistic evidence dating back long before the arrival of Columbus's have been found in North America. The Davenport calendar, a stone tablet (*stele*) found in a burial mound in Iowa in 1877, contained a carving of the "Opening the Mouth Ceremony" (Djed Festival) a ritual meant to enable the deceased to use their senses in the afterlife to help the living. This ritual is of Nubian/Egyptian origin going back thousands of years. Written on stone were Egyptian, Iberian and Libyan scripts. Dr. Barry Fell, known for his archeological research of ancient America discovered hundreds of Egyptian words in the dialect of the Algonquian tribal groups and Micmac, Wabanaki and Etchemis of Northern New England.[17]

The Olmec / Xi were another African group found in the Americas. They inhabited the Southern coast of the Gulf of Mexico in Central America in the present states of Tabasco and Veracruz. It was the Olmec who fashioned the huge heads with African features at theses location. Studies done by Dr. Clyde, Winters African American educator, anthropologist and linguist showed that the writing on the Olmec monuments was in the Mende script, a writing system used among the Mandinkas and other West Africans. The Olmec are thought to have influenced many of the cultural designs displayed by American Indian cultures of Mexico and Central America.[18]

Cocaine and nicotine found in Egyptian mummies indicate trade with the Americas. These substances are known only to the Americas....The Mayans, Aztecs and Incas all worshiped Black gods....Quetzalcoatl, a messiah serpent god, and Ek–ahua, the god of war are unquestionably Negro, with dark skin and wooly hair. Why would Native Americans venerate images unmistakably African if they had never seen them?[19]

Garaikai Chengu quotes the late Michael Coe, a leading historian on Mexico:

> "There is not the slightest doubt that all later civilization in Mexico and Central America rest ultimately on an Olmec base." [ibid19a]

Thor Heyerdahl, a Norwegian ethnologist, makes clear the possibility that ancient Africans were making transatlantic voyages. On May 17, 1970, he and his crew set out in a papyrus sailing craft modeled after the ancient sailing ships of Egypt on a journey from Morocco to Barbados. He accomplished the four-thousand-mile trip in fifty-seven days. [20]

The Black Californians were an ancient civilization that lived in Khalifians, today known as California. They were a matriarchal society trading with their sisters and brothers in West Africa and other parts of the world, thousands of years before European contact. These civilizations were not simply hunter-gatherers. They were advanced cultures with science, art, architecture and technological skills. They supported thriving cities with populations in the thousands. They maintained trade and commerce with other like-minded cultures in and outside North America. [21]

According to historian and linguist Leo Weiner of Harvard University, author of *Africa and the Discovery of America* (1920), Columbus in his own journals recorded what he learned from Native Americans: "Black skinned people had come from the south-east in boats trading in gold tipped spears."

To learn more about ancient America before 1492 consult the following internet resources:

Hotep.org
Kurimeo part 1 (From Indigenous American to African American)
Black Washitaw Nation of America
Washitaw Civilization of Mound Builders
African Civilizations of Ancient America
We are the Washitaw, by Dr. R.A. Umar Shabazz Bey, 2006.

This is a sample of the wealth of information now available thanks to researchers not afraid to offend the status quo.

The old guards of racism which included fourteen of the twenty one prominent Founding Fathers who owned slaves and those who continue the legacy of racism have seen it, as their duty to maintain racial dominance because they suffer from the delusion of a racial superiority complex.[22] Persons who seem to believe they are better than others to escape feelings of insecurity. These people are often obnoxious and hurtful...In most cases, a superiority complex hides an inferiority complex...They have little tolerance for reality...It is impossible for them to accept failure, instead they will project their inadequacies on others.[23] Other characteristics of a superiority complex include a pretentious attitude – intense mockery – a need to be admired, even if it means embellishing or lying – displaying a strong self-confidence – disregarding others opinions or contributions and placing excessive value on their own – overreacting to situations that dig deep into their insecurity.[24]

The delusions induced by the superiority complex I believe are at the core of the perpetual destruction of people of color.

Power brokers use multiple strategies to maintain the division and hostility among the races; misinformation, economic division, and political underhandedness. Pseudoscience and historical falsehoods prop up the delusion of racial superiority in order to justify ongoing carnage of people of color and the theft of their lands. This is a worldwide system of those in power, duplicated by those they raise and train for positions of leadership.

All those who do not fit their white supremacist paradigm are in jeopardy but those who do are also in danger. They fail to see, blinded by the division caused by racial stereotypes, that what has been done to others will eventually be done to them.

While the world speeds toward global annihilation, those in power continue to suck its blood, making the rich richer and the poor poorer.

Slavery in the Western Hemisphere & Black Origins

Slavery in America did not have its beginnings with Blacks taken from Africa. Indigenous peoples of all hues were taken from their own indigenous lands here in America. Alan Gallay reports in his book *The Indian Slave Trade,* 2002 that "between 1670 and 1715, more Indians were exported into slavery through Charles Town, (now Charleston South Carolina) than Africans were imported." The words Indian, Black, or Negro were often used to describe any person of color in the Americas.

Andres Resendez, in his work *The Other Slavery: the Uncovered Story of Indian Enslavement in America,* 2016, estimated that two to five million "Indian" aboriginals were enslaved in the Americas.

Brown University historian, Linford D. Fisher in his essay, *"Colonial enslavement of Native Americans included those who surrendered, too,"* 2/2017 concurs with Resendez. Fisher reports "Between 1492 and 1880, between 2 and 5.5 million Native American's were enslaved in the Americas." Henry Lewis Gates Jr. explains that 12.7 million Blacks were shipped to the New World from Africa but only 10.7 million survived. Of these only 388,000 were shipped directly to North America.[25] In addition to this "85% of the Blacks in America were already here before the slave trade. Only 15% of Blacks come from Africa."[26]

When Black people claim they are of Indian heritage or indigenous to America, they are often not taken seriously. This is because the only information we have been taught in the average American public schools is that all so-called Negros, colored, Blacks, or African Americans came to the New World by way of slave ships; and that most natives of America are those of fair skin and straight hair as past and present day portrayals display them. Such images and statements are inaccurate.

Europeans were surprised to find people actually living in peace, not simply mouthing a doctrine of peace. Benjamin Franklin states in his remarkable essay, *"Remarks Concerning the Savages of North America"* "There was no force, there were no prisons, and no officers to compel obedience or inflict punishment".[27] Franklin, throughout his essay, is awestruck by the kindness, intelligence, civility and hospitality of the indigenous people. Indigenous Blacks were apart of America before the arrival of African slaves. Instead of learning from the peaceful ways of indigenous people Europeans chose to destroy them.

Italian, Explorer Giovanni Verrazano explored the East Coast of North America in 1524. He described the inhabitants as thus: "They are of dark color not much unlike the Ethiopian, and hair black and thick, and not very long, it is worn tied back upon the head in the form of a little tail."[28]

In 1920 Carlos Cuervo Marquez, ethnologist, military general, and historian authored the *Study of Archaeology and Ethnography* He wrote:

> The Negro type is seen in the most ancient Mexican sculptures. The Negroes figure frequently is in the most remote tradition of some American Pueblos. It is to this race doubtlessly belongs the most ancient skeletons distinct from the Red American race. These skeletons have been found in various places from Bolivia to Mexico. It is likely that, we repeat, ***America was a Negro continent.***[29]

In 1832 Professor Constantine Samuel Rafinesque in his essay "The Primitive Black Nations of America" identified the Black and Brown indigenous groups found on Turtle Island which was renamed America. See pictures of the descendants of the first people in America at hcblackheritage.com/ancient-america, Houston County Black Heritage.

The Y Chromosome

The fact the human origins had their beginnings in Africa has been substantiated through intense academic research. It has become common knowledge. The discovery of a distinctive Y chromosome in the DNA of a descendent of Albert Perry a formerly enslaved man helped to revise the thinking of the human origin story. Perry's Y-chromosome did not originate from "Y-chromosomal of Adam" whose Y-chromosome was thought to be our most recent common ancestor. Perry's Y chromosome is estimated to be more than 100,000 years older than that of Adam's. The Y chromosome was found among the Mbo in Cameroon Central Africa, while the rest of the men in world have only been shown to contain the Y chromosome of Adam. This suggests that our revised Adam may have lived in Central Africa.[30] Additional information can be gathered regarding the discovery of man's new age at the following site:

> Colin Barras, *The Father of All Men is 340,000 Years Old*, newscientist.com, 03/06/2013.

> We know now that Luzia was a member of the Olmec civilization. Her skull matches the African facial features of the Olmec heads. Leslie Freeman, of the University of Chicago, states Luzia, is just one of many South American Paleo-Indian skulls I have been investigating since the end of 1980s. All studies preceding and subsequent to the analysis of Luzia have generated the same result: The first South Americans

have a marked morphological affinity
with present – day Africans and
Australians, showing no resemblance to
present Asian Mongoloids or American
Indians.[31]

Why is so little known about the slavery of Black
and Brown people before the start of the transatlantic
slave trade? That truth would expose the fact that
Blacks were enslaved in their own homeland. If that was
understood, Blacks would be demanding in addition
to financial reparation, the return of Black lands stolen
from them here in America; as in the case of the land
returned to the Black Washitaw Nation of America
described earlier in this chapter. Looking to Africa is
away to divert attention away from the Black holocaust,
land theft and slavery that took place in America before
the importing of Africans. The holocaust of Black and
Brown people and theft of their lands by Europeans is
a consistent theme around the world.

"Between 1492 and 1550 overwork and famine
killed more Indians in the Caribbean than smallpox,
Influenza and malaria… Slavery has emerged as a
major killer."[32] Resendez reports a dramatic decrease
in the population: by 1517, only eleven thousand had
survived.[33] Russell Schimmer of the Yale University,
Genocide Studies Program, draws a similar conclusion
regarding the population of Hispaniola (Haiti and the
Dominican Republic): The depopulation of the Taino
Indian in Hispaniola was the result of enslavement,

massacre or disease… "Estimates of the population range from several hundred thousand to over a million… By 1514 only 32,000 Taino survived in Hispaniola."[34]

The Hispaniola decimation by the Spanish is not unique. The transport of African slaves began as a consequence of the depopulation of the aboriginal people in the Americas.

Black Indigenous North Americans

My DNA results as stated in chapter three showed 1% Native American blood;[35] this would seem to contradict my grandmother's claim that her husband's father was Native American. These findings would tend to substantiate what Professor Gates has concluded, that Blacks usually have little to no Native American blood.[36] Indigenous Americans, as commonly portrayed were not the only inhabitants of North America. Black and Brown people also comprised much of the population of the America's just as they do today. Elijah M Haines, American Democratic Party politician 1822-1889 reported in his book, "The American Indian":

> The aboriginal of America is tall, straight of stature, and muscular, having coarse black hair, well-formed limbs, deep chests, brown or copper colored complexion, head a little flat prominent nose, compressed lips, dark

eyes, and possessed of a great power of endurance.[37]

Haines, left the Democratic Party and became a Republican because of his anti- slavery stance. His book "The American Indian" is considered an important historical document.

Captain Bartholomew Gosnold, on the fourteenth of May of 1602 describes the natives of Cape Neddock Maine as such "These people are tall of stature, broad a grim visage, of a black swart complexion."[38]

References, 37 and 38 are from Kimberly R. Norton's, book *"Black People are Indigenous to the Americas: Research Material for the Inquisitive."*

Blacks who claim to be Indian are often dismissed because of the racial characteristics commonly associated with American Indians. Once we understand that the Indigenous population of North America comprised a range of complexions there is no need to accept the narrow racial and DNA stereotypes that deny indigenous Blacks in America their Native American identity. When I speak to Black indigenous Americans I am not referring to Africans or African Americans who have lived among Indians or those who may have been in servitude in some tribes. Instead I am referring to Browns and Blacks who are indigenous to the North American continent.

Of course, fair skinned "White looking Indians" are the prominent versions representing Indian leadership. Often these Indians rejected dark skinned indigenous inhabitants or African Americans who have become a part of an Indian tribe. This is a consistent tactic wherever colonizers go. They put other Whites, those who are very fair, look White or indigenous locals who will serve their interest to lord over the dark populations. For additional information refer to the following sites:

> 98% of African Americans Are In Fact Native Indians and Owed Millions, D. Calloway, 7/ 2/2019. 103 Amazing Facts about the Black Indian by: Whanstachanah P. Kanyon a non-reservationist, 2003. Deception Hidden Behind the Feathers, Marsha Stewart, 2017.

Native Americans and Slavery of African Americans

Slaves did not always find solace seeking refuge among some Indians tribes, notably the "five civilized tribes" (Creek, Cherokee, Choctaw, Chickasaw and the Seminole). This may have been the exception rather than the rule. Professor of History Roy E. Finkenbine, *"The Native Americans Who Assisted the Underground Railroad",* The Potawatomi, Wyandot, Ottawa, Ojibway, Shawnee and Odawa were those who assisted in helping runaway slaves to freedom at great personal

risk.[39] "The first path to freedom taken by runaway
slaves led to American Indian villages, where Black men
and women found acceptance and friendship among
the original inhabitants of Turtle Island",an indigenous
name for North America.[40] William Katz, states, there
was solidarity between Africans and American Indians
who were not slave holders.[41]

Escaped slaves and the freedmen, formally enslaved
Black persons who had been released from slavery
usually by "legal" means who found refuge in Indian
tribes, were in a much better condition than those
under the hands of Europeans; unless they found
themselves in the clutches of tribes who adopted a form
of bondage that was restrictive and punitive, emulating
the laws of the Deep South; though, to be fair racist
laws were nationwide.[42] Even in cases where Indians
had slaves there was variety: free African Americans and
those of mixed African-Choctaw descent lived in the
eastern Mississippi part of the Choctaw nation. These
communities were common in Indian Territory before
and after the Trail of Tears. African Americans could
settle alongside the thousands of free African-Native
Americans (also known as, indigenous Blacks) that were
citizens of the Five Tribes. justiceforgreenwood.org.[43]
The "Five Civilized Tribes" may have seen themselves
distinct from African Americans but the slave system in
America and those who were a part of it saw all people
of color as fair game. Either to be enslaved or killed.

The total number of Black slaves held by the "Five
Civilized Tribes" (Cherokee, Choctaw, Chickasaw,

Creek and Seminole) has been assessed at 5000 to 15,000.

In Creek society "enslaved Blacks were not housed in separate villages or communities but lived in close contact with the Creek who held them captive"…"they were allowed much more freedom than their counter parts enslaved by White people." Mixed race children were considered Creek.[44]

Many in the Cherokee Nation who held positions of authority were of mixed blood as a result of White traders living among Native Americans and taking wives. Their presence affected ideas and cultural life styles of Indian settlements. The closer contact Indian tribes had with Europeans, the greater influence and pressure to adopt European values.[45]

In 1827 the Cherokee wrote their own constitution reflecting many of the racist values of southern slave laws; Cherokee hierarchy stressed separation between African Americans and Cherokee. African Americans had no part in Cherokee affairs even if they were part Cherokee. Adopting a constitution reflecting southern values attests to the institutionalization of Black chattel slavery in the Cherokee Nation.[46]

Most Cherokee did not have slaves as was the case with American Whites but the attitudes and ideas of those in control (the slave holders) infected the societies of both Indian and Whites. Those who escaped the destructive mindset of racism where, I believe a minority; a minority of the wisest. Despite the Cherokee and the other "Civilized Tribes" attempts to placate Whites by emulating the White lifestyle, they could not prevent the American government from taking their land and setting them on the "Trail of Tears" to Oklahoma.

"Between 1830 and 1850 about 100,000 American Indians living between Michigan, Louisiana and Florida" were forced on the genocidal trek to Oklahoma. Some journeys were done during the winter months "Contemporary historians believe, that between 4,000 and 8,000 Cherokee perished during the forced removals in 1838 and 1839, as well as 4,000 Choctaw (a third of the entire tribe) and 3,500 Creek Indians." Men women and children died from starvation, exposure and disease;[47] these figures don't include the Chickasaw, Seminole and Black slaves of the five "Civilized Tribes." These additions would probably bring the total of deaths on the trail of Tears to 17,000 -18,000 or more.[48]

Tiya Miles professor of history and North American studies at the University of Michigan in her article," *Pain of 'Trail of Tears' Shared by Blacks as Well as Native Americans,"* gives accounts told to her by people whose Cherokee grandparents along with their Negro slaves traveled the Trail of Tears: "faithful Negro slaves who… went ahead of the wagons and killed any wild beast that came along." Sadly these slaves are not named. In the 1930s Eliza Whitmore, former slave of Cherokee's stated: "The weeks that followed General Scott's order to move the Cherokee were filled with horror and suffering for the unfortunate Cherokee and their slaves."

The presence of Black slaves on the "Trail of Tears" owned by Native Americans is not a commonly known historical fact. Another interviewee expressed anger that sympathy is only reserved for Indians portrayed as victims while their racist policies hide the fact that they had slaves who also suffered on the Trail of Tears. This interviewee goes on to say "I was prepared to pounce on any African American who felt compelled to express pride in their Native American heritage at the expense of their African blood;"[49] a pride expressed because of an ignorance of the truth.

Seminoles and Black Seminoles

Black Seminoles consisted of indigenous Blacks, African who were never enslaved, mulattos, freed slaves, and escape slaves. Beginning in the Seventeenth century many Blacks fled plantations in the South to join Indigenous Seminoles who also fled to Florida to evade European extermination. The term "Estelusti" is a Muskogee word for black. It was a tribal name given to non-indigenous Seminoles.

Seminoles, unlike some other tribes welcomed runaway slaves. Race was not taken into consideration. They held on to their traditions and welcomed outsiders. Seminole country was a place where Blacks sought refuge. African Americans were valued for their intellectual knowledge of White Society and their fighting ability which in turn provided greater numbers as Seminoles fought the European invaders.[50] The increased numbers and intelligence provided by escaped slaves laid the foundation for the largest slave rebellion in U.S. history; one you may have never heard of. In 1835 – 1838. An estimated 465 plantation slaves joined forces with the Black Seminoles and Maroons (Blacks who lived outside of slave society and fought to retain that existence) together equaling an estimated 1,200 or more. They struck against the slave system of their mutual enemy. In the months during 1836 twenty one plantations were laid waste.[51]

Some Black Seminoles were fully integrated into the tribe through the marriage line of the mother or by adoption while others formed independent communities and paid a tribute to the Seminoles. There were also slave and master relationships. The numerical breakdown of these categories is not clear; but it is evident that there was a distinction between Seminoles and Estelusti. Humane treatment of slaves was seemingly the case among the Seminoles. Bondage nevertheless subjects one to the humiliation of being someone else's property.[52]

1866 Treaties

The U.S. Seminole Treaty of March 1866 Article (2) gave citizenship to Black Seminoles. Part of the settlement states, "… the number of Oklahoma Seminoles having African ancestry was so large that the language of the

1866 Seminole Treaty reflect that the Seminole ceded their "entire domain" an excess of 2 million acres for the location of Indians and Freedmen.

The 1866 treaty forged by the U.S. government and the 5 tribes did not prevent the Creek and Texas slave holders from attempting to take freed Blacks into slavery. The well-armed Freedmen, Black Seminoles and Kickapoo tribe members fought together to maintain their freedom. Once it became clear that the United States government was not going to help honor the treaty plans were devised to escape to Mexico. In Mexico they were received as free Blacks and given land and provisions to start their own colony.[53]

Even before the 1866 treaty, the aforementioned tribes had been retreating to Mexico where slavery had been outlawed since 1829. In that same year after Mexico outlawed slavery, an estimated 5,000 African Americans escaped to Mexico; many through the Southern Underground Railroad. They formed a community. Just across the border, in current times, this Mexican community celebrates Juneteenth, the celebration of the emancipation of Black slaves.[54]

Black Seminoles experienced antagonism from Seminoles when the U.S government proposed to give $56 million to Seminoles for their lost lands in Florida. On July 1, 2000, through illegal means, the Seminoles disenfranchised Black Seminoles and Freedmen by denying their votes on an issue that impacted their citizenship, making Black Seminoles and Freed men ineligible for federal financial compensation that was allowed for in the U.S. Seminole Treaty of 1866.[55] For addition Information regarding Black Seminoles and Seminoles interaction see *"Seminole Freedmen and Black Native Citizenship"*.

Black Seminoles continue to be denied financial compensation by Seminoles who use discriminatory tactics to reject the legitimate claims of Black Seminoles. These discriminatory policies impacted Black Seminoles access to vaccinations during the COVID 19 pandemic.[56]

A historical note: In the late 1500's most Africans Americans came to Florida as slaves but there were some who settled in St. Augustine as free Africans. In 1693 slaves were considered free by the King of Spain if they converted to Christianity and declared loyalty to Spain. In 1738 a separate town was established for free Blacks; it was named Fort Mose, the first free African American settlement in America.[57] Since the 1500's African American have had a presence in Florida; predating the Seminole migration in the 1700s.[58]

Research reveals complexity in the Indian, African American relationship. It was risky for escaped slaves regardless from whom they sought help because the Caucasian slave system in America contaminated every facet of life for people of color.

The five tribes are a minuscule number of the hundreds of indigenous groups who struggled to hold on to their land and way of life through; armed resistance, political negotiation, compromise, and treaties, even buying into the White man's life style as the Five tribes did could not protect Indian nations from Europeans' intolerance, self-righteousness, arrogance and greed for land and power.

The history of the Seminoles and other indigenous groups has been either minimized or simply ignored particularly in public school history books. The recent interest in genealogy and the ability to find information through the internet have created a hunger for historical and genealogical information that was not easily accessible in the past.

Massacres of Indigenous Peoples

The abuse and murder of indigenous people in the Americas spans hundreds of years to the present. It is a miracle that any survived. Many indigenous cultures have become extinct. Historian David E. Stannard writes:

> The destruction of the Indigenous cultures of the America's was, far and away, the most massive act of genocide in the history of the world. Eventually more than 100 million natives fell under European rule. Their extermination would follow. As the natives died out, they were replaced by slaves brought from Africa.[59]

Historian Benjamin Manley's *American Genocide*, reports from 1846 – 1873, 370 sites were discovered in California where unarmed men woman and children were massacred by non-Indians. The murders were committed by vigilantes and roaming White gangs. Manley concludes that officials created and managed a "well-funded killing machine." Manley cites Senator John B. Weller of California who served as the fifth governor of California from 1858 – 1860, referring to the indigenous people, "Humanity may forbid, but the interest of White men demands their extinction." This has been the attitude of many in positions of power at that time. Their hostile quotes are easy to find in historical records. "Between 1846 and 1873 California's Indian population plunged from perhaps 150,000 to 30,000" Manley says.[60]

George Washington during his presidency sought to ameliorate relations with Indians but ultimately followed the pattern of destruction of those who came before him. Washington instructed Major John Sullivan to "totally destroy the Iroquois settlements and do not listen to any overtures of peace before the total ruin of their settlements is affected."[61]

In 1783 Washington again made clear his anti-Indian sentiment; comparing indigenous people to wolves, "Both being beast of prey, tho' they differ in shape." He called for their total destruction. Washington's troops would skin the bodies of Iroquois from the hip down to make boot tops or leggings. The Iroquois called Washington "Town Destroyer." Within five years twenty-eight of thirty Seneca towns had been destroyed.[62]

In 1787 the Northwest Ordinance was enacted, opening up the Ohio Valley to new American settlers. Indigenous inhabitants fought to keep their land. In an attempt to resolve the problem, Washington approved treaties with seven northern tribes. These treaties were meaningless without the U.S. government preventing incursions onto tribal lands. Indigenous peoples had to fight in order to protect themselves and prevent their land from being seized. Washington warred against those trying to keep their land Instead of enforcing the treaties; a pattern the United States has followed ever since. In 1796 Washington, concluded: "I believe scarcely anything short of a Chinese wall, or a line of troops, will restrain land jobbers and the encroachment of settlers upon the Indian Territory."[63]

Describing Indians as "savages" was always a ploy to justify the killings. Indians were not the savages. English explorers Arthur Barlowe in July 1584 stated: "We found the people most gentle loving and faithful, void of all guile and treason and such as lived after the manner of the Golden Age … A more kind and loving people there cannot be found in the world;"[64] similar sentiment were also echoed by Benjamin Franklin.

Today indigenous Americans continue their century's old fight for what little land they have left. This is in the face of ongoing efforts by the U.S. Government, aligned with corporate forces to confiscate indigenous people's land. Indigenous Americans are at the forefront of the current environmental movement. They have been crying in the wilderness for a long time; finally their cry is being heard.

The atrocities against indigenous Brown and Black people in the Americas are the foundations on which Europeans have built their empires. Building societies on the destruction of other cultures is a poor foundation for long term sustainability. Cultures in the past thought their lofty positions of power and weaponry would preserve them. Their assumptions proved to be wrong. There is a greater power beyond materialism that materialistic cultures do no respect. That power is the law of cause and effect or "Karma", "you reap what you sow". I fear for the American people.

Chapter Seven

The Big Lie from Black to White

Major characters in the Bible were men and women of color though you would probably not know that if you went by the pictures used in Bible references cited in most Bibles printed in America. Especially "children's" Bibles. A lot of Old Testament history takes place in Africa and in what is known today as the Middle East.

In medieval times when Europeans arrived in Africa they claimed they were bringing Christianity to a benighted continent, but something like Christianity had arrived in Africa nearly two thousand years earlier. The ancient Egyptians were no stranger to the teaching of a monotheistic Creator God. Pharaoh Akhenaton (1352-1336 B.C or B.C.E) taught there was one creator of the universe. Ankh, the cross with a loop on top represented life, death, power, immortality and water purification. After the demise of the Egyptian polytheistic religion the Christian Coptic church adopted the Ankh as a form of the Cross that also connected with their ancient African history. In the late 1900s the Ankh was slightly altered and adopted in

American culture as another depiction of the Christian Cross.[1]

Axum, Ethiopia adopted Christian tradition in the third century as consequence of King Ezana's conversion in A.D. 327.[2] In A.D. 362 Patriarch Athanasius ordained a bishop of Philae in Nubia.[3] The corrupted version of Christianity that most Europeans have spread has used a race-based ideology that subjects people of color to White rule.

Jesus, was not born in Europe, but in the Palestinian town of Bethlehem. I believe the depictions of a Caucasian Jesus and white main characters in the Bible was meant to propagate the agenda of white supremacy. What better way to propagate this lie than to make Jesus, the incarnate God, and make him white? To combat this white supremacist view, we need to look at what the Bible says about Jesus's appearance:

> Revelation 1:13-15 "And in the midst of the seven candlesticks one like the Son of Man … His head and his hairs were white like wool … His feet like unto fine brass, as if they burned in a furnace."

Jesus's family went to Egypt to hide from Herod because they could blend in with the Egyptians. This is a clear indication that Jesus was not Caucasian. The Bible gives other descriptions as to Jesus's true appearance:

Ezekiel 40:3 "And he brought me thither, and, **behold there was a man, whose appearance was like the appearance of brass."** Rev 2:18 ... "These things saith the Son of God who hath his eyes like unto a flame of fire, **and his feet are like fine brass.**"

Daniel 7:9 "... The ancient of days did sit, whose garment was white as snow, and **the hair on his head like pure wool**..." Daniel 10:5-6 "...and behold a certain man....**his arms and his feet like the <u>colour </u>to polished brass."**

One thing is clear, Jesus was not the pale face that Western culture has portrayed. Who is this European imposter called Jesus? One source says it is Cesare Borgia; the second illegitimate son fathered by Pope Alexander the Sixth of Rome.[4]

Europeans Claim to Israel

The present-day slaughter of Palestinians by Israeli security forces is often justified by the religious and political belief that God gave the land of Palestine to the Jews after their captivity in biblical Egypt. Justification for theft and murder has almost always historically been carried out in the name of some higher power.

Some scholars have questioned the Biblical Exodus

story. The evidence which has been cited on both sides of the argument seems to me, for the most part, irrelevant. Disputed evidence or not most believers believe the Exodus story by faith.

The late President Gamal Abdel Nasser stated in 1952: "The Europeans claiming to be Jews are nothing more than Hebrew speaking gentiles ... You left here Black and came back White. We cannot accept you."[5]

Now, while some question the validity of the Exodus story while others believe it by faith, the question for me is, why do these Europeans claim ownership of Israel?" They are seen by some as imposters who are using the religion of Judaism/Christianity to claim ownership of a land that is not theirs. It is clear that Nasser knew something that most seem ignorant of. As in the case of Jesus, the Bible tells us who the real Jesus was. The Bible also tells us who the real Hebrew were and they were certainly not Caucasians.

If I haven't been perfectly clear, I believe the Jews settling in the current territory of Israel are not ancestral Hebrews, but rather European who settled there as a result of British occupation of the once-Palestine controlled region.

Who are the Indigenous Hebrews?

Genesis 11:26-31 tells where Terah, Abram's father, raised Abram and his siblings. They were raised in Ur of the Chaldees in Southern Babylonia. The Chaldeans were in earliest times one of many Cushite (Black) tribes inhabiting the great alluvial plain.[6] "The whole of East Africa was called Cush by the Greeks and in modern times "Cushi" is a Hebrew term for Black person."[7] DNA studies have shown that Abraham and his ancestors were of African-Asiatic dominion. This dominion extended from West Africa to India.[8] In Genesis 14:13 the Black Cushite Abram is referred to as, *"Abram the Hebrew"*. In Genesis 17:5 Abram's name is changed to Abraham. Here begins, the long line of Black Hebrew messengers/prophets, continuing all the way to Jesus.

Abraham's father was Cushite and the family was born and raised in the Cushite Empire of Babylonia. There is no reason to suspect that Abraham was anything other than someone of Black Cushite descent. Historical data of that location in that time period of history points to a person of color. He was most certainly not a White or fair-skinned person as pseudo academics and religionists have portrayed him. This misrepresentation is a part of the foundation of white supremacy.

From the Beginning

Four rivers flowed from Eden. The first river is the Pishon that ran the entire land of Havilah, today known as Saudi Arabia, and is now dried up. Its gold spoken of in Genesis 2:11 is still being mined. The second river is the Gihon (Nile). It winds through the entire land of Cush (Ethiopia), according to Genesis 2:13. The former land of Cush is also identified with the country of Sudan. The Nile River and its tributaries run through Egypt, Sudan, and Ethiopia, with tributaries going through many other East African countries. The third river is the Tigris and the fourth is Euphrates says Genesis 2:14. The Euphrates and Tigris both run through Turkey, Iraq, and Syria.[9]

According to Genesis 2:10 -15 it appears that Eden covered a vast area in Africa. If the Christian ecclesiastical establishment; theologians, pastors and missionaries are taught the connection between Black African countries and the Bible/Christianity such information has been given at best sparingly to the flock. Disinformation has been the standard diet. Disassociating ancient Egypt from its African roots claiming that ancient Egyptians were White or fair skinned thus depriving Blacks the glory of their own history. This has been the classic disinformation campaign in the religious and secular domain. Whenever things of prominence point in the direction of Black greatness (as in the case of Abraham) some Whites particularly those in positions of influence often want to claim the glory for themselves and whitewash history. Those who are informed are aware of this deception.

Alkebulan is the oldest known indigenous name for Africa. It means *mother of humanity* or *Garden of Eden*.[10] If you remember In Chapter Six, Count Constantine de Volney makes a significant contribution regarding the

Black identity of ancient Egyptians. Thank you, Count de Volney, for being truthful.

The Black Connection - Dispelling the Delusion of Biblical White Supremacy

In the *Unger's Bible Dictionary* 1981 edition page 442 refers to Ham's four Black sons it states "Cush, Mizraim, and Phut were the progenitors of the tribes that peopled Africa, and Ham's forth son Canaan became the father of those that principally occupied Phoenicia and Palestine. Ham's father Noah had two other sons Shem and Japheth." Genesis 10:6–32 reinforces the Black lineage of Noah and his three sons. Ask yourself this question. If Ham fathered the sons who populated Africa, Phoenicia and Palestine obviously Ham's father Noah had to be Black.

After the flood in Genesis 9:1 Noah and his sons were told to be fruitful and multiply and replenish the earth. For hundreds of years the Caucasian creators of an alternate reality have convinced Whites and Blacks that Black people had no history of note; when in reality Black people laid the foundations of history and are the ancestral race that largely populated the ancient world.

The truth has been hidden in plain sight. According to Unger's Bible Dictionary, Moody Press third edition, it states on page 442; "The Hamitic people are presented in Genesis 10:8-10 as developing earthly imperial power in their first appearance in human history.... They were among the earliest great capitals of the civilized world and were located in the land of Shinar." Shinar "denotes the entire alluvial plain of Babylon between the Tigris River and the Euphrates ....This was the cradle of ancient civilization."

Cush was Ham's eldest son. The kingdom of Cush was also the ancient name of present day Ethiopia in Northeast Africa. Mizraim was Ham's second son. His name was the ancient Hebrew name of Egypt. Phut was Ham's third son. His descendants are those of the North African Amazigh commonly known as the Berbers, a Roman insult meaning Barbarian. The Amazigh are the original inhabitants of Northern Africa. Today these nations include Algeria, Morocco, Tunisia and Libya which is thought to be founded by Phut. At that time the land of Phut was called Phoenicia.[11] Canaan the ancient name of Palestine was named after Ham's fourth son Cannan the father of those who principally occupied Phoenicia and Palestine.[12]

Ur of Chaldeans was in Southern Babylonia, where Tehar, Abraham's father was born, (Genesis 11:26–28). Abraham was the ninth generation from Shem. Shem and Ham were sons of Noah, (Genesis 6:10). Abraham's father was Cushite and the family was born and raised in the Cushite Empire of Babylonia. Moses was married to a Cushite (Ethiopian) woman, Numbers 12:1. As stated, DNA studies have shown that Abraham and his ancestors were of Afro-Asiatic dominion. The Chaldeans were one of many Cushite tribes.[13]

The story of Genesis is the story of Black people and the repopulating of the earth by Noah and his sons; an earth that existed according to archeological findings, millions of years before the flood referenced in the Bible.

Bone fragments at least 35,000 years old were found in a cave in the south region of Romania's Carpathian Mountains. Forensic artist Richard Neave reconstructed the remains into a complete skull. Dating by radiocarbon analysis indicate they may be 36,000 years old. The remains found were much earlier than remains previously found, thought to be white. It would appear from the recreation of the skull that Europe was originally settled by African People.[14]

Some like to repeat the delusion that color does not matter. We know it does matter because for centuries segments of the Caucasian elite, have lied, denied, distorted, ignored, co-opted the history and stole lands of Black and Brown people. *Today, In Israel the killing of unarmed Palestinians and the theft of the land is in plain sight.*

Texe Marrs, one of the world's foremost symbolists and scholar of ancient history and Mystery religions states:

> "According to Christian Evangelicals, Jews are the descendants of Abraham. Those living today who profess to be "Jews" are not of the ancient Israelites, and they are not the seed of Abraham. In fact, DNA research shows that the

> Palestinians actually have more Israelite
> blood than do the "Jews!"[15]

The DNA evidence that Marrs is referring to is the research done by Dr. Eran Elhaik, genetic researcher at the Johns Hopkins University School of Medicine. Elhaik's has "pinpointed the biogeographic origin of the European Jews to the South of Khazaria and not Israel.[16] They are not the seed of Abraham. Today Khazaria would be a part Southern Russia.

Alfred Lilienthal, was a Jewish American, Attorney, writer and anti-Zionist. He stated in the Midwest Magazine on January 6, 1975 "We, the so-called Jewish people, forgot the basic facts of history. In 1948 the Israelis ... drove out tens of thousands from their homeland with Zionist propaganda. Zionist overlook the fact that Judaism (which none of the original Hebrews knew) was a proselytizing religion after Christ. Many of the Europeans were converted to the Jewish faith in places far from Palestine and therefore, were not ethnic to the Holy land."

Other writings by Alfred Lilienthal - *Patriotic American Jew Fought against Zionism,* Justice4poland. com/2019/10/08/Alfred-lilienthal-*patrotic-american-jew-fought against- Zionism.*

George P. Friedman, was a Jewish French sociologist and philosopher. In his book, *The End of the Jewish People,* pointedly states that the European claiming to be Jews, are nothing more than "Hebrew speaking

Gentiles…" Friedman mirrored the views of the late president of Egypt, Gamal Abdel Nasser.[17]

As with all grand deceptions they are spearheaded from the top. For the most part the citizenry accept what they are told and blindly follow. Whitewashed history needs to be exposed for the deception that it is, so that people can build on a foundation of truth.

The Curse

In Genesis 9:25 the curse of Canaan came into play. The Curse had nothing to do with race because at this time it was all about family. This story has been manipulated by the white supremacist elite (the Doctrine of Discovery) and used as a rationalization to kill people of color, steal their land and enslave them; a scheme the wicked continue to use even to this day. Ham in Ancient Hebrew means "Black, hot, burnt". Ham was Black and the logical conclusion would be to assume all others related to Ham were also Black. The deception comes into play by using the so-called Curse on Canaan to represent a curse on all people of color. Of course this is absurd but if you tell a lie long enough it becomes the standard means of operation. Why would Noah curse all people of color because of what his grandson Canaan did or didn't do? This would be like Noah cursing his own Black self. Noah was not cursing people of color. The Bible makes that clear. Gen. 9:25 states "... Cursed be Canaan a servant of servants shall <u>he</u> be unto his brethren." *His brethren were not white.* Noah was referring to Canaan the individual and or the Canaanite nation; a nation that has not existed from around 2300 BC.[17a] The enemies of people of color have skillfully and diabolically used and continue to use Gen 9:25 to rationalize and justify the global destruction of Black and Brown people. The lie of perpetual servitude for people of color to serve White people has been a clever deception crafted and perpetuated for centuries.

The origin of this deception transpired during the leadership of Pope Urban the Second in 1095. He gave his blessing to European kings to "discover" and claim land of non-Christians. Also In 1452 Pope Nicholas V declared war on all non- Christians. He promoted the plundering, stealing of land, killing and perpetual enslavement of indigenous people. Columbus and others carried out their acts of barbarism under the cover of the Doctrine of Discovery, Manifest Destiny and other barbaric mandates coined by their religious and political leaders.[18] Robert Morales is the chief negotiator for the Hui'qumi'nu treaty group in Vancouver Island in British Columbia Canada. He writes regarding some of the intricacies of the Doctrine of Discovery as he works to regain indigenous lands. The treaty group consist of six indigenous first nations working to end the legacy of colonialism, and regain title and rights to their land.[19]

Catholic, Protestant and Jewish Religions,
have been the heart of an age old system

of subterfuge, designed to steal land from
indigenous people, enslaves and kill them.
- Sterling Anderson

The North African Amazigh / "Berber"

Today North African countries are ruled by fair skinned inhabitances a part of the worldwide cabal that suppresses dark skinned people. The fair skinned leaders of Egypt, Algeria, Morocco, Tunisia, and Libya including Arabia suppress millions of the indigenous populations.

The Berbers are 35% of the total population in Morocco's 28,000,000. In Algeria they are 15% of the total population of 10,000,000 – Libya 470,000 - Tunisia 86,000, Egypt has a population of 10,000 Berbers and also has its indigenous Black population of three to four million Nubians. Outside of North Africa there are about 2.5 million Berbers in Mali, Niger and Burkina Faso.[20] Dr. Moses Ochone, of Vanderbilt University states:

> Arab racism is so deep it is inscribed in the semantics of the Arab language. To this day, the generic word for Black is "abd" which translates to slave, this among many other racially-loaded ones, applies though out the Arab speaking world, regardless of dialect and

orthography… The only way for Blacks
to gain social mobility in the Arab world
is to become a soccer star…[21]

Before the Ottoman Empire there was no such thing
as the Middle East; it was all Africa (atruearab.blogspot.
com). Egyptologists/archeologists have brought to light
the wonders of ancient Egyptian civilization, but also
that of the Nubians who were contemporaries of the
ancient Egyptians. Alongside Egypt, the Nubians had
developed their own civilization. Nubians pharaohs also
reigned in Egypt. They along with the Egyptians and
Amazigh are indigenous to North Africa, inhabiting
this area for thousands of years before European or
Arab, Islamic contact.[22]

Corippus, in the 6th century used the phrase "facies
nigroque colorus" meaning "faces or appearances of
black color" to describe the North African Berbers in
his book *Johannis.* Procopius in Book IV of *History of
War* says that the Vandals who settled in North Africa
were not black – skinned like the Mauri (Moors) also
classified as ancient Amazigh/Berbers.[23]

"Westerns have chosen to concentrate on the most
recent world of the Arab and Berber speaking people
and present it as if it is a world that has always been. It
is like comparing the Aztecs of five-hundred years ago
with the ethnic mix of America today."[24]

The Amazigh are the descendants of the pre-Arab
inhabitants of North Africa. They are the name of
a race descended from Noah. They belong to the

Afro-Asiatic family; related to ancient Egyptian.[25] The name Berber is a insult the Romans coined for Barbarian who by original definition the Romans were barbarians themselves. Late in the Roman Empire, the word barbarian came to refer to all foreigners who lacked Greek and Roman traditions.[26] The Berber's proper cultural name is Amazigh which historically was identified as meaning "free-man," to be purified of excess...[27]

The Ancient Story of the So-Called African American

In 2019, Blacks in America with the surnames of their ex-slave masters would have had a history of captivity in America for exactly 400 years counting from 1619 the widely accepted date of African slaves being brought over to the Americas via the Trans-Atlantic slave trade. Genesis 15:13 "They shall afflict them for four hundred years." Some believe this is referring to the 400 year period of time that Blacks will be in bondage in America, symbolized by the Israelites bondage in Egypt. Deuteronomy 28:63, "So it will please him to ruin and destroy you. You will be uprooted from the land you are entering to possess..." As part of the warning, God says in Deuteronomy 28:68, "The Lord will send you back to Egypt in ships." – which I suspected is a reference to the Trans-Atlantic Slave Trade that brought Africans to the "New World" with

Egypt used to symbolize America. Could it be more than symbolism?

The following story as fantastic as it may sound indicates the presence of ancient Egyptians in North America. The finding of the Ten Commandments written in ancient Paleo – Hebrew on an 80 ton stone in Los Lunas, New Mexico is an indication that there was a Hebrew presence in this part of the world. According to Harvard scholar Robert Pfeiffer, expert in Semitic languages, this form of writing was used over a thousand years ago.[28] The Bat Creek Stone is another indication that ancient Hebrews were in North America long before Columbus.[29] Mainstream archeologists and religionist refute such notions. Deuteronomy 28:64, "And the Lord shall scatter thee among all people, from the one end of the earth even unto the other…." It would not surprise me that Hebrews were in ancient America. The Bible is the "wonderful word of God" as long as it is being manipulated to back up the lies of white supremacy. The existence of ancient Hebrew and Egyptians in America would give a new meaning to the scripture "I'll send you back to Egypt in ships"… Deuteronomy 28:68

Egyptians, Grand Canyon and American Mounds

On April 5, 1909, a front page article in the Arizona Gazette reported a detailed account of an archaeological expedition led by G.E Kinkaid that described an extraordinary cave site in the Grand Canyon. Kinkaid's expedition had been funded by the Smithsonian to investigate information that was reported by John Wesley Powell. Powell was the Director of the U.S. Geological Survey 1881-1884. In 1869 he reported an underground network of a great citadel of well-constructed rooms; one large enough to hold a population of 50,000 people. Mummies and various artifacts of Egyptian and Oriental origin were found; some displaying exquisite workmanship. The article however, was written anonymously. When the Smithsonian was questioned about the discovery, they said, they could not find any records of the Kinkaid and Jordan expedition that was sent to investigate the information given by Powell. On March, 12, 1909, the Gazette had reported an earlier phase of Kinkaid's explorations, *"G.E. Kinkaid Reaches Yuma."* How is it that the Smithsonian had no information on these individuals when it was the Smithsonian that hired them? Remember, the article was written anonymously. It is quite possible the writer was putting him or herself in jeopardy for leaking the story to the Gazette. During that time, certain information, much like today, was not meant for public consumption. I believe the mainstream academics and selected elites have a time line of history that they have a vested interest in maintaining. They do not want to hear opposition to their orthodoxy, or questioning of their beliefs and their legitimacy.

The Smithsonian is governed by a 17 − member board of officials as specified in the Smithsonian

Charter: Eight regents are government officials and
nine are from the general public chosen by a board and
approved by a joint resolution of Congress. This board
also administers the Smithsonian's budget. The denial
of the caves existence and of those men who explored
them seems consistent when you consider the powers
that ultimately control the Smithsonian. The Elites
have always told us their version of history and only
what they want us to know.

The public knows little regarding the history
of America prior to European arrival. Thousands
of mounds and pyramids of various sizes and styles
covered by centuries of vegetation dotted the North
American landscape. Once uncovered, they were
found to be gravesites and living quarters of an ancient
people. Many were looted and destroyed by settlers.
Others, the Smithsonian examined. Their contents held
valuable information about the past and even items
of priceless monetary value. Some of these structures
remain today; Cahokia Mound in Missouri, Monks
Mound in Illinois and the Poverty Point Mound sites
in Louisiana are just a few examples. Some historical
sites and monuments rival the great pyramids of Egypt.
This amazing information is not generally known but
has been made known through the internet.[30]

Is there a cover-up? Do your research! I encourage
those drawn to videos not to ignore the written word.
From Babylon to Timbuktu by Rudolph R. Windsor and
Dr. Clyde Winters's, *African Empires in Ancient America*
are historical gems. Both writers are African American

Scholars. *Rasta Livewire.com* is another great resource that addresses concerns of people of color.

The further you go back in time, the closer you get to the truth. - Sterling Anderson

Chapter Eight

Systems of Suppression

Unions, Politicians, and Prevailing Wage

Parents want what's best for their children. Nana and her parents were no exception. Opportunity is crucial in one's ability to succeed. I was told in the 60's that predominantly White youth were recruited from in the inner-city schools by White tradesmen to become apprentices in the building trade unions. Black youth were discriminated against. Whether or not this was true, the fact remained that very few Blacks were in unions at this time.

The Bacon Davis Act was passed by Congress in 1934 with the strong support of labor unions. This Act required construction firms contracting for the federal government to pay their workers locally prevailing wages. It was passed by lawmakers with the explicit intention of keeping African American workers out of federal construction projects. The American Federation of Labor (the "AFL" of today's AFL- CIO) president William Green testified that "Colored labor is being sought to demoralize wage rates."[1] When African American tradesmen left the South to get work in the North, they were competition for White workers. Their rates were cheaper, and their quality of work was equal if not superior to their White counterparts. As a means to eliminate the competition, unions were formed, establishing a set wage for labor, the prevailing wage. This was an attempt to prevent being underbid. Federal government and often state government construction contracts adhered to prevailing wage law and often hired only union workers. Minorities suffered on both counts. They were not union workers and they could not underbid other contractors because of prevailing wage laws. Eliminating prevailing wage would even the playing field so that minority craftspeople could bid on public projects.[2]

Professor David E. Bernstein reported:

> "Many New York construction unions, led by the electrical workers Local 3 and the plumbers Local 2, adamantly refused to admit African American members. The electricians' charter specifically limited membership to White males. For decades, some officials tried to open union membership to minority workers…. For example, in 1971, Mayor John Lindsay of New York shut down hundreds of millions of dollars in city construction for seven months to try to

force minority-hiring concessions from
the building trades. The results proved
to be minimal.

Today, 50 years after historic civil-rights legislation
broke barriers in public accommodations, voting,
education, housing and employment, New York
building trade unions remain subject to persistent
complaints from African-Americans about lingering
discrimination by construction unions – as evidenced
by historic fines levied against the sheet-metal workers
after a 44-year litigation."[3]

Recent Advancements

For centuries, road blocks have impeded Black
advancement in the building trades. In New York, from
2006 to 2015 apprenticeships rose from 18.3 percent
in 1994 to 35.1 percent in 2014. The share of total
jobs went up to 21.2 percent in the New York Union
construction sector. It was a positive trend for New
York. Was it a positive trend for the nation?[4]

According to, Cherrie Bucknor, during a
progressive think tank meeting in Washington D.C.,
"Black workers are more likely than workers of any
other race or ethnicity to be unionized." Research The
numbers in New York give credence to the Center
for Economic Policy and Research (CEPR) findings.[5]
Workers in the Northeast and Pacific region were likely
to be unionized. Twenty eight states in the Southern,

Midwestern and interior Western states are, however, Right–to-Work states. Unions are discouraged and wages are lower. President Obama said this about Right-to-Work supporters, "What they are really talking about is giving you the right to work for less money." Unions are the prime vehicles that enabled Black Americans and others to be able to move into the middle class. The struggle of workers and unions won the 8 hour work day, work breaks, sick time, and time and a half, paid vacations, increased wages and work place safety. When necessary unions fought on behalf of workers job security. Without the organizing power of unions, workers were at the mercy of their employers.

Unions provide a balance between the interest of employers and their employees. According to Saharra Griffin and Malkie Wall, research assistants for Economic Policy at the Center for American Progress Action Fund, some of the unionized progress is threatened by President Trump's anti-labor policies; weakening gains by not requiring employers to pay overtime for work done over 40 hours - awarding billions in federal contracts to companies that violated wage laws – "tip pooling," (not allowing people to keep their individual tips) - canceling of the requirement of employer's need to report workplace injuries or illnesses to the Occupational Safety and Health Administration (OSHA) - The Fair Play and Safe Workplace rule - the banning of government contracts from going to companies with poor safety or labor records – Restricting worker power and attacking unions making it more difficult for workers to unionize – threatening worker's retirement savings and undermining anti-discrimination. Rescinding these policies not only weaken unions but also negatively affect the lives of citizens. It seems that another Trump presidency or a president similar to him may benefit business owners but will diminish gains made by workers and unions.[6]

Teacher strikes in 2018 and the September 2019 GM strike of 48,000 workers may have been a wakeup call for their employers. Workers would no longer accept employer's rules of the game. Wage inequality, corporate greed and Medicare for all were the rallying cries among the public and Democrats attempting to get their party's 2020 nomination. Would Democrats play it safe and pick a moderated candidate? This was one of the reasons I believe that Hilary Clinton was defeated and Donald Trump was elected president. He was a contrast to the status quo. Many like myself now think he was not the contrast America needed. I think it is safe to say that almost any Democrat presently running for the presidency would be an improvement over the present state of affairs.

Substance Abuse

There are multitudes of racially targeted schemes devised by those in power. The saturation of liquor stores in low-income Black communities are one of them. In a June 2000 study by John Hopkins School of

Public Health, researchers showed that "predominantly Black, low income neighborhoods in Baltimore were eight times more likely to have carry-out liquor stores than in White or racially integrated neighborhoods."[7]

Drugs have also been a plague in Black communities but it has been a boondoggle for states and local governments. The passing of the Harrison Narcotics Tax Act on December 17, 1914 could be seen as the genius of once again rationalizing the abuse of Black citizens. Months before its passing into law there was a propaganda campaign by those who had an interest in its passing the tax act. On February 8, 1914 the New York Times posted a racist diatribe, "Negro Cocaine Fiends" echoing southern racist sentiments. The myth of the "cocaine crazed Negro" was used in the south to justify heinous acts against African American; it was also used by proponents as ammunition to see to it that the Harrison Act became law. The Harrison Act required all persons involved with the handling of Opium and Coca products to register with collectors of the internal revenue. The Act and those policies that have followed have simply morphed into systems that fund state and local governments at the expense of Black communities where hundreds of thousands are criminalized and imprisoned for using the smallest amount of drugs often as a pretexts to acquire government funds.[8]

The Religious Scheme

Liquor stores are not the only things on the corners of Black communities. Churches are equally as prevalent. I believe that they are another system of suppression. Religion seems to me to be just another tool in the toolbox of the White capitalist system. I think religion has been used to keep the masses in a dream state filled with hopes, wishes, and magical thinking. People in power have used this method for eons because it works so well. On the internet estimates are rampant regarding the billions of dollars religious leaders have fleeced from their flocks and selfishly misused for lavish lifestyles. These accusations include both White and Black churches. What else is new? Misallocation of funds by businesses seems to be a common practice in America. The only difference is that some churches prey on the people in the name of God. Money is not the only concern regarding the failings of the religious community. The churches moral failing are often glaring in the mainstream press, thus further diminishing confidence in religious institutions.

The billions of dollars I am referencing is not talking about the Church as a whole in America. In general church members are usually encouraged to give 10 percent in tithes including other offerings often requested during church meetings. Rent / mortgage, upkeep, salaries, utilities and other miscellaneous expensive are taken out of these weekly totals. Most churches in America are small to moderate size run by men and woman who I believe for the most part feel called to what they are doing and aren't trying to swindle anybody. If they are making a profit they are fortunate. The concerns have been among leaders of mega churches where lavish personal spending has been found. Accountability is a real issue; since the money is not taxed funds can be easily compromised. In most churches, the ushers and/or deacons collect the money usually by "passing the plate." It is then given to the pastor, after which there may be little or no accountability particularly in churches not connected to a higher governing authority.

It is crucial to have accounting systems in place that are transparent to the members. This diminishes the possibility of misuse of funds but by no means eradicates it. Honest leadership is the key to corruption free organizations.

First Corinthians 9:11 asks, "If we have sown spiritual seed among you, is it too much if we reap a material harvest from you?" First Timothy 5:17–18 …"The worker deserves his/her wages." Other verses have been used to manipulate the faithful into giving beyond their means and feeling justified in doing so. It is not uncommon to hear church members making excuses for over-the-top lifestyles and building projects of their leaders while using these and other scriptures for justification. If you give people an emotional high once or twice a week combined with a guilt trip, the money pours in. Until profits are taxed, accountability is difficult, perhaps even impossible.

If we have not learned to chart our own spiritual paths, others will chart it and sometimes profit at our expense. Multitudes chase after individuals looking for a "touch from God", fawning over and idolizing so-called "men and woman of God" looking for emotions and external stimuli to guide them.

The late Dr. Love Henry Whelchel, professor of church history at the Interdenominational Theological Center (ITC) stated in a class on YouTube, "The church has gotten caught up in materialism and greed. Many ministers today want to live like celebrities. In other words, instead of the church standing with the community, the church has become self-serving. It has turned away from its mission."

Professor Whelchel's point is well made. Black churches however have been at the forefront of social change for Black Americans and have also laid a foundation for how social movements in general approach societal and cultural change. We must remember that the Black church is not a monolith. It is comprised of many separate entities. One must be careful not to insinuate that all Black churches are in some sort of financial or moral quandary and have fallen away from their perceived mission. These concerns are not unique to the Black church. They are of concern for all churches. There are those that propose that churches should pay taxes. It would bring in billions in tax revenue and decrease the temptation of financial mismanagement. It would also limit the hold that the government has over churches by eliminating the threat of withholding their tax exempt status if churches do not conform to government expectations. Taxing religious institutions, in my opinion, is long overdue.

Dr. Whelchel, April 6, 2013 at (ITC) lecturing on African American Church History said of those who concentrate their loyalty to a church or an individual:

> "Black people are the most spiritual people in America…because of our struggle. I didn't say religious, spiritual. I don't need to go to church; all these institutions, church will mess you up. They will confuse you. I don't need all that. You need spirituality. That's where it is." "God is a spirit. They who worship, worship Him in spirit and truth."

Repression through Highway Construction and City Destruction;

The construction of the highway systems across America was another weapon used in the suppression and destruction of African American communities. These construction projects were always in the name of "improving transportation efficiency."

"When policy makers and highway engineers determined that the new interstate highway system should penetrate to the heart of the central cities, they made a fateful decision, but also a purposeful one. Indeed, the interstate system's urban expressways, or freeways, not only penetrated the cities but they ripped through residential neighborhoods and leveled wide swaths of urban territory, ostensibly to facilitate auto mobility. In retrospect, it now seems apparent that public officials and policy makers, especially at the state and local level, used expressway construction to destroy low-income and especially black neighborhoods in an effort to reshape the physical and racial landscapes of the postwar American cities."[9]

Transportation Secretary Anthony Foxx, under President Obama acknowledged the destruction that highway systems across America had brought upon African American communities:

> "We now know—overwhelmingly—that our urban freeways were almost always routed through low-income and minority neighborhoods, creating disconnections from opportunity that exist to this day. Between highway construction and urban renewal, roughly two-thirds of the families displaced were poor and mostly African American."

Urban renewal and highway construction was rampant throughout Boston in the 1950's and 60's. I grew up in Roxbury, a predominantly African American section of Boston. I remember rows of tenement housing on Tremont Street being demolished. Many years later, Tremont Street was expanded into a four lane thruway and the site of the MBTA's (Massachusetts Bay Transportation Authority) underground public transportation system. What became of the Black residents who lived on Tremont Street? Other communities destroyed in the name of transportation improvement are as follows;

- Miami: "I-95 cut the heart out of Overtown, a thriving black community."
- New York City: "They call the Staten Island Expressway the Mason-Dixon Line."
- Los Angeles: "The Century Expressway was one of seven freeways that led to decay in African American and Latino communities."
- Seattle: "I-5 was built through the city's oldest blue-collar community, despite residents' concerns they'd be isolated from the rest of the city."
- Baltimore: Urban Planner "Robert Moses wanted to plow through a West Baltimore community known as Harlem Park, a then-thriving middle-class African American neighborhood. Harlem Park was destroyed before the project was stopped."[10]

Highway systems all over the country created physical barriers between the races. In Milwaukee, Highway 41 and Interstate 94, along with railways and other barriers, effectively separated the races from one another. There are other places where highways were used to segregate the races, including Pittsburgh, Pennsylvania - Shreveport, Louisiana - Hartford, Connecticut and Tampa, Florida. Lower standards of living resulted from these barriers, cutting off communities from the economic vibrancy of shopping centers, job availability, transportation routes, etc.[11]

Emily Badger reports:

> After the police shooting and death of Philando Castile, activists occupied a highway that, a half-century ago, was constructed at the expense of St. Paul's historically Black community. Interstate 94, like urban highways throughout the country, was built by erasing what had been Black homes, dispersing their residents, severing their neighborhoods and separating them from Whites who would pass through at high speed.[12]

Rampage against Black Cities:

The Wilmington Coup

The destruction of Black communities caused by racist highway planning has its historical partner-in-crime by violent invasions into Black communities. On November 10, 1898 in the thriving seaport town of Wilmington, North Carolina, a massacre occurred. Blacks were doing well economically; they along with White progressive Republicans gained control of the political levers of power. Democrats pledged to change that in the upcoming election. The Democrat vote prevailed and voted in their mayor and city councilors. Emboldened by their victory they demanded the Black owned Wilmington Daily Record newspaper be shut down. Alexander Manly the owner was hated; because he would respond to the racist writings in the White owned Observer Newspaper. The day after their victory on November 10, 1898, White Democrats formed a coup to violently take over Wilmington. A mob of approximately a 1000 or more, led by Alfred M. Waddell, a former U.S. military officer and Congressmen included clergymen, lawyers, bankers, merchants and a white supremacist group called the Red Shirts, burned down the Wilmington Daily Record, destroyed and confiscated Black homes and forced 1400 or more Black citizens to flee. It was reported that twenty-five Blacks were killed though it is suspected that hundreds of Black people were killed and dumped into the Cape Fear River.[13]

The 1919 Rampage against Black Chicagoans

In Chicago, Illinois from July 27 to August 3, 1919, after eight days of violence, upwards of 1000 Black families lost their homes as Whites rampaged through segregated Black neighborhoods. Five hundred were injured. Fifteen Whites and twenty-three Blacks were allegedly killed. The violence was sparked by the death of Eugene Williams, an African-American teenager who accidently crossed a segregated boundary at the beach where he was swimming. Some White beach goers threw rocks at the young man. One hit him in the head causing him to drown. This incident incited a commotion as knowledge of it spread throughout the city. White gangs took advantage of the situation and started accosting Black men. This started the worst racially relate violence in Chicago's history. President Woodrow Wilson in a rare rebuke castigated the Whites as "the aggressor" in the Chicago Uprising.[14]

The Tulsa Oklahoma Massacre of Blacks

The Greenwood area in Tulsa, Oklahoma flourished in 1910 as a result of the oil boom. Blacks enjoyed an above average standard of living. Blacks having anything of value had always been disturbing for some Whites. On June 1, 1921 in the Black Community of Tulsa, a Massacre occurred. Over 800 people were treated for injuries, an estimated 300 Black residents were killed and more than 1000 homes and businesses were destroyed. Over thirty-five city blocks were ravaged. Homes and business including those in Black Wall Street (the most prominent Black business area in the country) were looted and burned. This catastrophe took place as a result of an unsuccessful attempt by an armed White mob to lynch a Black man being held by authorities for an alleged assault of a White woman. A group of Black men went to the local jail to assist in the protection of the accused man. Authorities turned them away. As they were leaving, a White man attempted to disarm a Black veteran. A shot rang out and a riot ensued. This was only a pretense to commit the acts that followed. Thousands of Whites gathered as a result of the incident. Outnumbered Blacks tried to defend their community but did not stand a chance. Instead of trying to stop the violence against the Black community, local police officers joined in the carnage. The community was destroyed.[15]

Elaine Massacre of 1919

When you consider what was happening to people of color all over America in the 18th century the following slaughter was probably not as unusual as one might think. In Elaine, Arkansas in 1919, a White mob began shooting into a Black church. In the process of this criminal act, one of the perpetrators was killed.

Vigilantes, police and military personnel armed with seven machine guns gathered. From Oct. 1st through the 7th hundreds of men woman and children were slaughtered, property was confiscated and destroyed. Black people were hunted over a 200 – mile radius. There are multitudes of similar stories fueled by the evil delusions of white superiority: these are just a few examples.[16]

Now You Have It, Now You Don't (the Subprime Scandal)

There are those who break free of some of the systemized suppression and are able to buy their own homes. There is indeed a Black middle class, though they are at the mercy of those who rig the economy for their own benefit. In the last economic disaster beginning in 2000-2008 Subprime loans had been issued to those with credit scores in the 600's or below. It was estimated that the total loss of wealth for minorities was $164 to $213 billion. This is believed to have represented the greatest loss of wealth for people of color in modern history. Black/African Americans lost approximately $71 billion to $92 billion, while Latino borrowers lost between $75 billion to $98 billion. Whites would have been 44.5% higher and losses for people of color would have been about 24% lower if subprime loans had been distributed fairly.[17]

Borrowers do have to take responsibility for their loans however the ultimate cause for the subprime loan crisis lay squarely on the shoulders of financial institutions who in their quest for profits made risky loans. According to Emily Badger, *The Dramatic Racial Bias of Subprime Lending During the Housing Boom*, Bloomberg 08/16/2013, minority customers who were financially qualified for a prime mortgage rate were shifted into a subprime mortgage that had higher closing costs, adjustable interest rates and other fees designed to protect banks from default. Minorities were more than two times more likely than whites to receive high cost loans. Banks who fraudulently put qualified minorities in subprime loans were guaranteed they would get a mortgage payment without fear of default while charging unwarranted fees; a windfall for lending institutions. Minority families were susceptible to this scam because for so long minorities communities had been ignored by banks. Now they were being targeted "because they weren't risky", a practice referred to as "reverse-redlining." "In 2006.... Black and Hispanic families making more than $200,000 a year were more likely on average to be given a subprime loan than a white family making less than $30,000 a year."[17a] This is additional proof that structural, systematic racism was in play and there is no reason to suspect that such practices have stopped.

A Common Response

It is common to hear those of European decent speak of the prejudice their forbearers experienced when they came to America. In some circumstances they do so as a way to distract from or minimize the African American responses to present-day injustices. When I hear this response from some Europeans, I believe it is their way of equating their experience to the African American experience. When was the last time you heard descendants of Europeans fighting for civil rights, protesting against police brutality and decrying frequent murders of unarmed White men?

The Scourge of Racism

Blacks, despite the intentional historical roadblocks previously mentioned, are told to "Pick yourself up by your bootstraps." When Blacks attempted to overcome systematic racism by developing their own communities, they were punished. "You're damned if you do and damned if you don't."

Little will change in current-day America until the American leadership class, politicians, law enforcement, church leaders and others in positions of authority can acknowledge and rectify their own deep-rooted racist views of the world. Until such a resolution occurs, minorities will continue to pay a price; in many cases a severe one. Sadly, many of those in authority will pass on the scourge of racism to others as they have done until this day. It seems like a never-ending cycle. In the 2020's, racism is not only alive, but it is thriving; spurred on once again by the "leaders."

It is easy to fall into cynicism as a result of the anti-minority sentiment that exists in America. That is exactly what some politicians want; folks to give up the fight for progress. Politicians continue to use lies and fear to ignite hostility between Whites and Blacks. For many this is their bread and butter; it is how they have achieved power and maintain it. In 2022 you continue to see the champions of division in full force trying to turn back the clock on racial equity, woman's rights, and democracy, by interfering with free and fair elections.

I think to some degree all have been infected by the scourge of racism. Centuries of divisive volatile rhetoric spewed from the mouth of influencers, particularly politicians have created an uneasy and even toxic environment between the races. Finally, it is the individual's responsibility to oppose propaganda that is designed to foster division and hostility. Examine stories you are told. Are they true? Seeking answers earnestly can lead to a greater understanding of self and others. Ask yourself do my feelings line up with my faith and values?

Protests initiated by the Black Lives Matter Movement were crucial in stirring the conscience of a nation that minimizes racial injustice. The police killing of George Floyd on May 25, 2020 and the voices of protesters have made it clear to at least a part of White America the seriousness of racism in this country. Some in positions of power have given more than lip service to the reasonable demands of protesters. It is questionable whether or not Floyd's death will be a catalyst for real change i.e. dismantling the mechanisms of structural racism. There is a lot of heat and fire in the midst of traumatic events that eventually cools and reverts back to business as usual. Structural racism has been a fundamental part of the operation of America. Changing it will require a Herculean effort and spirit. In my opinion there seemed to be no such desire in the Trump administration. To be fair, racism has been left to fester in American society for centuries. As I work on this section of the book in 2020 we are still in the throes of racial protest in response to the killing of George Floyd, the COVID-19 pandemic is raging, historic unemployment and a contentious presidential campaign heading into the November 2020 election are all in play.

The Kenosha Shootings

In the Kenosha, Wisconsin August 25, 2020 armed white supremacist groups gathered in opposition to unarmed peaceful protesters. Two White protesters; Joseph Rosenbaum, 36 and Anthony Huber, 26 were killed by Kyle Rittenhouse, a 17 year old gun totting alleged supremacist: Gaige Grosskreutz was injured. President Trump's focus was on law and order instead of on the shootings. He referenced the sporadic looting and the setting of fires which was taking place separate from the peaceful protest. The unspoken assumption was that these acts of criminality were committed by the protesters. It is suspected however that these were not connected with the peaceful protest but were instead opportunistic acts or acts committed intentionally to discredit the protest movement. Peaceful protesters were lumped together with the rioters while gun toting white supremacist were given a pass by the president. Even the killing of unarmed protesters has been excused by many on the left.

The Unite the Right Rally

President Trump's action were similar when describing far-right attackers who on August 12, 2017 in Charlottesville, Virginia carried guns and assaulted the anti-Trump protesters. At that protest, 32 year old Heather Heyer was killed by a driver intentionally running into the anti-Trump protesters. Instead of condemning and calling out by name the white supremacist groups who incited the violence, the President stated, "there were very fine people on both sides". Even Republicans called out the president for not taking a stronger stance against white supremacist groups. I believe far right extremist groups and their sympathizers have been emboldened during the Trump administration as a result of him not doing enough to condemn them.

The neo-Nazi website the Daily Stormer, reacting to Trump's words on the Saturday after the incident in Charlottesville, praised the President's comments as "good." "He didn't attack us. He just said the nation should come together. Nothing specific against us" wrote Andrew Anglin, the website's founder. "No condemnation at all" Anglin continued. "When asked to condemn, he just walked out of the room. Really, really good, God bless him."[18]

Investigative Journalist Jason Wilson reported that hate groups have grown 55% in the Trump era. He goes on to explain the President's indifference to the appeals of protesters for an end to police killings of unarmed Black people portends increased dangers for Blacks in America.[19,20]

I believe indifference to civil, human rights and disrespect for the rule of law will continue long after Trump's presidency.

Chapter Nine

Killing the Leaders and Destroying Alkebulan Civilizations

Alkebulan is the oldest known indigenous name for Africa. It was called this before Europeans knew of Africa's existence. African scholar Dr. Cheikh Anah Diop explains, the ancient name of Africa was "Alkebulan meaning "Mother of Mankind" or "garden of Eden."[1]

Killing the Leaders

In "Redemption Song", Bob Marley Bob asked "How long shall they kill our prophets while we stand aside and look?" When will enough be enough?

"Patrice Lumumba, prime minister of newly independent Congo, was the second of five leaders of independence movements in African countries to be assassinated in the 1960s by their former colonial masters, or their agents."[2]

Scores of African leaders have since been assassinated. Africa's disarray is directly connected to the discrediting and killing of African leaders. Their names should not be forgotten. In this chapter I want to remember some of those leaders who have sacrificed their lives for their people and their country. The following is a brief acknowledgement:

> **Sekou Toure,** became the first African president of Guinea. His, was the only country who voted "no" to French rule

After the Algerian revolution against French rule (1954-1962), the French, in order to avoid other revolutions devised a strategy that would allow French colonies to vote for or against remaining a member in the "French Community". A "yes" vote would mean that France would continue their over 100 year rule in Guinea. A "no" vote represented independence from French rule. On October 2, 1958, Guinea was the first and only African colony that voted to reject General Charles de Gaulle's plea for them to remain under French rule. The French made an immediate withdrawal from Guinea but before they left they destroyed government records and infrastructure. Toure is famously known for being the first African leader to say "no" to France. He set the stage along with the Algerian revolution for other French colonies to have the courage to seek their independence.[3]

Sylvanus Olympio

Togo, a West African country, had been under European domination since the beginning of the slave trade in the 16th century. Sylvanus Olympio was the first elected president of Togo. He came from a prestigious family; graduated from the London School of Economics, and used his abilities in the service of the Togolese people. He was elected prime minister in 1958 and led his country to independence from France in 1960. In 1961 he was elected president.

President Olympio, in an attempt to avoid the destruction that France had unleashed in Guinea, agreed to pay forty percent of his country's budget to France. This made it impossible for Togo to become self-sufficient. Togo began printing its own currency in an attempt to break away from France's strangle hold.

On January 13, 1963, three days after printing started President Olympio was assassinated in what was speculated a French supported coup. Gnassingbe Eyadema one of the killers involved with the assassination installed himself as dictator. He remained in power until his death in 2005. Today Togo "is ruled by the most repressive totalitarian neocolonial puppet regime aided and abetted by France, USA, Israel and the UK."[4]

Thomas Sankara, became president of Upper Volta, a land locked West African country in August 1983, after the breakup of the Ouedraogo government. He renamed the country Burkina Faso (land of upright people). Sankara had a love for his people, a quality not admired by the French colonial powers and those they used to enforce their rule. During his four years as president, his accomplishments were extraordinary. He vaccinated 2.5 million against meningitis, yellow fever, and measles. There was more than a 50 percent increase in literacy from 1983 to 1987. He placed women in positions of power, banned the practice of female genital mutilation, and eliminated forced marriage and polygamy in support of women's rights. He eliminated the use of expensive government vehicles, switching from Mercedes -Benz cars to Renaults. He refused air conditioning and other amenities because the people did not have them. He rejected help from ex-colonizers. He instead pooled the resources of the people so they could produce their own food, build roads, and care for themselves. President Sankara set a high standard for other African leaders. In October 1987 he was assassinated. His death profited France and those who France used to enforce its will; while the rest of the population suffered.[5]

Patrice Lumumba, is one of the most recognized revolutionary African leaders. He was the first democratically elected prime minister of the Democratic Republic of the Congo in Central Africa. Lumumba's resistance to Belgium rule and the United States in the affairs of his country made him an obstacle to their continued extraction of natural resources and exploitation of the Congolese people. The mining of uranium from Congolese mines enabled the United States to construct the first atomic bombs that destroyed Hiroshima and Nagasaki.

America's use of these weapons under the leadership of President Harry S. Truman triggered the worldwide arms race, which has continued to this day. It was in this climate that Lumumba sought independence from Belgium and the U.S. He was assassinated on June 17, 1961 approximately six months after Congolese independence. Fifty years after his death, the name Lumumba resonates as a symbol of independence and freedom for Africans.[6]

Muammar Qaddafi, became another victim of the western empires; America and (NATO) the North American Treaty Organization. We were told by President Obama the invasion of Libya was because of Human Rights violations and Qaddafi's military adventurism. "Adventurism.", America's hypocrisy is breath-taking. I think America's creation and continued existence is based on the exploitation of the weak. Those who complain about Qaddafi have and continue to use Africa as their feeding grounds to prop up their own economies. The historic and ongoing exploitation of Africa by Western powers cast serious doubt on the claim they want to "help" Libya. It seems that every time American politicians claim they want to "help the people" millions of unarmed poor civilians die in the wake of their actions.

America's sophisticated system of Propaganda can make you believe almost anything if you're unwilling to question what your being told. The so-called free and independent media often simply echo what they are told by the government; the news coverage of Vietnam, Iraq, and Afghanistan are just a few examples of how the government used the media to purvey its propaganda and sway public opinion to justify their actions. In chapter fifteen Major General Smedley Butler, opens up a Pandora's Box of truth; detailing his part in America's destruction of countries to maintain and advance America's so-called "exceptionalism".

On September 1, 1969 Qaddafi overthrew King Idris the Libyan puppet leader for the West, resulting in America's being tossed out of Libya; losing its largest military base abroad.

In 1971 with the demise of the Gold Standard, Saudi Arabia and the United States agreed the petrodollar would be used as the reserve currency. This meant that all oil transactions had to be done in dollars. Libya had freed itself from the petrodollar and western debt; both means by which western powers control Africa.

RASCOM (Regional African Satellite Communication Organization) spear headed by Qaddafi was formed in 1992; 45 African nations with the aim to bring down the cost of communication on the African Continent. Africa was paying a total of $500 million a year in satellite fees to French and other European companies and paying the highest call charges in the world. In December of 2007 after 15 years of work,

Africa brought its vision of its own telecommunication system into being. This required bypassing the World Bank and the International Monetary Fund (IMF) because of their high interest rates.[7]

2011: On the 19th of March 2011 a multi-state military intervention was led by NATO against Libya and Qaddafi's regime. Initial reports from the United Nations Security Council stated that the intervention was to prevent Islamist extremism and terrorism going on in the state, citing "crimes against humanity." The U.N. forced a no-fly zone, a travel ban, and froze the assets of Qaddafi and other Libyan officials. President Obama ordered air strikes on the country. On October 20, of 2011 Qaddafi was brutally killed by forces of the National Transitional Council – a group which was recognized by the U.N. A formal review of the military intervention in 2016 by the British Parliament Affairs Select Committee determined that the western nations had outright exaggerated the talks of crimes against humanity, and played up the threat of Islamist Extremism in the country to justify their war. The intervention was criticized to have been about resources, and caused a political and humanitarian crisis in Libya – which the "intervention" was supposed to have solved.[8] The Libyan, Qaddafi overthrow is a part of the centuries old playbook to deny Africans their own land and their right to self-determination.

Libya had achieved economic independence, with its water, its food, its oil, and its state-owned bank. It had arisen under Qaddafi from one of the poorest of countries to the richest in Africa. Education and medical treatment were free; having a home was considered a human right, and Libyans participated in a Libyan form of democracy. Qaddafi had developed the world's largest irrigation system dubbed "The Great Man-Made River Project" and planned to spread the model throughout Africa. He also planned to create an independent hard currency in Africa that would free the continent from economic bondage under the dollar, the IMF, and the French African Franc, shaking off the last heavy chains of colonial exploitation."[9] I believe the western powers have come to view the exploitation of Blacks as their natural order of things. Any attempt to get free from their clutches is faced with stiff resistance; as shown in the following paragraphs:

Wikipedia had listed 44 African countries out of the 54 that exist and have calculated the number of leader's who have been assassinated in each country. I looked at the 44 countries stretching back from 1942 –2008 and counted approximately 170 killings of African leaders. Incredible. Between 1961 and 1973 there has been, 22 African leaders assassinated. Alleged for asserting their independence and refusal to be subservient to colonial powers. The following is a list of the 22 most recent.

1963: Sylvanus Olympio, President of the Rep. of Togo
1966: John-Aguiyi Ironsi, President of Rep. of Nigeria
1969: Abdirachid-Ali Shermake, President of the Rep. of Somalia

1972: Abeid-Amani Karume, President of the Rep. of Zanzibar

1975: Richard Ratimandrava, President of the Rep. of Madagascar

1975: Francois – Ngarta Tombalbaye, President of the Rep. Chad

1976: Murtala – Ramat Mohammed, President of the Rep. of Nigeria

1977: Marien Ngouabi, President of the Rep. of Congo – Brazzaville

1977: Teferi Bante, President of the Rep. of Ethiopia

1981: Anouar El-Sadate, President of the Rep. of Egypt

1981: William – Richard Tolbert President of the Rep. Liberia

1987: Thomas Sankara, President of the of Burkina-Faso

1989: Ahmed Abdallah, President of the Rep. of Comoros

1989: Samuel – Kanyon Doe President of the Rep. of Liberia

1992: Mohammed Boudiaf, President of the Rep. of Algeria

1993: Melchior Ndadaye, President of the Rep. of Burundi

1994: Cyprien Ntaryamira, President of the Rep. of Burundi

1994: Juvenal Habyarimana President of the Rep. of Rwanda

1999: Ibrahim Barre – Mainassara, President of the Rep. of Niger

2001: Laurent Barre-Mainassara, President of the Rep. of Congo-Kinshasa

2009: Joao Bernardo Vieira, President of Guinea-Bissau

2011: Mouammar Khadafi, President of the Rep. of Libya[10]

The Hidden Hand of Colonialism

Many think that the colonial era has ended, but nothing could be further from the truth. Since 1961, fifteen African nations continue to pay tribute to France in amounts upward of hundreds of billions of dollars. They are: Benin, Burkina Faso, Ivory Coast, Mali, Niger, Senegal, Togo, Cameroon, Central African Republic, Guinea Bissau, Equatorial Guinea, Chad, Congo-Brazzaville and Gabon. It is estimated that France holds $500 billion of African money. These African countries have no independent access to their money. It belongs to France. The Africans primarily benefiting financially from the French presences are those who are well connected, the governing class and security forces that help France to maintain control.

For centuries Africa has been ruled by ruthless Europeans and African puppets paid by Western backers. The puppet's job is to keep the doors open for foreign interest. Africans leaders whose intent is to free the people from oppression are politically neutralized, slandered and demonized by propaganda, or killed. This has left Africa and its people in shambles. Leaders who do rise are at the mercy of western powers who have financial sway over African countries. The Arab Spring uprising and others around the world are often attempts to overthrow leaders that do not represent the interest of the people. Hopefully I've helped you understand how Africa continues to be exploited by Western countries as they help themselves to the abundant natural resources (gold, diamonds, lithium, uranium oil, gas, timber, etc.) of Africa to sustain their countries. The people of France and other nations are often not aware of how much their economies depend on the exploitation of Africa.[11]

For further information see: How Europe under developed Africa by Walter Rodney – Dr. Taimur Rahman@Laal – Europe and the People without History by Eric R. Wolf.

In March 2008, President Jacques Chirac stated, "Without Africa, France will slide down into the rank of a third world power."[12] In 1957, Chirac's predecessor, Francois Mitterrand said; "Without Africa, France will have no history in the 21st century."[12a] This quote can be found at (Politique Francaise et Abandon 1958) translated on reddit.com.

"We have to speak the language of truth. African growth pulls us along. Its dynamism supports us and its vitality is stimulating for us …. We need Africa" said Finance Minister Pierre Moscovici, during an opening statement at the Franco-African Economic Conference 12/04/2013.[13] Moscovici left out France's most obvious need for Africa; its resources.

The colonialist system is akin to a worldwide organization of gangsters whose stock and trade is deception, theft and violence to maintain its global positioning. It is the means by which the globalist elite powers have captured the world and govern it. France's colonial structure in African countries is a microcosm of this world-wide system.

Other countries, Australia, United Kingdom and the United States are a few who have territories separate from their countries boundaries. Lands often seized for their own use. "A territory is a geographic area (such as colonial possession) dependent on an external government but having some degree of autonomy" *Merriam Webster*. The US has eleven territories that are uninhabited and five colonies: Guam, Puerto Rico, American Samoa, US Virgin Island and the Northern Mariana Islands all of which have little say in self-determination. These locations are exploited for their natural resources, cheap labor, and strategic military locations.[14]

In America and else were we see poverty, homelessness and the shrinking of the middle class caused by job loss and inadequate compensation. Wages have not kept pace with the cost of living making it difficult for the individuals and families to get by. What is happening? Greed is happening. Economically advanced industrialized countries continue to inhale the riches from poorer ones. These advanced countries and the corporate elite are now doing the same to their own citizens as wages are suppressed, jobs are cut and exported, people are being replaced with machines and benefits to citizens are being cut. Corporate elites get subsidies for their businesses, kickbacks, tax breaks or even pay no taxes. These are accommodations given to the rich by the rich. Corporate America rakes in huge profits while workers are paid less than a living wage. The federal minimum wage of 7.25 per hour is not livable by any stretch of the imagination. It could be considered a modern day slave wage.

During the Trump era some top-tier companies got tax breaks, or even paid no taxes. Among them are Amazon, Chevron, Netflix, Eli Lilly, IBM, and General Motors. This practice is not unique to President Trump, it has been going on for decades under Republican and Democrat administrations. We can hope, as of the writing of this in 2022 that the new administration under President Biden can address this practice and at least put a dent in this injustice.[15]

As Americans we don't perceive ourselves a colonized people, but we are. A dictionary's definition of colonization is "the action of appropriating a place or domain for one's own use." Is this not exactly what the big banks and corporations have done in America and around the world; appropriated the world as their private domain and those in it their subjects? Populations are at the mercy of governments, banks and corporate whims.

These institutions, banks and corporations that control governments have no concern for the people: it is all about profit and control. Nothing so clearly illustrates this is that while individual and mass murders by gun violence are an epidemic in the United States, the government and their corporate gun lobby supporters have bonded together to resist gun laws that would end the daily slaughter of Americans. A majority of the population, 71% in a University of Chicago Harris School of Public Policy and the Associated Press–NORC Center Public Affairs Research poll in usnews.com, Aug.23, 2022, agreed that tougher gun laws should be enacted yet the slaughter continues in states across America.

"The selfish spirit of commerce knows no country, and feels no passion or principle but that of gain." (Thomas Jefferson, April 15th 1809). "I hope we shall crush… in its birth the aristocracy of our moneyed corporations, which dare already to challenge our government to a trial of strength and bid defiance to the laws of our country." (Jefferson, November 12, 1816). Jefferson feared that government, banks, and corporation would ultimately exploit the people and control all. Are we not there today; colonized and don't know it?[16]

The Real Africa before European Desolation

The name Ashanti has Hebrew origins, the "ti" at the end means race of or people of, Asha. Ashan was the name of a city located in southern Israel, Judah (Joshua 15:42, 19:7/ 1st Chronicles 4:32, 6:59). The word Ashan in Hebrew means smoke city or burning city. Ashanti means the people (sons) of Ashan or the people of the smoke city. This was the reference to the city of Ashan after the Romans destroyed it in 70 C.E. The sons of Ashan escaped into West Africa and developed the Ashanti Kingdom.[17]

In 1819 English traveler and author Thomas Edward Bowdich, described the Ashanti Royal Palace in Kumasi the capital of the Ashanti Kingdom:

> ...an immense building of a variety of oblong courts and regular squares [with] entablatures exuberantly adorned with bold fan and trellis work of Egyptian character. They have a suite of rooms over them, with small windows of wooden lattice, of intricate but regular carved work, and some have frames cased with thin gold. The squares have a large apartment on each side, open in front, with two supporting pillars, which break the view and give it all the appearance of the proscenium or front of the stage of the older Italian theaters. They are lofty and regular, and the cornices of a very bold cane-work in alto-relievo. A drop-curtain of curiously plaited cane is suspended in front, and in each, we observed chairs

and stools embossed with gold, and beds
of silk, with scattered regalia.[18]

The following research regarding African History
is derived from Pan Africanist Robin Walker and PD
Lawton both heavily quoting pan Africanist Walter
Rodney. The following information is found in the
*100 African Cities That Were Completely Destroyed by
Europeans* article by Earl Brooks found at corespirit.
com. Excerpts by Robin Walker and PD Lawton.

William Winwood Reade, the British historian,
explorer, and philosopher, described his visit to the
Ashanti Royal Palace of Kumasi in 1874:

> "We went to the king's palace which
> consist of many courtyards, each
> surrounded with alcoves and verandahs,
> and having two gates or doors, so that
> each yard was a thoroughfare … But the
> part of the palace fronting the street was
> a stone house, Moorish in its style …
> with a flat roof and a parapet, and suites
> of apartments on the first floor. It was
> built by Fanti masons' decades ago. The
> rooms upstairs remind me of Wardour
> Roads. Each was a perfect Old Curiosity
> Shop. Books in many languages,
> Bohemian glass, clocks, silver plate, old
> furniture, Persian rugs, Kidderminster
> carpets, pictures and engravings,

numberless chests and coffers. A sword bearing the inscription From Queen Victoria to the King of Ashanti. A copy of the Times, 17 October 1843. With these were many specimens of Moorish and Ashanti art". –Robin Walter.

Toward the end of the 19th century the British looted and destroyed the city of Kumasi with explosives.

Kilwa

In 1331, Ibn Battuta, described the Tanzanian city of Kilwa, of the Zanj, Swahili speaking people, as follows: "One of the most beautiful and well-constructed cities in the world, the whole of it is elegantly built." - excerpt from "The Invisible Empire" by PD Lawton. In 1505, Portuguese forces destroyed and burned down the Swahili cities of Kilwa and Mombasa."

Vaida

In the 15th century when the Portuguese, the first Europeans to sail the Atlantic coasts of Africa "arrived in the coast of Guinea and landed at Vaida in West Africa. The captains were astonished to find streets well laid out, bordered on either side for several leagues by two rows of trees, for days they travelled through a country of magnificent fields, inhabited by men clad in richly colored garments of their own weaving! Further south in the Kingdom of the Kongo, a swarming crowd dressed in fine silks' and velvet; great states well ordered, down to the smallest detail; powerful rulers, flourishing industries-civilized to the marrow of their bones. The condition of the countries of the eastern coast-Mozambique, for example-was quite the same." (excerpt from "The Invisible Empire" PD Lawton.)

Until the end of the 16 century, Africa was far more advanced than Europe in terms of political organization, science, technology and culture. That prosperity continued, despite the European slavery ravages, until the 17th and 18th century.

The continent was crowded with tens of great and prosperous cities, empires and kingdoms with King Askia Toure of Songhay, King Behanzin Hossu Bowelle of Benin, and Emperor Menelik of Ethiopia, King Shaka ka Sezangakhona of South Africa, Queen Nzinga of Angola, Queen Yaa Asantewaa of Ghana, and Queen Amina of Nigeria.", PD Lawton.

P.D Lawton historian, writer and researcher of South African affairs, born in Kwa Zulu Natal South Africa illuminated some of the hidden history of Africa. Lawton is the editor of Africanagenda.net.

For further information see: Africa-facts. org/ *interesting facts about Africa/−* & thenigerialawyer. com>historical-reminiscences.

These nations are a sample of civilizations across the continent of Alkebulan (if you remember, the translation of this word means "Mother of Mankind"), the ancient name of Africa. The defaming of Africa is an intentional strategy used to rationalize the ceaseless plunder of Africa's resources by the colonizers who use the "religions of peace"; Judaism, Christianity and Islam as a part of their assault. Alkebulan has never needed these hostile groups to teach them anything. They had their own religion and culture. Africans and other people of color around the world were forced by violence and deception to conform to western and middle-eastern religious ideologies:

> Numbers **33:52-53** Drive out all the inhabitants of the land before you. Destroy all their carved images and their cast idols, and demolish all their high places.

Take possession of the land and settle in it, for I have given you the land to possess it.

I think the leaders of Judaism, Christianity and Islam, in cahoots with governments, continue to use their holy books as their rational to do what they have always done so well: kill, steal and destroy those who are different from them, in the name of their "gods." Their violence continues to run rampant across the world today, each one blaming the other for their blood thirsty barbarianism. Despite their ongoing violence, all three claim to be religions of peace. Tell that to the people and nations they have destroyed.

Permission to Destroy
The Doctrine of Discovery (DoD)

Papal Bull Dum Diversas 18 June, 14, 1452

Pope Nicholas V issued the papal bull (edict) Dum Diversas on 18 June, 1452. It authorized Alfonso V of Portugal to reduce any "Saracens (Muslims) and pagans and any other unbelievers" to perpetual slavery. This facilitated the Portuguese slave trade from West Africa. The same pope wrote the bull Romanus Pontifex on January 5, 1455 to the same Alfonso. As a follow-up to the Dum Diversas, it extended to the Catholic nations of Europe dominion over discovered lands during the Age of Discovery. Along with sanctifying the seizure of non-Christian lands, it encouraged the enslavement of native, non-Christian peoples in Africa and the New World."[19]

The majority of the non-European world was colonized under an international law that is known as the Doctrine of Discovery (DoD). Under this legal principle, European countries claimed superior rights over Indigenous nations. When European explorers planted flags and crosses in the lands of native peoples, they were making legal claims of ownership and domination over the lands, assets, and peoples they had "discovered." These claims were justified by racial, ethnocentric, and religious ideas of the alleged superiority of European Christians.[20] The *"religions of peace"* claim to get their mandate from their "God of peace." This religious mandate to murder and steal from others, frees them from guilt of moral and criminal responsibility. The hypocrisy is mind-boggling.

The European elites did not need the (DoD) to give them permission to destroy and steal land from indigenous people, they had been doing that to each other for centuries. The DoD simply gave them the religious and legal cover to continue to perpetrate their genocidal crimes against *all* of humanity. There is no place on earth exempt from their destruction.

A mandate issued by Pope Paul the Third In 1537 attempted to restrain European governments from their rampage of barbarianisms that had started in Europe centuries before the discovery of the new worlds and other continents of color. Other such mandates were issued in an attempt to restrain the violence, but it was to no avail. The trend of destruction was irreversible. The spoils of such undertakings were immensely profitable. It is the reason why I believe it continues until this day.

Chapter Ten

Delusions and the Moral Universe

Rev. Martin Luther King Jr. observed that the triple evils of racism, economic exploitation and militarism continue to deteriorate life on earth. These evils are fueled by delusion. Webster defines a delusion as "a belief or altered reality that is persistently held despite evidence or agreement to the contrary, generally in reference to a mental disorder."

What is this belief that causes nations to seek dominance over others? It is the lie of superiority. We have seen it at work across the planet but most strikingly in Manifest Destiny (MD). This Ideology convinces people they have the right to engage in any horror they choose because of their "religious and or cultural superiority." Hundreds of millions of people have been destroyed because of this delusion. It is really scary because anyone can be subjected to its madness.

Evidence contradicts the delusional belief of superiority. Benjamin Franklin in his essay "*Remarks Concerning the Savages of North America*" makes clear that the Indians lived by a moral code. They did not just talk about peace but actually put it into practice. Franklin concurs with English explorer Arthur Barlowe that indigenous people of the New World were civilized. The same sentiment was expressed by other European explorers and travelers. These accounts of civilized Brown and Black inhabitants of the New World – which was called "Turtle Island" by indigenous people are instead replaced by accounts of indigenous people as savages. Their subsequent rationalizations for the deeds done in the name of Manifest Destiny, Doctrine of Discovery, white supremacy and the like are used as justification by the governing powers involved.

Around the world indigenous peoples continue to experience injustice by governments, states, and corporate entities; as these collective powers steal indigenous lands for their own use. For example since 2014 the Sioux people have resisted the Keystone pipe line being installed on their land at the Standing Rock Sioux Reservation in North Dakota; I think this is an example of the continued theft of indigenous people's lands for corporate and state use. The refusal to refrain from these acts is an outward sign of the delusional mindset that has no respect for indigenous people's property, and sees certain people as expendable in the furtherance of state and corporate goals. I believe this mindset trickles down from the leaders in their speeches and propaganda and gets into the heads of the masses creating conscious as well as unconscious biases.

What seems to be a daily shooting of unarmed African American men has also become an American way of death for other citizens by killers armed with weapons of war. The profits from the sales of these weapons flow into the hands of gun manufactures and into the hands of GOP elected politicians who support the gun lobbies agenda. In general all Americans lives have become secondary and expendable. Gun profits and gun rights are prioritized over human life. Unbelievable as it may seem it appears that some Americans have bought the delusion that gun rights take precedent over human life. Those who are in delusional states of mind cannot tell what is real from what is imagined, from what is true or from what is false.

The antipathy we see in toxic cultures was nurtured for centuries by their leaders to maintain the belief systems of superiority over individuals and groups; simultaneously these leaders gain power and further separate the elite ruling class from the general populace.

There is no incentive to change for those who profit from the brainwashing of their followers. So, here we are, century after century reliving the same old delusional hatreds. Mass media, particularly the internet, has provided the opportunity to expose toxic beliefs and behaviors as well as propagating them. The eradication of destructive belief systems is ultimately in the minds of the people as they wake up from delusions. The internet is without question a significant part of that awakening. The awareness and willingness to heed the messages of truth from within is equally important and a crucial part of that awakening.

"The arc of the moral universe is long but it bends toward justice" originally said by Theodore Parker, nineteenth-century abolitionist and Unitarian Minister. What are we to learn from his statement? Those with power seemingly beyond the reach of justice must be confronted and held accountable. We are part of that force that will bend this moral universe toward justice. Changes that will enhance and respect life will not occur without our participation.

Chapter Eleven

Bacon's Rebellion, Infant Mortality, Stoking the fire, Hope

Bacon's Rebellion of 1676

Between 1500 and 1600, the English elite began to gobble up the land for commerce capitalist pursuits. Laws were passed that dealt harshly with the poor. Thousands became homeless; sounds like the situation we are in to today. In an attempt to address the situation the government exiled multitudes to the New World promising them a better life. Ships were packed with men, woman, and children. During the 6-8 week journey to America, many died from starvation and sickness due to the horrendous conditions on the ships. Once in America, the people found themselves in no better conditions and often worse than what they had left. They were once again under the yoke of those in power. Indentured servitude, slavery, high taxes and poverty was their fate. The promises of land and opportunity for wealth were just tricks to get them off the streets of England. Those who were fortunate to get land had to battle the original inhabitants whose land they were stealing. There was no help from England or from William Berkeley, the governor of Virginia. As a result of these conditions, frustration grew. The needs of the people were ignored, while the government catered to themselves and those with wealth and power.

Nathanial Bacon, a man of privilege was in opposition to Governor Berkeley concerning the handling of the Indian population. The inequality between the rich and the poor was another point of contention the two shared. These disagreements pitted Bacon and Berkley against one another. This set the stage for Bacon's Rebellion of 1676. The rebellion brought together factions of the disenfranchised; hundreds of Englishmen, Negros, and a mixture of freemen, servants, indentured servants, and slaves. Before the rebellion, distinctions between Whites and Blacks had not become ingrained. All had the same oppressor.

The rebellion was unsuccessful in changing the balance of power. It was, however, a wake-up call for those in power. They understood that solidarity among the "lesser" classes threatened their authority. Schemes were devised and implemented to create division among people, using color as the dividing line. Soon after the rebellion, a system of divide and conquer was devised and implemented. Whites were given greater opportunity for social and economic advancement, while Blacks were kept in subservient roles. Laws were passed that locked Blacks into a system of perpetual slavery. This made sure that coordinated Black and White rebellion would no longer be a threat. Equally or more important for the land owners was the guarantee of an endless legion of free labor.[1]

This system of racial superiority has been carried over to the present day; with most of the low paying wage jobs being held by people of color. The government system historically thrived on division, as it does today. I believe portions of the White community have learned to blame Blacks and the poor when there standard of living is threatened. Cutting services that benefit the less fortunate is often the cry; thus shielding the elites from the responsibility for the disorder they have created.

The division between the races has been maintained throughout the centuries by written and unwritten laws that solidify white supremacy. Racism is a part of the psychological makeup of many Americans. It is in full bloom when leaders sanction racist feelings and actions.

Inequity continues to widen between the "haves" and the "have-nots." Some Whites today are beginning to see that their adversary has never been people of color. Their adversary has been and continues to be, their leaders. This is a reality that those in Bacon's rebellion clearly understood. Today some have become aware of the schemes of those in power, but far too many are still drinking the "Kool-Aid", as in, accepting the skewed reality without question, and worse, defending that perversion.

"An ideological basis for explicit racism came into unique fruition in the West during the

Modern period (1500 - 1800's). No clear evidence of racism has been found in other cultures or in Europe before the Middle Ages."[2] "Race, while not a valid biological concept, is a real social construction that gives or denies benefits and privileges. American society developed the notion of race early in its formation to justify its new economic system of Capitalism, which depended on the institution of forced labor, especially the enslavement of African people."[3] Although the persistent claim is that America became a great nation because of Capitalism the foundational truth is that America became a great nation because of 400 years of free labor.

The impact of slavery and race continues today, through systems that negatively impact Black people. Educational and job disparities with the low paying labor and service jobs filled mostly by minorities is not an accident. Health disparities are also significant between Blacks and Whites.

Infant Mortality

The U.S. health care system spends more than all other countries according to The Organization for Economic Co-operation and Development (OECD). Thirty six developed member countries comprise the organization. The U.S. ranked No. 33 for infant mortality. For over 50 years the U.S. has not advanced at the rate of other

(OECD) countries and Black babies and mothers are facing the greatest impact.[4]

Currently In the US, there has been a decline in infant mortality, but Black infants are observed to have about 2.1 times the infant mortality rate of White infants. Black infants are 3.8 times more likely to die from low birth weight complications, and Black mothers are more likely than White mothers to receive late or no prenatal care… Even among college-educated parents, different rates of low and very-low birth weight babies account for higher Black Infant Mortality Rate (IMR) when compared to White populations.[5]

Racism, has always been the metric under which Black people suffer in America. I have no reason not to conclude that infant and maternal mortality is not just another symptom of an institutionalized racist mind-set.

Stoking the Fire

President Trump, in a speech addressing police officers on July 31, 2017, instructed police to not be "too nice" during arrest, and suggested not worrying about protecting the head of arrestees when being placed in squad cars. I saw that police responded enthusiastically by clapping, cheering and doing fist pumps, suggesting to me they like to be rough. Police already have a reputation for brutality in minority communities, and I think this is an example of both the president and the police condoning such actions. This kind of rhetoric particularly from the president will only encourage abuse not only by police but also by those who sympathize with the president's rhetoric.

Segments of this country's population are in denial even to the existence of racism; in fact some believe White people are the ones being discriminated against. Many who have been indoctrinated by overt and covert systematic racism simply have learned to blame the victims of racism instead of the corrupt systems in place. We need leadership that does not stoke the fires of hatred; instead, we need leaders that seek resolutions that will bring people together. These resolutions when possible should be geared toward win–win outcomes for both. If our leaders are unable and or unwilling to govern evenhandedly for the best interest of all the people, they should be replaced. If elections can't remedy the situation, the framers gave us a solution in The Declaration of Independence, "The people have the right to alter or abolish it and institute new government." They however were not addressing or referring to the needs of people of color, but the intent of the people themselves having the right to change the government in the advent of corruption is there.

Attempting to alter or abolish the present government, with the country as divided as it is, would cause greater division, unrest, chaos and in our present state of affairs violence. Is America going down the path of extinction like past empires? "A great civilization is not conquered from without until it has destroyed itself from within."[6]

Hope

There are individuals in our society that seek to enflame racial tension as in the case of those in Charlottesville, Virginia and Kenosha, Wisconsin. There are also multi-racial groups; Blacks, Brown and Whites coming together all over the country peacefully resisting forces of division and violence. It is with these the hope for systemic change can occur. As Lincoln said, if we lose our freedom it will come from within; conversely if we are to keep our freedom it will also come from within.

My condolences to the Heyer family whose daughter Heather was killed on August 12, 2017 at the Charlottesville, Virginia protest and also to the families of Joseph Rosenbaum and Anthony Huber both killed at the Kenosha Protest in Kenosha Wisconsin on August 25, 2020. It is my wish that peace envelops all families who have lost loved ones in the seeming unending struggle for civil and human rights.

This is the hope for America. We will no longer allow the divide-and-conquer tactics of leaders to continue to separate us. As more Americans suffer under the hands of the politicians and their billionaire bosses, hopefully some will come to realize that it's not the poor and minorities that pose a threat to America, it is rather the system and those who control it.

Chapter Twelve

The Political Billionaire's System

Corrupt Politicians and Greedy Business Owners

One rarely hears politicians talk about cutting corporate welfare, which was estimated in 2012 to be $100 billion annually and is no doubt considerably higher today.[1] Corporations have lobbyists fighting for their welfare. They finance politicians to ensure it. We, the American public, do not have lobbyist fighting on our behalf. Some believe that welfare fraud is extensive simply because television has shown some individuals getting caught scamming the system. It is estimated that only one percent of those receiving welfare may be taking advantage of it. Politicians and citizens ignore the estimated $100 billion a year of our tax money that is given in the form of tax breaks to corporate America by both Democrat and Republican politicians. In 2018 Corporate giants, Amazon, Chevron, Netflix, and IBM were among sixty Fortune 500 companies that avoided all Federal income taxes.[2] In 2020 fifty five big name corporations, despite millions of dollars made in profit paid no federal taxes. Among them were FedEx, Nike and Dish Network.[3]

Walmart, McDonald's, and others with profits in the billions are recipients of subsidies, yet, they do not pay their employees enough for them to take care of their basic needs. This forces employees to seek government assistance. McDonald's average net income from 2017 to 2021 was approximately 5.88 billion dollars.[4] Is it not possible with those kinds of profits to boost hourly wages to at least $15.00 an hour? That would give workers a yearly income of about 31,200 per year; the average cost of living for an individual. This cost can differ considerably depending on where you live. The federal government's minimum wage is $7.25 an hour. This amounts to about $15, 000 per year, where the average cost of living for a single person is $31,104.[5] That is a shortfall of $16,104. If the minimum hourly wage was $13.00 per hour that would bring an average yearly earnings to $26,000, which is still below an individual's average cost of living but far better than $15,000. The minimum wage should be at least 15.00 per hour, equaling $31,200 a year about $96 over the cost of living. The alliance between politicians and corporations is predicated on keeping the minimum wage low. The hiring of part-time employees to avoid paying benefits does not bode well for American workers.

Austerity for the Poor Prosperity for the Rich

The Trump budget for 2020 will continue to cut domestic programs that help millions of Americans to survive. People of moderate means and the poor will suffer. It proposes cutting $777 billion over ten years; this includes Medicaid and the Affordable Care Act (ACT), subsidies that help people afford market place health coverage. This will cause millions to become uninsured.[6]

People are calling for a Medicare for all health-care system that will cover the cost of health care for *all* Americans. It would be paid for by eliminating health insurance payments and co-pays. An increase in taxes would also be enacted to fund this system. This request falls on the deaf ears of politicians in the House and Senate who between them in 2017-2018 received 28,486,079 million dollars from the insurance sector.[6a] for additional information on businesses distributing fat checks to politicians go to (OpenSecret.org) and (wewantadeal.com).

$220 billion over the next ten years is slated to be cut from a variety of domestic programs; SNAP (food stamps), Social Security Disability Insurance and Supplemental Social Security Income, Temporary Assistance for Needy Families (TANF), and the elimination of Social Service Block Grants. The Trump budget calls for deep cuts in public housing, a critical source of affordable housing.[7] With the transition to the Biden presidency, it is anticipated these cuts will be reevaluated and hopefully overturned but past statements by Biden have favored cuts in Social Security. We shall see.

Prosperity for the rich through tax cuts and other government means continues, while austerity for the average American is being implemented. Martin Luther King Jr. stated "Socialism for the rich, rugged Individualism for everyone else." We're marching towards, if not already there, a feudal system where a few lords will own everything while the serfs will toil to barely survive.

Environmental Cuts Increase Corporate Profits

The Environmental Protection Agency (EPA) received a $2.5 billion dollar / 23% cut in the 2019 budget. This cut reduced funding for enforcing pollution laws by 11%. 72% of all greenhouse gases are produced from the use of electricity, heating and transportation. These are all sources of energy that are generated by fossil fuels. Agriculture, forestry and land use contribute 18.4 % toward global emissions.[8] Spending less money on environmental safe may increase corporate profits but it will decrease the health of citizens as air quality deteriorates.

I grew up in the late 50s and early 60s when air quality was much worse. Vehicle exhaust and cigarette smoke were everywhere. We do not need to return to those days of relaxed standards.

EPA cuts will also put our water supply in a state of continuous peril. Water supplies in some states are already contaminated. In parts of the state of North Carolina where I currently reside, water supplies are already in danger. "GenX" Polyfluoroalkyl substances (PFAS), a man made chemical that does not break down in the environment has been found in N.C.'s drinking water along with other chemicals. PFAS is linked to cancer, thyroid and immune disorders. Recent reports have found (PFAS) substances everywhere even in the rain water.[9] Offshore deep-sea oil exploration and extraction will negatively impact our oceans. EPA cuts will only contribute to increased ocean degradation.

The April 2010 Deep Water Horizon oil spill emitted 134 million gallons of crude oil into the Gulf of Mexico, contaminating over a 1000 miles of coastlines. In March of 1989 the Exxon Valdez spilled 11 million gallons of oil contaminating 1300 miles of Alaska coastline. Both spills killed hundreds of thousands of birds and countless forms of ocean life. These are a couple of examples of the worldwide destruction unleashed by oil spills as described by Laura Moss, journalist writing on environment and cultural issues.[10] The last thing we need, as suggested by the Trump administration, is unrestrained oil drilling up and down the coastlines of the United States. If President Trump or someone of his ilk gets back in office in 2024 and seeks similar policies, then the environment will experience increased risk of industry-related disaster.

Taxes

In 2018 Corporate America got permanent tax cuts, decreasing their rate from 35 percent to 21 percent. That is, coupled with the tax loopholes they have been exploiting for decades. Americans got temporary tax relief lasting for only eight years. The Trump administration wants to give $100 billion more in tax cuts to those who need it the least, the rich. Trump said, "If we cannot do it through legislation, we will look at other ways to get it passed."[11]

During President Eisenhower's administration, the tax rate was 90 % for the rich. Adjusting for inflation, today's tax rate on individuals making $413,200 would be 72%. A couple making $464,850 would be in a 75% tax bracket. Senator Bernie Sanders made this point during the 2019 Democratic presidential nomination debates. It was fact checked by editorial sources and found to be true.[12]

Here is a side of the tax story that the public rarely hears. 238 corporations paid an effective tax rate of 2% over an eight-year period from 2008 through 2015. Eighteen of the corporations paid no federal income tax over the eight-year period. A fifth of them (forty-eight) paid less than 10%. One hundred paid no federal tax in at least one year from 2008 to 2015. These 238 companies are Fortune 500 companies that have shown consistent profits over the eight-year period from 2008 to 2015.[13] Equitable tax laws are needed so that Americans are not picking up the financial slack that corporate America is evading. As long as the rich and the super-rich write the tax laws or influence those who do, the tax system will continued to be skewed in their favor, and so will everything else that is influenced by money.

Protecting their Masters and the Indiscriminate Killing of Palestinians

The deaths of unarmed men, women, and children continue globally as populations protest for economic equality, human and civil rights. Elites care only about keeping their authority and expanding their power. Those that do their bidding - military, police and other security forces are subservient to the wishes of government officials, religious and military leaders. They are driven by misplaced loyalties and dependence on a paycheck. There seems to be no limit to what they will do for their masters. Many military operations and police departments have followed bad orders because of bad politics lording over them.

A stark example of violence against unarmed men, women, and children can be seen in current-day Palestine. More than 250 people were shot dead and it is estimated that more than 29,000 were wounded as Israeli soldiers shot unarmed civilians during the Great

March of Return protest, which started on March 31, 2018 and continued every Friday for a year. It was organized by grassroots organizations in the city of Gaza, which has the largest population in the State of Palestine. The March commemorates the expulsion of an estimated 750,000 Palestinians from their homeland, the destruction of five hundred thirty villages and major Palestinian cities and the killing of Approximately 15,000 in mass atrocities and massacres in the 1947-1948 land grab by Zionist military forces.[14] Today there are 6 million refugees living in 58 camps throughout Palestine and nearby countries. Zionist believe in the establishment of a Jewish state in Israel. It was the 1947 invasion of Palestine that triggered the first Arab-Israeli war.[15] Zionist, do not represent all Jews.

UN Resolution 194 paragraph 11 calls for compensation and immediate return of Palestinians to their villages and towns from which they were forcibly removed. Forcible removal from and destruction of Palestinian property, abuse and killings of Palestinian citizens is never ending and this led to Hamas launching rockets into Israel on May 10, 2021. In response Israelis hit Gaza with air strikes killing 213 people, with an estimated 1500 wounded, 132 buildings were destroyed, and 316 were severely damaged including six hospitals and nine health centers. More than 52,000 Palestinians were in need of appropriate shelter. In the 2014 conflict the Israeli military killed 2,100 Palestinians. More than 11,000 people were injured and over 20,000 houses destroyed that year. Only seventy three Israelis were killed and only 720 were injured during that same year. According to Human Rights Watch Israel, the Jewish state is committing "crimes against humanity of apartheid and persecution" against Palestinians.[16]

Israel's disproportionate response to conflicts they provoke has been Israel's trademark since the invasion of Palestine in 1947- 48.

The Palestinian struggle is reflected all over the world with people who are fed up with corrupt governments controlling their destiny. Citizens are demanding their government respond to the will of the people or step down. As I'm writing this section in November of 2019 these are some of the countries in civil revolt; Bolivia, Chile, Lebanon, Iraq, Sudan, Algeria, and Nigeria, and even the French had a bone to pick with their leaders. It is a foreboding sign that greater unrest will continue, as people resist the present order. These corrupt governments that oppress people are protected by their military, police, and other security forces that enable them to continue policies that hurt the citizens. It is long past time for these security forces to serve the *people* instead of the small group of elites that pay them.

Chapter Thirteen

Freedom and Beyond

Boundaries and the Freedom to Explore

Parents want the best for their children. Parents however need to consider as the child matures not only what *they want* but also take into consideration the gifts and skills that the child may exhibit. These talents may diverge from the vision and direction a parent may have imagined. This may be difficult for a parent to accept. Parents may deny that they want to see reflections of themselves in their children, but nevertheless they go to some lengths to make sure their children reflect their values; that is their role. When does that duty end? At some point, the boundary between parent and child must be respected. Parents, to some degree, must give their youth the freedom to explore life for themselves otherwise they may find themselves in the uncomfortable position of trying to force-feed their sons and daughters something they do not want. Balance between guidance and authority is the key. My father encouraged me to go into the electrical trade which I did but eventually I left because my interest was in the human services. He accepted my wishes with grace.

Support and guidance are necessary as our young people explore the great unknown. Guilt, fear, and frustration from parents only complicate the child's journey. Setting our children free from our own believes and ideological points of view can be agonizing. If parents are not careful, conflicting points of view can tear a family apart. Parents must mature as their children mature. This means allowing our young people to choose their own way: with our guidance of course. Parents should not act as dictators. We need to be patient as young people grow. This is often easier said than done, but the effort will be rewarded. It is unfortunate that too often parents are stuck in belief systems and ideologies that do not allow for freedom of thought. They confine perceptions to narrow parameters making it difficult for the young person to explore and develop a vision of their own. These parameters can easily be breeding grounds for intolerance and bigotry if they are not challenged by opposing ideas that can open their mind to other perspectives. Parents must do the often difficult task of being open to other points of view therefore enabling their children to grow into balanced and thoughtful people.

I think if parents give their offspring the needed space, they may be surprised when their young people return with answers to questions the parents themselves may or may not have asked but should have.

Grandma Evelyn Anderson

Personality is an interesting thing. It is always much deeper and more complex than can be perceived by casual observation. You *really* cannot tell a book by its cover. Grandma Evelyn, called Nana by her grandchildren, was a short woman between 4'6 to 5 feet in height. Don't let stature fool you, in many ways, Nana was a maverick; strong willed with a mind of her own. She was not slavishly subject to the whims and demands of cultural norms that most follow without question. She was curious, questioning and I believe suspicious of the status quo. These characteristics were not particularly endearing for a Black woman in the nineteenth century. She was liked by some, but she had her share of detractors, even in her own family. I always got the impression that Nana did not concern herself about what others thought of her. She was going to do what she thought was best regardless if those around her agreed or not.

From my perspective, Nana never seemed to force her will on those around her, at least not in an overt sort of way. She did not have to say much to make her point. She had an expression that made it clear when she did not agree with an idea or particular point of view. I remember her quizzical expression whenever I expressed something that she found questionable. That look would give me the feeling that I should rethink whatever I was saying. When you were around Nana it was wise to be thoughtful. She was a serious, contemplative, individual but if you spent time with her you found a friendly person to converse with. In depth conversations with her was an opportunity I wish I had taken advantage of.

Grandma - Beyond the Norms

As a child and into her teen years, Grandmother Evelyn Anderson (Nana) sang soprano in the church choir. She was often given opportunities to sing solos. From a very young age, I remember hearing Nana singing in her high operatic soprano voice. I heard it mentioned that Nana was disappointed that she did not have the opportunity to develop a singing career. That dream would have required a variety of support systems, single-mindedness on her part and of course talent. Even with all these things going for her, opportunity and some luck were crucial determining factors. Both were in relatively short supply for Black Americans at that time. Once Nana was married and was responsible for a family, a musical career was beyond her grasp.

Independence was a strong theme in Nana's character, and it got her into areas that some considered taboo. Nana was a psychic: one who demonstrated abilities inexplicable by natural law. She became aware of this ability when she was around five years old. She told my sister Paulette that she was able to see events before they happened. I think physic ability is most often strongest in the young, probably because their minds are not cluttered with the ideas of their given culture. These abilities are varied and may be inherited. Both of my sisters Evelyn and Paulette have shared with me experiences that they could not explain. Most were dreams and visions relating to future and or past events that were often expressed symbolically. Some of which were useful while others were too abstract to understand. For my sisters these incidents were rare. For Nana, these experiences were common and she was able to utilize them in service to others.

The Tearoom

Boston has the oldest psychic tearoom in the country. The Original Tremont Tearoom opened in 1936. Nana worked there during the 1960s. It was on Tremont Street across the road from the Boston Commons. There, Nana would give readings (telling individuals things regarding their lives). In my teens, I remember family members talking about my grandmother working there. The conversations were not positive. Her daughters were Christians and they believed their mother's activity went against their faith. Of course like most religious people I've seen, they rigidly believed their way was the only true way, and were not accepting of other points of view. I ashamedly admit, that much later I became among those who thought they had a lock on truth. Once I started exploring outside my religious tradition I gradually came to a much more expansive view of the world. My exploration was a major contributing factor to my writing this book.

During my lengthy Christian experience I have observed so-called religious persons predicting events, none of which came to fruition. Equally unimpressive were their attempts at healing. I have seen ministers go through rituals week after week while desperate people clung to their every word in the hope of healing. There was none! Instead parishioners were told to "wait on God" or "God works in mysterious ways." My grandmother surely could do no worse than those hoaxers pretending to be something they were not, prophets or healers. According to the stories I heard Nana was quite successful in her readings. She had a following. The owner of the tearoom thought highly of her abilities. In fact, the owner of the Tearoom encouraged Nana to stay on after she made a decision to retire. I have come to the conclusion that folks need to mind their own business; if people's ideas and beliefs do not harm themselves or others they should be allowed to be free to live their life without judgment or condemnation; there is already much too much of that.

Chapter Fourteen

Free Will? Albert Einstein, Unjust Laws and the UFOs/ UAF Phenomenon

Free Will?

We learn our values, beliefs, attitudes, and reactions from our environment. In turn these values, beliefs, and such, are the building blocks of our personalities. These can also include innate traits passed down and inherited through genetics. While other traits are absorbed consciously others to a great extent are acquired unconsciously. A process that starts at a very young age when we are too young to make conscious decisions to accept or reject those things that impact our personality. They are simply unconsciously absorbed from one's surroundings.

Where does free will come into play? Is it more of an illusion than a reality? Could it be that most of the so-called free will we display is simply prewired reactions reflecting the environmental influences that helped form us? On the surface, the things we do appear to be driven by free will as we make conscious decisions. How many of these decisions are driven by our experiences? How many are conscious decisions driven by unconscious motivations? That is decisions made without really understanding why we make them.

Those in authority have long understood the power of unconscious learning. For centuries, they have used it and twisted it to their advantage. How else do you get individuals to enthusiastically fight and die for any reason deemed necessary by their leaders? Many consent without question, thought, or consideration for their own safety. Following orders is a knee-jerk response for the indoctrinated ones.

This type of cultural programming of unbounded loyalty to country, individuals, and religion begins at a very young age with school, church, movies, toys, friends, parents, etc. all conveying the same message of blind allegiance. Moms and dads are convinced that military service, even when it leads to the death of a child, is an honor simply because somebody in authority says it is. Some would call this patriotism.

This type of programming is not only restricted to patriotic indoctrination, but also directly correlates to racism, sexism and cultural divisions, all of which are unconsciously learned behaviors. For the most part, it seems, these things have nothing to do with free will.

When does free will start and cultural environmental programming end? In the previously outlined examples, I don't think there is any free will. Patriotism, racism and sexism are commonly learned and programmed responses from a very young age. Until someone is awakened from their proverbial stupor, they will continue to do what they have been programmed to do, create robotic reactions to their environment.

Albert Einstein

Albert Einstein said, "He who joyfully marches to music in rank and file has already earned my contempt. He has been given a large brain by mistake, since for him the spinal cord would fully suffice. This disgrace to civilization should be done away with at once. Heroism at command, senseless brutality, deplorable love of country stance, how violently I hate all this, how despicable and ignoble war is; I would rather be torn to shreds than be a part of so base an action! It is my conviction that killing under the cloak of war is nothing but an act of murder." Einstein's depiction of war and those who participate in it may be offensive to some; truth usually is. It is this kind of outrage that needs to be expressed if the carnage is ever to end.[1]

Science's Influence in Countering Unjust Laws and Tradition

Propaganda has often disguised itself in "god talk." Religion has a long history of influencing the thinking and actions of others, for better or worse. For the most part, those who control the flow of religious information, along with their political counterparts, have gone unchallenged in their contrived view of the world. Science has helped to change that.

The work toward the invention of the microscope by Malpighi, Robert Hooke, Leeuwenhoek, and Zacharias Jebsen who often gets the credit but all contributed to its development.[2] They made it possible for the invisible world of microbes to become visible. This discovery eventually shattered the religious myth that evil spirits or certain infractions that the religious elite saw as sinful were the causes of sickness.

Religions of all sorts are at the forefront when it comes to marginalizing and destroying those who disagree with their tenets. Many would argue that religion has served humans admirably. That may be the case depending on your point of view; but at what cost? The destruction of civilizations in the name of religion is commonplace. Conflicts continue overtly and covertly with the delusions of religious and / or cultural superiority at their root. These two warped motivations often go hand in hand.

For years, officials of The Inquisition (the arm of the Catholic Church responsible for punishing those who deviated from church doctrine) harassed Galileo. They eventually placed him under house arrest for his discovery and assertion that the earth revolved around the sun. Galileo died in 1642 while still confined.[3] Fifty-six years prior to Galileo's discovery, Giordano Bruno an Italian Dominican friar, philosopher, mathematician, poet, and cosmological theorist theorized that the earth revolved around the sun. In 1586 authorities burned him at the stake because of his views of an infinite universe inhabited by many other intelligent beings.[4]

Delving into the sciences precipitated the persecution of Galileo and the execution of Giordano Bruno. Millions all over the planet have suffered and died under the heavy hand of religious fanaticism. Protestantism also had its persecutory counterpart in John Calvin who persecuted and killed those who dared to think for themselves by not parroting the dogma of the day. Renaissance man, Michel Servetus, a theologian and physician, skilled in many of the sciences, was among the many caught in the web of the Protestant witch-hunt. In Geneva, Switzerland, on October 27, 1553, Servetus was burned at a stake for not adhering to the doctrine of the Trinity.[5] It is regrettable that intolerance, violence, and murder in the name of religion was and is still common.

Science has put the fear of "God" in the religious hierarchy. They fear that their hold on power and their revenue streams will dry up; as science pulls the covers off many of the myths they hold dear. Religion and superiority these Siamese twins, "power on" because people love their delusions: the truth is often too painful to tolerate and for many impossible to accept.

UFOs /UAF (Unidentified Aerial Phenomenon)

Ever since the United States detonated the first atomic bomb in July of 1945 UFO sightings have increased.[6] Occasionally throughout 2022 mainstream media with information given to them from high ranking government officials have released sightings of UFOs/UAF. The government admits these vehicles are faster and out maneuver our most advanced air craft.

Since the crash and military recovery of a "flying disc" that went down in Roswell New Mexico on July 2, 1947 and the thousands of sightings seen since, the government in response has circulated misinformation regarding the existence of UFOs.[7] Not only ordinary citizens but military and commercial air plane pilots have also seen these objects. Behind the smoke and mirrors the US government, because of UFO intrusion into US air space UFOs have been taken very serious. Over the 75 year period since Roswell, there has been approximately twelve government funded investigations into UFOs, most notably Project Blue Book.[8] Most of these projects were designed to maintain the cover-up of the UFO reality. In April of 2020 the Pentagon released videos of UFOs that were tracked by radar; some were going into and coming up from the ocean and traveling at speeds and making maneuvers unexplainable with our knowledge of physics.[9] For me what is also unexplainable is why after 75 years of UFO deception is the government suddenly openly admitting there existence? You can be sure that after 75 years the powers that be have a whole lot of information regarding "Unidentified Flying Objects" that they are not telling us. You don't designate something multiple levels "Above Top Secret" which is the designation for UFO, if you don't have something extraordinary to hide. In 2022 President Biden backed intelligence investigations into UFOs. Past presidents have not been able to access these files. If Biden is successful in accessing them it will indicate a change in a decade's year old policy of strict secrecy.

Type, UFO whistle blowers, in your search box for additional information.

UFOs (Unidentified Flying Objects) are nothing new. They've been around for a long time. Indigenous people have known of their existence for hundreds even thousands of years. In some cases they also knew the beings who manned the vehicles. From all over the earth indigenous peoples have spoken of beings coming from the sky. It is possible that Giordano Bruno who I spoke of in the above section got his belief of life beyond earth from the indigenous people of his day and / or from the appearances of vehicles in the sky that he observed. Both the Hopi and the Dakota point to the Pleiades from where their ancestors came. Black Elk, in his book *The Sacred Ways of the Lakota*, speaks of his interaction with the disks and his communication with the beings that operated them; who he says were short in stature but human. Other Indian tribes also point to the heavens as their origins. The Dogon tribe in West Africa, living in Mali have ancient petroglyphs of the solar system. The Dogon also possess and have passed down ancient knowledge of Sirius B a companion star of the star Sirius. The existence of Sirius B was not known by Western scientists until 1970. The Dogon say that this knowledge was given to them thousands of years ago by the Nommos who came from Sirius B in an "ark" that came spinning down from the sky.[10] 15th Century paintings and a medieval tapestry of the Virgin Mary shows an unknown vehicle in the background sky; this is among other medieval artistic renderings displaying what is assumed to be non-human vehicles in the sky. These were portrayed hundreds of years before the modern discovery of human flight.

I think the truth about extraterrestrial life has been known for centuries and has been hidden from the world's populations. Such knowledge would crush the believe systems of those in power.

In the 1980's under a FOIA (Freedom of Information Act) the CIA released 1000 pages of UFO records pointing to the existence of extraterrestrial life. Other countries have also opened their files for the public to view. These revelations affirm what Giordano Bruno asserted more than four centuries ago and what indigenous people have known for far longer. Ardy Sixkiller Clarke, in her book *Sky People,* interviewed indigenous people living in Mesoamerica (Mexico, Guatemala, Haiti, Honduras and Belize) and tells of their contact with the "Sky People." Some of these contacts are long standing until the present.[11] "Sky People" gives answers to a topic that only seems to have questions. The documentary titled "Unacknowledged" by Dr. Steven Greer is an informative documentary regarding extraterrestrial existence; he's one of the world's foremost authorities on the subject.

Chapter Fifteen

Berta Caceres, the Generals and Modern Day Manifest Destiny

Berta

On March 2, 2016, Berta Caceres was murdered. She was a forty-four year old grassroots environmental leader fighting on behalf of her people, the Lenca, the indigenous people of Honduras. Between 2010 and 2014, 101 environmental activists were killed in Honduras.[1] These killings continue because of the Lenca's resistances to government and corporate takeover of their land. Berta, before her death, was awarded the Goldman Environmental Prize, an award given annually to noteworthy work done by environmental activists.

A report in November of 2017 by the Honduran Attorney General's Office, concluded that executives of Desarrollos Energeticos S.A (DESA), along with individuals associated with the Honduran military were among eight suspects arrested for the slaying of Berta

Caceres. DESA was contracted to build a hydroelectric dam on Lenca land.[2]

The trial of those accused of taking part in Berta's murder began in September of 2018. Berta's daughter, Bertiza reported that the government, even after a court order, refused to provide information to the family's legal team. The government had information implicating high-level business and state officials for more than a year and a half, but did not act on it.[3] This resistance to share information was not a surprise. It was the government that gave permission for a dam to be built on Lenca land, without consulting the Lenca people. "On December 2, 2019 seven of the men involved with Berta's slaying were sentenced to 30 to 50 years in prison. None of the leaders have yet paid for their involvement."[4] This changed on July 6, 2021 as the Honduran Supreme Court convicted David Castillo, the former president of the hydroelectric corporation DESA as a co-perpetrator in Berta Caceres Murder.[5]

Since the 2009 coup against the democratically elected President Manuel Zelaya, subsequent leadership has thrown Honduras into chaos. Thousands of Hondurans have been killed while others have fled to the USA for asylum. These killings continue as the people stand up against corruption.

If the Trump administrations as well as others do not want to accept Honduran asylum seekers into the United States these administrations should stop supporting the military regime that is forcing Hondurans to flee. Some in Congress have called for the end of military support to Honduras as well as other parts of the world where military aid is used to murder unarmed civilians. Their call has not been heeded. America also has to answer for the number of unarmed civilians it kills in drone attacks around the world. President Biden's 2021 February announcement of ending the US backing of the Saudi war in Yemen is a game changer. "This war has to end", he stated, and to underscore our commitment, we're ending all American support for offensive operations in the war in Yemen, including relevant arm sales."[6] The devil is in the details. Only time will tell whether or not similar policies will extend to Honduras, Israel and other corrupt regimes that kill unarmed innocent men, women and children. One thing we know for sure, ending support for these regimes will not happen without intense pressure from American citizens.

The Generals

Major General Smedley D. Butler, a thirty-three-year active military soldier (1898–1931) and author of *War is a Racket,* had this to say about his military tenure:

> "I spent 33 years and four months in active military service and during that period I spent most of my time as a high class muscle man for Big Business, for Wall Street and the bankers. In short, I was a racketeer, a gangster for capitalism. I helped make Mexico and

especially Tampico safe for American oil interests in 1914. I helped make Haiti and Cuba a decent place for the National City Bank boys to collect revenues in. *I helped in the raping of half a dozen Central American republics for the benefit of Wall Street*. I helped purify Nicaragua for the International Banking House of Brown Brothers in 1902-1912. I brought light to the Dominican Republic for the American sugar interests in 1916. I helped make Honduras right for the American fruit companies in 1903. In China in 1927 I helped see to it that Standard Oil went on its way unmolested. Looking back on it, I might have given Al Capone a few hints. The best he could do was to operate his racket in three districts. I operated on three continents."[7]

In 1930 because of Franklin Delano Roosevelt's establishment of the New Deal the business elites were up in arms. The companies of Brown Brothers and J.P Morgan, both who increased and / or acquired their wealth through their involvement with the slave trade were among those who conspired to overthrow the government of the U.S.[8] General Butler was sought to lead the coup but by this time he understood the game being played by business elite's, bankers, and corrupt government officials. He understood that war was a racket to make many filthy rich at the expense of the thousands of lives and maimed bodies of brain washed naive young boys who bought the propaganda that they were fighting for something noble; nothing could be further from the truth. General Butler spoke before a congressional committee revealing the details of the plot. Others Included in the attempted insurrection were the businesses of Dupont, General Motors, Birds Eye, General Foods, Heinz, Goodtea, Maxwell House, Prescott Bush and others. As you would expect none of these entities were held accountable.[9]

Nothing much has changed since the death of Major General Butler in June of 1940. The bankers, big business, and government continues to have free reign. They are still seldom held accountable for their actions. Today, we continue to co-opt governments into doing our dirty work. These co-opted governments suppress the will of their people, thus allowing American interest to prevail.

The murder of environmentalist Berta Caceres's of Honduras is an example of the millions throughout Central, South, and North America and other parts of the world who have died and are dying so that the capitalist empires can flourish. This is how I think capitalism works on the grand scale. It is just, "business as usual."

According to four-star General Wesley Clark, the NATO supreme commander who served under President Bill Clinton, there was a plan under the

2001–2009 Bush administration to invade seven predominantly Muslim countries; Iraq, Syria, Lebanon, Libya, Somalia, Sudan, and Iran. The plan was devised shortly after the September 11, 2001 downing of the World Trade Center (WTC). A high-ranking military official relayed this information to General Clark when he visited the Pentagon in November 2001.[10] Iran is the last country to be destroyed as described in George Bush's administration invasion plan. In 2015 the Obama administration brokered the Iranian nuclear deal, (JCPOA) Join Comprehension Plan of Action. Under this agreement Iran would reduce its stock pile of uranium by 98%. In May of 2018 the Trump administration withdrew from the agreement only to place greater sanctions on Iran which in turn encouraged the Iranians to advance their nuclear program. Trump's goals were not clear. What he did accomplish was increased tensions between Iran the US and Israel. That would appear to be exactly what he intended. To what end? I think it would fulfill the wish list of the last country to be destroyed on the Bush administration's hit list; the last domino to fall in the Middle East.

According to General Clark there was no rational reason as to why this plan was set in motion. These countries had no link to the (WTC) destruction.[11] Clark also speaks to the above concerns on YouTube.

These Islamic countries border strategic waterways and are not in sync with the Western values; reason enough to gain dominance over them. Clark was beginning to understand what Major General Smedley Butler learned firsthand decades ago: everything is expendable except the maintenance and expansion of the empire.

In the Autumn of 2018, President Trump directed a lot of tough talk toward the North Korean President Kim Jong-un. Trump was only voicing publicly the frustrations of presidents before him. What should we do about North Korea's nuclear weapons program? In August of 2002, during a Bush administration planning meeting, under Secretary of State John Bolton, suggested North Korea be added to the list of countries to be invaded.[12]

Obama's call for a trillion-dollar upgrade to the US nuclear weapons program, and Trump's resistance to compromise makes it nonsensical for Kim Jong-un to consider nuclear disarmament. Unless the US is willing to make significant concessions, a denuclearized North Korea is nothing more than a pipe dream. The only thing preventing a US attack on North Korea is their possession of nuclear weapons. How lucky for them! I cannot say the same for Libya and Iraq.

America's, "Do what I say, but not as I do" policies do not encourage other leaders to put their trust in the words of an American president. With the Biden presidency a new effort is being made to revive the Iran agreement. As of December 2022 efforts for revival look doubtful.

Modern Day Manifest Destiny

Manifest Destiny has been called by different names in different times; colonialism, expansionism, imperialism, neocolonialism: the meaning has always been the same. It refers to the stealing of land, killing of its inhabitants and destroying their property, in the name of God, white supremacy or simply greed for land expansion. Obama said, "You can put lipstick on a pig, but it is still a pig." For thousands of years, this system of land theft has been in play. Western cultures have become quite adept at it and have used this system as a means to acquire land while amassing power.

Fanatical Christians, Jews, Muslims, and others make use of what I call "The God System." It is easy to get people motivated to do what you want in the name of a "higher power." The use of a higher power fused with political slogans for love of country etc.; have been woven together to create the mantra of "patriotism." Their ultimate game plan as previously stated is to ensure that citizens are willing to die in wars and in other vain pursuits designed to keep the powerful in power.

The day military big shots and those they manipulate stand up and refuse to fight and die for their masters in contrived wars, is the day that America *will* be great. Unfortunately, that day is unlikely because the military and the government are fused at the hip, it seems, they serve each other.

Chapter Sixteen

The Call - Breaking through - The Eyes

The Call

In 1965, shortly after graduating from high school, I got "The Call." I was informed I needed to appear at the Commonwealth Armory on Commonwealth Avenue in Boston. There were hundreds of young men already there when I arrived. The Vietnam War was raging and the draft was the law of the land. The military was looking for bodies. Fifty years have passed, and being interviewed at the Armory is still one of my most vivid memories.

My dad asked as I was preparing to go to the Armory, "What are you going to do?" The Nation of Islam had already shaped my attitude about fighting in America's wars. I told him I was not sure. I would figure it out when I got there.

As I sat in a large room among hundreds of other young men, I was thinking of a way to express my refusal to fight. When I received a form to fill out I wrote my opposition to the war on it. The next move was theirs. I remember waiting calmly. Shortly after, an officer came before the group holding a form and yelling, "Who wrote this?" I knew he was referring to me. I stood. He beckoned me to follow. I expected hostility. To my surprise, his demeanor became friendly once we were in his office. He calmly said, "I understand." Understand what I thought? Was his statement a short hand way of saying that he understood the truth about this war? I was pleasantly caught off guard. He explained that filling out the form did not obligate me to do anything. He told me from this day forward, I would not be hearing from the military. I took him at his word and completed the form. His word was true. I never heard from the draft board again other than to notify me I was rejected from military service. Some of my homeboys died in the war; others were injured physically and psychologically.

Without alternative sources of information to broaden the ability to make informed decisions, one is stuck with information from mainstream and corporate media outlets whose primary interest is to make money for their investors. They are bound by their investors and what government officials are willing to reveal. Some information is prohibited from going public because of national security: a catch all for anything the government does not want us to know. As Americans, we must educate ourselves beyond the talking points of the traditional corporate news media; otherwise, we may be making decisions that are not in our own best interest.

My advice is do not be a sheep led to the slaughter. Ask questions, and do some investigation before committing yourself to any cause or ideology; particularly one that is going to put your life in danger. If you are going to put yourself in harm's way, at the beck and call of some leader, at least know why! Gaining insight will lift the hypnotic trance of those who say, "Do what you're told, and don't ask questions." As a result of inquiry you will gradually be able to make rational decisions based on fact rather than psychological and emotional fantasies.

Breaking Through

From time immemorial men, women, and children have been harassed, abused, tortured, and sacrificed on ideological alters of those in power. The Salem Witch Trials in Massachusetts are a stunning example of this type of religious and political maliciousness.

Had my grandmother (Nana) lived during the time of those trials, she could have been a prime target of scrutiny because of her unconventional views. Living in Lynn on the border of Salem would have been much too close for comfort. In fact, according to historical records, there were people from Lynn and many other towns in Massachusetts who were accused and slain for witchcraft.[1]

Fear is a common human response to things not understood. Evil is easily attributed to things that are strange and unfamiliar. For those in positions of authority, individuals with psychic ability can easily represent a threat to their authority.

Researchers are working to understand the world beyond our five senses in an attempt to unlock its mysteries. Much like the discoveries into the world of the microbe that exposed the religious superstition of sickness new discoveries beyond the five senses may also affect the world as we know it.

The Eyes

For a number of years, Nana lived on the first-floor apartment on Woodbine Street in Roxbury, Boston Massachusetts. That was the last house my father bought and the house my sisters and I grew up in during our teen years. I lived there until 1967 before I left to live on my own.

My grandmother had the opportunity to observe my comings and goings, adding another pair of eyes to monitor me. I never brought trouble home, so that was never a concern for my parents. My mother once told Vernice after we had married, "Tommy (my nickname) was always such a good boy." I'm glad my mother thought so.

The guys I hung out with were party animals. We would party until the last record spun. For the most part that was the extent of our frivolous behavior.

I met Eric a tall heavy set outgoing young man while we were both members of the Nation of Islam. I met James through Eric. James was tall, slim and on the reserved side. The three of us were inseparable during our mid-teen years. We would walk the city streets at a blistering pace following information leading to the parties for that weekend. Not having a car did not stop us. Eric's parents owned a cleaning business. Party central was at "Care Cleaners"; were Eric worked with his parents. Eric had all the information regarding the party locations for the night. I remember Mr. S's, (Eric's father) hearty laugh. He was funny yet serious. He and his son Eric had a reputation of being individuals you did not want to mess with. Eric's mom, Mrs. S. was kind and sweet. She always had a pleasant word. She would remind us to behave ourselves before we went out on the weekends. She knew young men's tendency toward mischief.

Nana never commented on my comings and goings; at least not to me. On the weekends, I never knew what time I would be home because I never knew what time the last party would end. Coming home was particularly uncomfortable when I didn't have my key and had to ring the doorbell; announcing my arrival time to the whole household. I would occasionally throw pebbles at my sister Evelyn's third floor bedroom window to get her attention. This would be the signal that I did not have my key and wanted her to open the front door. Evelyn reminded me of an occasion when she did not wake up and I was forced to ring the doorbell. She said I blamed *her* for my getting in trouble. I can't believe I reacted that way. I smile thinking about it. If Sis said I blamed her, then I am sure I did. Her memory is far better than mine.

Chapter Seventeen

Holy Trinity D&B Corp, Music, Introvert or Extrovert?, The Family & Religion, Commitment

Holy Trinity Drum and Bugle Corp

From 1959 to 1962 my sister Evelyn and I were members of the Holy Trinity (Troubadours and Cadets) Drum and Bugle Marching Corps, located in Boston's South End. We had the opportunity to see the Cadets for the first time while doing errands with our mother in the South End. We were around thirteen years old. The Cadets were marching up Tremont Street, not far from the University of Massachusetts on Arlington Street. My sister and I were attracted to their music, precision and stately appearance as they marched by us. Sis recalls we ran after them to find out their name. We saw the name "Holy Trinity Cadets" written on their bass drum. It was not long after that we became members of the junior corps, the Troubadours. That chance encounter began for me a lifetime of musical involvement.

The corps was the creation of Father Carr, a Catholic priest at the Holy Trinity Church on Shawmut Avenue in the South End of Boston. His hand was central in the development and sustaining of the drum corps. My guess is at the time we were in the corps he would have been in his mid-fifties; he was around 6'5" with the sturdy build of an athlete. He was a no nonsense kind of a guy and had to be, considering some of the characters he had to deal with. He would pop in on some of our music rehearsals and walk around the facility making sure things were in order. The buck stopped at Father Carr. If there was anything that could not be resolved by the instructors he would take charge; that would include discipline. Father Carr's love for the drum corps was shown through his tireless efforts to maintain the many facets of the corps functioning; such as the horns, drums, uniforms, instructors, fund raising etc. He marched with us in all our parades and attended all the competitions. The drum corps mothers were Father Carr's foot soldiers. They were the unsung individuals. Without them the drum corps would probably have ground to a halt. We owe Father Carr and all the mothers a debt of gratitude. Thank you!

Playing the baritone horn in the junior corps and singing with the guys in the neighborhood were my first opportunities to work with others toward a common goal. Being part of these groups, particularly the drum and bugle corps, which had nearly a hundred members helped me to learn social skills that carried over into adulthood. I learned to work with all different types of personalities. Some were individuals I had to tolerate, and a few I preferred to steer clear of. All in all, it was a great group to be associated with. The drum corps helped me develop patience. Patience was needed to learn the musical parts and the assigned marching maneuvers. I was encouraged by reminding myself that by practicing I was getting closer to mastering my musical and marching assignments.

Those who graduated from the Troubadours (the junior corps) to the Cadets (the senior corps) were usually in their mid-teens. They had proven their ability as musicians as well as their ability to execute marching and maneuvering patterns. In the Troubadours Ricky Rogers was our drill instructor. He was a hard task master. He would holler and even throw a drum stick at you if you continued to make mistakes while he was trying to teach the basic steps of marching and maneuvering. He was strict but also caring, which made him special. If you made it through *his* boot camp you could probably make it in the Cadets'. Ricky was the drum major in the Cadets and a darn good one. He had won multiple awards for his marching and performance skills. He and Mr. Whitney, our horn instructor, determined who was ready to graduate to the Cadets. Advancement to the senior corps was based on your proficiency in both marching and musicality.

In both the junior and senior corps competitions were judged on musical articulation and marching and maneuvering proficiency. In both, the judges would frantically run around the field looking for flaws in the performance. For errors in both marching and musical articulation one tenth of a point was subtracted from a beginning perfect score of one hundred. Because of the high bar set by the judges, absolute perfection was required of each corps member. Competition was fierce. You could be knocked out of 1st or 2nd place by one tenth of a point.

In the Cadets you were expected to learn the music and marching patterns quickly. Meeting the expectations of the instructors and some of the Cadet members who were years older than us recruits from the Troubadours, proved stressful enough for some to forfeit their dream of marching with their long-admired Cadets. Those who hung in there were my sister Evelyn who was in the color guard, Peter Rodriquez., the Gillory brothers, "Little" Woo, Carl Finley and David Roderick who years later would be my best man at my wedding.

As far as I can remember, Holy Trinity was the only corps in Massachusetts that was comprised of a significant number of non-white members. We competed in the junior and senior drum corps divisions in Massachusetts and beyond. True to form, there were the haters among other drum corps groups who would unleash their racial epithets. My sister Evelyn recalled an incident that went beyond name-calling. She was riding with Father Carr, leaving the competition grounds when his car got bogged down in traffic. Another car pulled up alongside him. Those in the other car pretended to be friendly as they acknowledged Father Carr's return home from the hospital after a heart attack. One of them threw ice water in his face. Blacks were not the only ones harassed and attacked. Some Whites who associated with us were also targets. My sister's story made me realize that Father Carr was a trailblazer. He was a hero, courageously putting his faith into action, despite the racism that was prevalent during the 50's and the 60's. Thank you, Father Carr, from all of us.

Despite the negative racial climate of the times, the Cadets forged on and were a force to be reckoned with on the competition field. I may never have had the opportunity to develop my musical skills had it not been for Father Carr's refusal to not let racism deter him from his vision to organize an inner city drum and bugle corps. Of the hundreds who benefited from his efforts, we are grateful.

Holy Trinity Cadets
(Father Carr is in front in Black)

In 1962, the corps disbanded. Father Carr was relocated to Jamaica. His predecessor had no interest in continuing the drum corps. I joined other senior corps, but their style of music left me unfulfilled. As far as I was concerned, no one could arrange music like Mr. Bergdahl, the Cadet's musical director. He knew how to arrange music that touched your soul. I eventually fell away from the drum corps scene. Playing music however had become part of me. I learned to play the slide trombone. It was a smooth transition from the baritone horn that I had played in the drum corps because the size of mouthpieces were the same.

Music

Before I go much further I have to give props to my Grandmother Evelyn (Nana) she introduced me to Tony Bennett when I was a teenager. She gave me a 45 record of his hit, *I Left my Heart in San Francisco*. To this day, Tony Bennett and his genre of music inspires and excites me. It was this style of music that the Cadets played, and why I enjoyed it so much.

Playing the trombone eventually helped me transition into a new peer group of musicians. It gave me an opportunity to play professionally in jazz and rock bands. In 1968 I started playing trombone with the

Bacchanalians, an Afro Cuban jazz band. This was my first opportunity to leave the seclusion of my practice room at home and start playing with others. The group consisted of seven core members. At times it expanded to as many as ten.

Thanks to Bertram Alleyne, who founded the Bacchanalians in the mid-1960s, we novice musicians got the opportunity to strut our stuff. We performed at local community events and numerous colleges in the Boston area. Performing at the Playhouse in the Park was the venue the group highly anticipated. This was a huge community event. It was at Franklin Park which borders Roxbury, Dorchester, and Jamaica Plain. Hundreds attended. It was a feather in your cap to perform there. Our personnel consisted of two saxophones, Gregory O'Byant on tenor, Cyril Chapman on alto sax, yours truly Sterling Anderson on slide trombone, Curtis Jones on vibes, Bertram Alleyne on conga drum, Charles Holly on bongos and various small axes, Ralph Kimball (aka Tuffy) on trap drums and Hassan Requib formally known as James Hogg on upright bass. The group produced a sound that drove the crowd wild!

Elma Lewis sponsored the Playhouse in the Park event. When it came to the performing arts, she was the driving force in the Roxbury Community. She had started the Elma School of Fine Arts in 1950. The school's mission was to provide for the social, cultural and artistic needs for African Americans living in the Boston area. In 1968 the Jewish community donated to Elma Lewis an enormous long abandoned Jewish synagogue. Now it was going to be put to good use. It sat on the corner of Elm Hill Avenue and Seaver Street in Roxbury. Varieties of artistic expressions were taught; dance, music, the painting arts and sculpture to name a few.

The Bacchanalians began for me a life long odyssey of playing music with a variety of groups. The Bacchanalians never formally disbanded. Gigs gradually dried up. In the back of the book, I name those with whom I had the privilege of performing with over the years. The following are pictures of the groups with whom I have played.

Bacchanalians – Afro Cuban Jazz Band
From left to right top row– Cyril Chapman (alto sax), Sterling Anderson (slide trombone), Richard

Harris (bass guitar), Stan Cleveland (trumpet), Gregory O'Bryant (tenor sax), bottom row – Dorian Magee (drums), Sid Simmons (piano), Bertram Alleyne (conga drum) founder and leader.

Kilimanjaro
from left to right – Yusif Harlim (bass guitar), Cyril Chapman (alto sax), Marlik Farced (drums), Sterling Anderson (slide trombone)and Elliot Slaughter on piano.

The Contemporary jazz quartet Kilimanjaro was organized in 1975 by Cyril Chapman ex- member of the Bacchanalian. Kilimanjaro's music was a step up in complexity from the music performed in the Bacchanalians. Thanks to Cyril we were given the opportunity to stretch our music making capabilities. Our performances at the defunct Western Front Jazz Club in Cambridge, Massachusetts were for me the most memorable. We were really on those nights and the crowd acknowledged it. Between playing with the Bacchanalians and Kilimanjaro I also had the opportunity of playing in a rhythm and blues band, backing up a consummate entertainer, Ralph Graham. This gave me the opportunity to expand my musical horizons.

After a lengthy hiatus from playing music, I started playing again in 2007. This was after we moved from Boston to North Carolina in 2005. I was invited to play music again by Tracy Love the piano player in the picture. I was excited to start playing again. We played jazz standards, something I had always wanted to do. To get myself up to speed I began woodshedding. We named ourselves The Love Connection the above personal were as follows: From left to right; Wayne Webster (tenor sax organizer and leader), Tracy Love (piano), Janci Hartley featured singer and MC and yours truly Sterling Anderson on trombone and vocals. We rehearsed for about a year to get our repertoire tight then began gigging here and there. It was a great seven-year run. We disbanded when members relocated.

Introvert or Extrovert?

In previous attempts to describe my mother and father's temperaments, I tended to lean toward the narrow but commonly used definitions of "introvert and extrovert." These definitions are limited and misleading when not properly understood. The psychological definition of introvert and extrovert refers to how people gain and lose energy; not necessarily how ones behaves. Introverts gain energy from solitude. They lose energy from being around others for extended periods of time. Extroverts gain energy from being around people. Their energy is sapped when they spend too much time alone. They recharge by being social while introverts recharge with solitude.[1]

My dad and mom were both introverts. They enjoyed their solitude. That is how they recharged themselves after being around people for extended periods of time. Dad enjoyed solitude and used much of his time working on creative pursuits, with the intention of becoming independent from the daily grind. He enjoyed psychology and information geared toward personal growth and self-awareness.

Once or twice a week Ma would joyfully take her bus ride over the MIT Bridge that connects Cambridge to Boston. She would refuse a ride when offered. Ma would go to Wendy's to eat, and then go shopping afterward. At the time I did not understand this was my mother's way of getting her alone time for the purpose of recharging herself.

Introverts can appear to be extroverts and vice versa; this confusion is understandable when these terms are used only to gage outward personality traits. No one is totally an introvert or extrovert; both have the same needs but in varying degrees. Individual tendencies may lean towards one more than the other. After researching these temperaments, I have become aware of the likeness between myself and my parents. Now I understand my need for extended periods of alone time due to my own tendency towards introversion.

This type of awareness can enlighten ones understanding for those who have a strong need for social interaction as opposed to those who may not. It has given me more insight regarding those I interact with. Discovering the similarities between my parents and myself makes me feel closer to them even though they've both passed. Thinking about this feeling of closeness brings tears to my eyes.

From the perspective of temperament, my parents were much more alike than they may have realized. Their difference though, was evident in their view of the world. Ma was more apt to accept traditions, though she was more complicated than that. She did not blanketly adhere to the status quo programming. In fact at the time Obama was running, Ma was intelligent enough to support Obama while I was still brainwashed by religion and the political status quo and voted for his republican opponent.

Understanding the meanings of introvert and extrovert has given me a deeper understanding and appreciation for my parents. Ma was an "introvert", but not to be confused with characteristics of passivity, shyness, or being reserved or withdrawn; no, Ma was none of these. She was outgoing and knew how to stand up for herself and the family when she saw the need. Ma blasted a teacher at Sister Paulette's middle school because of what she saw as unfair treatment. At times we viewed Ma as stubborn. I now believe what we viewed as pigheadedness was simply Ma standing for what she believed; not simply accepting things because she was expected to.

After a fall, Ma wore a halo for months; when it was removed the doctor recommended surgery. Ma refused the surgery and nothing was going to change her mind. She was willing to get a second opinion. The second doctor said there was no need for an operation;

confirming Ma's stance. When her primary doctor was told she had elected not to have the surgery his once friendly demeanor switched to something other than friendly. Again, Ma's so-called stubbornness was simply her conviction of what she knew was best for her. As I look back, I realize Ma's resistance to other's points of view was simply her right to have her own. Ma's tendency toward introversion had nothing to do with passivity or being withdrawn but instead her need for alone time to recharge herself to reengage in the world.

Family & Religion

Ma would see to it that my sister, Evelyn and I attended the Catholic Church that was not far from where we lived on Suffolk Street in Lynn, Massachusetts. This was part of Ma's traditional upbringing that she held on to. She was not excited about the church, but without knowledge of other spiritual alternatives, the church would have to do. I don't remember Dad attending church. It is my guess he came with us on some occasions. Dad was not a fan of religion but he did not discourage us from attending church. He attended church with his family when he was young. Dad was practical and probably saw the church as a means of instilling positive moral values. To my knowledge, religion never became an issue between my parents.

Until editing this section of the book I had not thought of how Dad who was not a fan of organized religion must have felt when my mother, sister and I became members of the Nation of Islam (the Muslim religion). I was about thirteen when I joined the Nation. We had lived in Boston for about three years before moving to the house Dad bought on Intervale Street. Dad became friends with our next door neighbor Mr. K. Both attended some of the Muslim meetings together. Mr. K and his whole family eventually joined the Nation of Islam. With friends and immediate family joining the Nation, my father must have felt a sense of abandonment, sadness and maybe a little anger as friends and loved ones became members of an organization that he wasn't interested in becoming a part of. I felt ashamed that it took writing a book to consider how Dad may have felt during those times of change. I decided to call Evelyn to get more insight on Dad's state of mind at that time. I was surprised when Sis told me that Dad had encouraged Ma to join the Nation. Dad thought that joining the Nation would give Ma a social outlet and the mosque was conveniently located on our street. That understanding helped put my feelings in a proper perspective.

Ideologically Dad had no problem with the Nation but he did not want to be involved with the demands of religion. The Nation wanted the men to sell the Muhammad Speaks newspaper and attend the mosque a couple of times a week; that was definitely not Dad's style. Dad had his own interests and wasn't willing to have his time consumed with outside demands. One thing Dad did have a problem with regarding the Nation was my selling the Muhammad Speaks Newspaper. Dad never voiced why he didn't want me to sell the paper. I think he had an uneasiness about me being on the street selling the newspaper, which was at the time a very controversial publication.

Dad and Ma

Commitment

Ideologically my parent's interests diverged but maybe not as much as I thought. The recent finding that Dad encouraged Ma to join the Nation puts a different slant on things. Ma's struggle with depression did however present a challenge to their marriage. Commitment was the glue that held them together.

Inherent in all marriages is joy and struggle. This is inescapable as two grow together. Individual growth is also important. The need for acceptance of one another as growth takes place is essential. There must be commitment for the process of growth to take root and to eventually flourish. Commitment is marriage's life's blood. My parent's commitment to their marriage was an example for me in my marriage.

First Corinthians, (New International Version) chapter thirteen's description of love is exquisite. "Love is patient, love is kind. I does not envy, it does not boast, it is not proud or rude, it is not self- seeking (Love does not demand its own way). Love is not easily angered, it keeps no record of wrongs. Love does not delight in evil but rejoices with the truth. It always protects, always trust, always hopes, always and preserves. Love never fails. This is a very high standard. Few can measure up but if these qualities are to be developed commitment is a key component. Commitment keeps things from falling apart. It is an essential quality in any endeavor; marriage is no exception. The contemporary description of "feel good love" or infatuation is not sustainable; in life things change. Commitment allows the time needed for love to grow and blossom, through the good and not so good times. The expectation of "feel good love" is not prepared for the long haul.

According to a 2017 Pew report, 54% of Americans consider themselves religious and 75 % consider themselves spiritual. There are those who believe claiming religious involvement is enough to sustain their marriage. Studies have proven that there is no significant difference between the divorce rates of religious versus non- religious.

According to research by the Barna Research Group, an evangelical Christian polling firm based in Ventura, California "Over a decade ago, American divorce rates were highest among Baptist and nondenominational "Bible believing Christians and lower among more theologically liberal Christians like Methodist, with atheists at the bottom of the divorce pack ..."

In 2008, Barna sampled American divorce rates 30% of atheist reported ever being divorced, compared to 32% born again Christians.[2] The bottom line is, if you are not committed, regardless what you profess, the likelihood is that you *will not* stay married.

I have experienced a greater sense of freedom and fulfillment since redirecting my energy and commitment from the demands of religion and instead directing my energy and commitment to my personal and marital development. Commitment can make the difference between working things out, or, moving out. Commitment is love in action. It means doing what is needed to create a specific reality.

Chapter Eighteen

Civilized Humans?

Do we really need religion to drill into us what is right and what is wrong? This question is rarely asked because religion has become like the air we breathe, and we take it for granted. To what do other creatures subscribe that tells them how to live? Whatever it is, its effectiveness is undeniable. Animals fight to protect their food and their young. Alpha males may fight to protect their harem or dominance in their group. Some animals are territorial. Animals are not known to plan and execute annihilation of other animals because of hatred and greed for territory. When has separate species of the cat kingdom sought to destroy another? This is ridiculous, but we with human consciousness under sociopathic and psychotic leaders are perpetually destroying each other. We kill millions in wars and within the societies we live. It would behoove us to follow the example of animals. I think the balance of nature is maintained through their ability to co-exist.

Humans claim superiority over the animal kingdom. Until humans learn the fundamentals of how to live in peace with one another, the claim of superiority is hollow and to me without merit. Instead of trying to train animals, I think we should spend time observing and learning from them their secret of co-existence. This knowledge has eluded present day civilizations even with all the fancy religious rhetoric floating around.

We credit *instinct* to whatever intelligence animals display. If that is the case, what is it that both human and animal parents feel toward their offspring? Does either need religion to teach them to love and care for their offspring? No! Religions, though they claim love as their supreme virtue more often than not practice just the opposite. They have created endless sources of division and bondage.

If we would nurture love, which is our birthright, religion and its contrived rituals would be out of business. Humans have come to accept what religion and its proselytizers have trained us to believe, specifically, that we need them.

I don't think religion is what we need to embrace. It is instead the instinctual universal virtue of love which is displayed in both the animal and human kingdom. The cultural systems created by religion have served to divert humans from love of one another. Humans instead have been taught, to love their religions, proselytizers and their country at the expense of the innate love that is displayed between child and parent. The "faithful", those who are completely brainwashed, programmed and manipulated by their religion will follow blindly and do almost anything they are told. They will go to war against others, or even kill their family members if their leaders or "holy book" commands it. Nauseating!

The Universality of Love and Compassion

Psychologist Harry Harlow (October 31, 1905 – December 6, 1981) professor at the University of Wisconsin –Madison, through his research with monkeys, came to the following conclusion in the early 50's; "these animals loved, had affection, mattered to each other." "He used the word "love" very deliberately" says Deborah Blum, Professor of Journalism at University of Wisconsin – Madison. Blum adds, "even though his fellow psychologists were highly skeptical, not to say scornful, of that notion." Today, Harlow's understanding of animal emotions has come into its own.

Research by Charles Snowdon, a University of Wisconsin Madison professor of psychology who explored primate behavior for 35 years, offers this definition of love, "a preference for one other individual that is more or less exclusive and long lasting, and transcends other relationships." Snowdon says "that animal love is evident in species that form lifelong attachments, if a mate dies or disappears, often the remaining mate does not form a new pair bond at all." Franz D. Wall of the Emory University and Patricia McConnell behaviorist at the UW–Madison and others agree that the attachments that animals demonstrate when seen in humans is called love. Love is exemplified throughout the animal kingdom. It is not restricted to humans; though many would like to think it is, again harkening back to religious rhetoric many have been programmed to believe. The biological construction that elicits love is present in mammals; not only humans.[1]

The following are examples of an animal's ability to show love and compassion.

There are multiple substantiated cases where children had either been abandoned or lost and were raised by an animal that had been moved by compassion and took on the responsibility of caring and or raising the children as their own. Rev. J.A.L. Singh in 1920 tells the story of Amala and Kamala, two girls from Midnapore, India, who were raised by wolves from a very young age.[2]

Oxana Malaya, from Ukraine, was raised by dogs that cared for her from the age of three to eight. She probably had been abandoned or lost. She was found in 1991 and was able, with difficulty, to be integrated into human society.[3]

In 2008 Argentinean police found a 1 year old boy who had been separated from his father for a few days in the harsh winter cold. The police found that a group of cats had been keeping the boy warm by staying on top of him and bringing him bits of food.

Marina Chapman, after being abducted from her village in South America when she was four years old was left abandoned in the jungle where she was rescued by a troop of Capuchin monkeys. She lived with them for approximately 5 years. Her true life story is in the book "The Girl with No Name." These are a few of the amazing stories of animals caring for humans as their own.[4] They affirm what Harry Harlow discovered: animals love, care and have compassion not only for their own but also for humans.

The Cambridge Declaration on Consciousness

The Cambridge Declaration of Consciousness has formally affirmed what many in the scientific community have come to believe, that humans do not have exclusivity of consciousness or emotions. On July 7, 2012 a prominent international group of cognitive neuroscientists, encompassing a variety of specialties, gathered together at the University of Cambridge to reassess the neurobiological substrates (a base on which a process occurs) of conscious experience and related behavior in humans and animals. They concluded that human and animal emotional feelings arise from the same area in the brain. "Convergent evidence indicates that non-human animals have the neuroanatomical, neurochemical, and neurophysiological substrates of conscious states along with the capacity to exhibit intentional behaviors. Consequently, the weight of evidence indicates that humans are not unique in possessing the neurological substrates that generate consciousness. Non-human animals, including all mammals and birds, and many other creatures, including octopuses, also possess these neurological substrates.[5]

★ The Cambridge Declaration on Consciousness was written by Philip Low and edited by Jaak Panksepp, Diana Reiss, David Edelman, Bruno Van Swinderen, Philip Low and Christof Koch. The Declaration was publicly proclaimed in Cambridge, UK, on July 7, 2012, at the Francis Crick Memorial Conference on Consciousness in Human and non-Human Animals, at Churchill College, University of Cambridge, by Low, Edelman and Koch. The Declaration was signed by the conference participants that very evening, in the presence of Stephen Hawking, in the Balfour Room at the Hotel du Vin in Cambridge, UK. The signing ceremony was memorialized by CBS 60 Minutes.

African American scientist Charles H. Turner (1867-1923) was a pioneer in the understanding of animal behavior and cognition. Despite the severe racism of his times he was able to publish more than 70 papers on animal intelligence, behavior and learning competencies. The reinventing of animal cognition research in modern times is reestablishing the work that Turner had begun over a hundred years ago. Kudos to Science and the writers for acknowledging Turner and publishing some of his work; because all too often Black genius and accomplishments are ignored while others claim the credit. Again thank you.[6]

The Love Transfer

What is the greatest perpetual mass evil committed on the earth? I would say without question, it is war and the genocide of populations. I previously touched on the programming of humans and their willingness to die at the command of their leaders. Leaders have used love of country as an excuse for the evil of war. These leaders include the military industrial complex and much of corporate America. Religionists and politicians perpetuating the madness are at the foundation of this cabal. Their job is to manipulate humans to dance when they play the tune. They have managed to get humans to transfer a portion of their love energy to idols. These idols include love of country (patriotism), religion, vain objects and ideologies of worship. These things have stymied human evolution for ages. They are the bane on human existence.

Acceptance

Accepting differences is a good starting point for developing respectful, harmonious and civil interaction; especially with those with whom one may disagree. Trying to mold others into what we want them to be, or resenting them for not being the way we like, cannot foster healthy relationships. One should be on guard against rigidity and unwillingness to consider other points of view; resist the defensiveness that comes from the fear of being wrong. Sharing different points of view doesn't always mean that someone is right or wrong. Often there is a middle ground. Confrontation is avoidable if conversation is approached in a win–win non - confrontational style.

Individuals have a right to their own points of view. Listening is making an effort to hear and pay close attention to someone's perspective. Without it, conversation is superficial. Suspend your thought process, pay close attention to what is being said; resist the desire to block out and or prepare an oppositional point of view. Be not concerned about winning or losing, and instead just listen for the sake of understanding. This style of listening can produce friendships instead of adversaries. No one is saying it's going to be easy, but it is worth the effort. With the above attitude it is possible to overcome ideological gulfs that may appear irreconcilable. For instance:

> In the 80's while living in Boston I was a member of an Evangelical Conservative Christian Church. I was encouraged by the pastor to make a run for a senate seat. My wife Vernice was by my side. We were partners in all endeavors. While in the process of campaigning to get enough names on a petition to run

for senate I knocked on a door and meet a group of Gay gentlemen. They invited me in and we talked about the campaign and my positions on issues particularly my stance on homosexuality. We had an honest, frank and above all friendly discussion. I was up front with them and told them I was a Conservative Christian but I dealt with people as individuals and not as groups to be stereotyped or defamed because of who they are. I listened intently, not in a competitive spirit but in a spirit of friendship for the sake of understanding; employing instinctively the principles of acceptance. At the end of our conversation although we didn't agree on everything one of the guys said I could vote for you. He said something to the effect, because you're straight forward and easy to talk to. The others agreed. I would say acceptance is a prescription for positive outcomes.

Chapter Nineteen

Ma's Parents and Her Caretakers

My mother's mother, Imla (Kelly) Johnson, died when her children Frances (my mother), Consuela (Aunt Ann) and Thomas were barely school age. Sadly, there is no information about Imla's life in Kingston, Jamaica, where she was born. She attended school in England, where she trained to become a nurse. She came to the United States in her early to mid- twenties. Racism prevented her from acquiring her Nursing credentials. She had to settle for a job cleaning a doctor's office.

Grandma Imla Johnson's Wedding Day
Picture of Imla Kelly Johnson provided
by granddaughter, Evelyn Browne.

Around the late 1920s, early 1930s my mother's parents purchased a home on Michigan Avenue in Lynn, Massachusetts. Not long after the purchase, Grandma Johnson contracted pneumonia and died. My grandfather was left to raise the children without his partner but he was fortunate to be helped by friends, the Grandisons.

The Grandisons

My mother and her siblings stayed with Mrs. Sarah A. Grandison and her husband during the times my grandfather was serving in the Merchant Marines. My mother explained she saw very little of her father because he was usually at sea. Mrs. Grandison was originally from Nova Scotia, Canada. She lived most of her life in Lynn, Massachusetts. They lived on Timpson Street. Mr. Grandison was a contractor and owned rental property. Between his job and the rental property he was not seen that often. It was arranged that if anything happened to my grandfather while he was at sea the Grandisons would raise his children. Granddad Johnson's ship, The Effingham, sunk on 3/30/1942[1] – from that day on the Grandisons became the permanent caretakers of my mother Frances, Ann and Thomas. I remember Ma telling me, "Mrs. Grandison was the nicest person." The Grandisons had three adult daughters: one of them was not so nice. She would lock the children in the closet when Mrs. Grandison was not home. Luckily, she didn't live there and visited only once a week. Allegedly one of the daughters became the first Black lawyer in Lynn. Mrs. Grandison's son-in-law, David Fuller was a dental technician and made dentures. He would occasionally bring my sister to his place of work. She still remembers the smell of rubber in the air from the construction process of the dentures. This led to my sister's interest in attending school to make dentures, but she ended up pursuing other interests.

While living with the Grandisons, Ma's brother Thomas died in a tragic baseball accident. A bat was thrown behind the back of the batter after the ball was hit. The bat hit Thomas in the head. He died at the age of 12. Mrs. Sarah Grandison was 100 years old when she passed.

Before the death of my grandfather he and the children resided on Michigan Avenue in Lynn; where the family was terrorized by the Ku Klux Klan. They burned a cross on the family's lawn. My grandfather, Thomas Johnson exchanged gunfire with them as he defended himself and his three children. He eventually sold the house.

Grandfather Thomas Johnson

When I wrote the previous paragraph, a feeling of sadness and anger arose. The danger of racism became much more personal despite the years that had passed since the cross burning incident. I visualized my mother as a child, her brother Thomas, and her sister Consuela (Ann) being rushed to safety. Their father retrieving his gun to confront those who sought to harm them. I can feel the terror they felt, a terror not foreign to Blacks over a 100 years later in 2023. Over the centuries the systematic brainwashing of some Whites by their academic, political, social, and religious leaders has convinced them to believe the delusion of white superiority. These racist deceptions have helped to create Individuals of mindless anger and destructive capabilities directed toward anyone that does not fit their delusional profile. For some Whites, it has become second nature to hate people of color. Harboring feelings and ideas instilled in them by their local and national leaders, makes them feel justified in committing crimes against people of color. It is alarming for Blacks to know these types of individuals are among us and can strike without provocation. The murder, abuse, and discrimination of Blacks and others of color has been the "American way" for centuries. Evil cannot be contained if it is ignored. It has and will continue to metastasize and spread to unexpected places throughout society; as it has in unprovoked school, mall and church massacres; all of which have no end in sight.

The Depression

My mother experienced many losses at a young age— her mother, father, and brother. This may explain her lifelong battle with depression. I remember as a youth trying to encourage her. She said to me "I don't understand why I feel so low." There were no answers then. Todays, medical professionals attribute

Depression to a chemical imbalance in the brain. This was unknown most of my mother's life. Long after she raised her family, the sickness was understood and subsequent treatments were found. Mood disorder tends to run in certain predisposed families. It is believed there are genetic components. Two of our four children also suffer from mood disorders.

Ma's bouts of depression could last for a week or more. She had the opportunity to take medication but refused. When Ma was not depressed, she was funny; a delight to be around. She had a natural knack for comedy. "Man alive" was one of the old fashion comic expressions she often used to highlight surprise or pleasure. Another expression was "Land Sakes" which according to Wikipedia was an alternative to saying for "Oh My God." Ma's comedy was not so much in the things she said but an atmosphere of humor that she would naturally emit. Words escape me for a more precise explanation. Suffice to say, Ma was funny.

Chapter Twenty

Ongoing Injustice

Ongoing Injustice

According to the March 25, 2021 Pew Research Center there are 46.8 million people who self-identify as Black, roughly 14% of the population.[1] The statistics that follow are frightening; that is if you're a Black male in the US.

Black people were 24% of those killed last year, while, making up only 13% of the population. From 2013 to 2022, Black residents were three times more likely to be killed by police than White people. In 2022 police killing for the population reached a record high of 1,176.[2]

Blacks are 13 % of the population, but 28% of suspects arrested in the US in 2010 were Black, 28 - 32 % of people killed by police from 2003 to 2009 in arrest related incidents were Black.[3]

Black American males between fifteen and thirty-four are 2% of the US population; yet in 2015, 15% of the 1,134 persons killed by police were Black; that's five times higher than that of White men of the same age group.[4]

The deaths of Terence Crutcher, Alton Sterling, Stephon Clark, Rashaun Washington, Philando Castile, Walter Scott, Eric Garner, Michael Brown, Gregory Gunn, Anthony Hill, Brandon Washington and Quanice Hayes are some of the unarmed Black men murdered by police.

The 2020 shooting deaths of Ahmaud Arbery, Breonna Taylor and the asphyxiation death of George Floyd shown across the media, sparked not only nationwide, but worldwide outrage against the injustice committed against people of color. George Floyd's homicide occurred on May 25, 2020. Protests against police violence continued into the fall of 2020, with no end in sight. At that moment White America finally got an irrefutable picture of how law enforcement is often meted out to Blacks in America; in this case a knee on the neck for 9 minutes 26 seconds until death. Cell phone footage made this revelation possible. This wasn't the first time White America had seen the unjust killing of a Black American. Will this time make a difference? The Individual use of camera phones has been instrumental in exposing police killings of Black individuals across America.

Arguments exist that say Blacks are more prone to violence than other races. They point to statistics citing that 93% of Black crime is committed against other Blacks. 84% of White crime is White on White crime; when is the last time you heard that statistic?[5] It is an established fact that most crimes are committed among individuals living in the same communities and / or have some familiarity with one another. It is also a fact that crime is often higher in communities where poverty is rampant, education and housing is substandard and low wage jobs or no jobs are the norm. The reality of crime and violence is that it is experienced in all communities, but is often higher where deprivation exists.

The poverty and crime statistics prove that when people can meet their basic needs and have access to health services, then their standard of living improves. When jobs with living wages are offered, people are more likely to meet their needs through legitimate means.[6]

Why is it that Black-on-Black crime is so often highlighted while White on White crime is not? I think it's an attempt to minimize the murder of Black people by law enforcement. I believe it's another way of justifying racist assumptions. I believe It is code for saying "Blacks are killing Blacks, so what is the big deal if cops kill them?" The big deal is that police take an oath to enforce the law and protect citizens. When they kill in a calculated and deliberate manner, they need to suffer the consequences like any other criminal.

We hear the endless talking points about how there are only a few bad apples in the police force, if that is the case how do you explain the murder epidemic of Black men that goes on decade after decade. There are obviously a whole lot more than a few "bad apples" The figures we get from police departments are only the killings they have not been able to hide. According to K.L. Williams who has trained thousands of police around the country in the use of force "on any given day, in any police department in the nation, 15% of the officers will do the right thing no matter what is happening. Another 15% will abuse their authority at every opportunity. The remaining 70% could go either way depending on whom they are working with." If only 10% of that 70% are rogue officers you are then faced with a 25% rate of unfit officers. Redditt Hudson is an ex–Black police officer and the writer of the article I am citing, *"I'm a black ex-cop, and this is the real truth about race and policing"* vox.com, 7/17/2016 makes it clear that no matter who you are that most officers will be influenced by the culture of violence if it exist in the department they are working at. Mr. Redditt also makes it clear that institutional racism exerted by police, displayed by their disrespect and extreme violence that Mr. Redditt has seen against Black people has caused the breakdown in police – community relations.

After you look at the statistics, the daily killing and brutality against Black people and others of color along with the testimony of an ex-police officer I think it is safe to say that you have a lot of narcissist and killers masquerading as police officers. America has never been honest by admitting the extent of the vicious abuse against Black people and unresponsiveness in taking steps to stop it; as a result high rates of Black murders and abuse continue despite the outrage of Black communities. The resistance by the Republican

Senate to passing the George Floyd Justice in Policing Act of 2021 is a continuation of the age old resistance to stopping abuse against Black people.

Lawsuits against Police

In July 2015, the Wall Street Journal, reported that lawsuits totaling more than 1 billion dollars were paid over a five-year period by ten cities for alleged beatings, shootings, and wrongful imprisonment committed against Black Americans. On August 17, 2014, a $5.9 million dollar settlement was paid to the family of Eric Garner for his strangulation death by New York City police officer Daniel Pantaleo.

On August 19, 2019 Pantaleo was thrown off the police force and denied his pension; a light penalty when you consider the fact if any other citizen committed this crime they would be in prison, probably for life.

In North Charleston, South Carolina, the shooting death of Walter Scott in April 2015 settled for $6.5 million. Michael Slager, the officer who shot Scott was sentenced to 20 years in prison after video footage showed him shooting Scott in the back five times as Scott ran.

Courts agreed to a $5 million dollar settlement for the October 20, 2014 murder of Laquan McDonald in Chicago. He was shot sixteen times as he walked away from an officer. McDonald was accused of lunging at an officer with a knife until the video from the dashboard camera revealed no such actions occurred.

In October 2018, Officer Jason Van Dyke was found guilty of the 2014 murder of McDonald. It was the first time in fifteen years that a Chicago police officer had been convicted of a shooting. These rare convictions may be a wake-up call, signaling a new attitude in the treatment of African Americans. But old attitudes, actions and habits are seldom reversed.

Chicago spent $709.3 million to pay for actions related to police brutality from 2010 to 2017. Surely, we are into the multiple billions of dollars in lawsuits if you include cities other than the ten alluded to by Zusha Elinson and Dan Frosch, in their article *Cost of Police-Misconduct Cases Soars in Big U.S. Cities*, Wall Street Journal, July 15, 2015.

For those who question the legitimacy of the Black protest movements against the killings of unarmed Black citizens, ask this question: "Why are cities paying out these huge sums of money if these claims are baseless?" Has law enforcement suddenly become a charitable organization? It is time to wake up. Stop defending what is indefensible!

From the foundation of America the destruction of people of color has been a source of recreation, profit and wealth for Individuals, families and businesses. I don't think that has changed. Blacks are used by some for recreational hunting for those who call themselves vigilantes, like in the Ahmaud Arbery case. From 2019-2020 there was a 49% increase in hate crimes against Black Americans, 2,871 that is an increase of approximately 1466. Blacks continue to be the largest victims of hate crimes solely because of their race.[7]

Police Departments have been accustom to getting away with practicing excessive force on its population. Black people have largely been their target. Some racist officers within their ranks have been satisfying their hatred and blood lust with virtually no consequences. In the unusual event where a family is compensated for the destruction of a loved one, the financial cost seems to have no impact on police policy; the killings continue.

Police Brutality Bonds

A bond in its simplest terms is an I.O.U between a lender and the borrower.

When a family is compensated for the death of a loved one the money obviously does not come from the individual officer; in fact the individual officer is most often not held fully or criminally accountable. The lack of severe punishment does not discourage future acts of violence. I think it condones them. The money that few are compensated comes from financial institutions where the money is borrowed from by the State / police departments. The lender profits through interest fees. How does the borrower pay these loans? By once again victimizing the same communities where the victims come from through various laws, fees, fines, and other "legal" but illegal methods of coercion to garner funds.[8]

Violence against Native Americans

The Native American population increased from 5.2 million to 9.7 million in the most recent 2020 census. They are one of the smallest minority groups in the United States. According to Lyndsey Gilpin, an independent freelance journalist whose work has appeared in The Atlantic, Huff Post and more. In her article she states that "Native Americans are 2.5 times more likely to experience sexual assault and rape than any other ethnic group in the United States." The highest rates of violence on record are against tribal women and men. Gilpin's study is one of the first national reports to include significant research on the race of the perpetrators. It showed that most were White.[9] Dr. Andre Rosay, director of the Justice Center for the University of Alaska, stated that "by far, the most glaring result was that almost every single victim experienced some sort of interracial violence." This understanding makes it important for laws to hold non-tribal members responsible for their acts, including those in authority.[10]

I have shown how police violence has been consistent and overwhelming against people of color. Native Americans are killed at a 12% higher rate than

Black Americans, making them the most endangered population of people killed by police.[11]

The government's historic and ongoing hostility against people of color is perceived by some as a permit to commit despicable crimes against these populations. Law enforcement and others believe they can get away with their crimes particularly against the Native American population because of their invisibility in the general population. Exposing crimes against Native Americans is the first step in stemming the wave of violence. Violence against indigenous people is the foundation from which America was built. The authorities would rather ignore it than to bring its present ugliness into the light.

Grandfather told his wife, Evelyn (Nana), that the reason his Father changed his Native American name to a White man's name was to escape the violence perpetrated against his people. He told my grandmother that the violence against his father's people was more severe than the violence against those of African descent. The above information supports his conclusion.

Chapter Twenty One

Ma

Ma's Beauty

For most of my life, I saw my mother going through depression. It really was a considerable part of her life, and something that was often present. I saw that it hampered her ability to engage life normally. Uncomfortable situations could throw Ma into a low state. Sister Evelyn surmised—and I agreed—that our mother's depression hindered her ability to be cognizant of the feelings and needs of others. Things had to be her way. Her refusal to take medication was a prime example; but even her "stubbornness" which I discuss in the section "Introvert or Extrovert" represented a legitimate point of view that may not have been known or taken serious by others. I pondered about Ma's strong resistance against taking medication for her depression. Ma had to be prompted to take medication even with her high blood pressure. She preferred using natural remedies and shied away from pharmaceutical medication. This would explain her resistance.

It was not until after our move to North Carolina in 2005 that I began to see my mother from a broader perspective, and not just centered around her depression. She was often depressed when Vernice (my wife) and I visited. Despite her mood, on more than a few occasions, our presence sparked within her the will to transcend her melancholy. She was very fond of Vernice and seeing her and myself helped lift my mother's spirit.

We tried to time our visits from North Carolina to Boston during the Juneteenth celebration at Franklin Park. Juneteenth is an annual gathering to commemorate the emancipation of African slaves. It is also known as Freedom Day. It draws people from the local area and others from out of state as well. Thousands attend the event. There is music, food, and family gatherings. Juneteenth was an opportunity to connect with old friends and meet new people. After the election of Joe Biden, Juneteenth was made a national holiday on June 19th 2021. Thank you Joe for your thoughtfulness.

On one occasion while getting prepared for the celebration, Vernice and I encouraged my mother to come with us. She was depressed at the time. We didn't have much hope she would come. I remember leaving her bedroom. When we returned, to our surprise, Ma was dressed and looking forward to having a good time.

I grew up in Roxbury, and knew many at the Juneteenth celebration. Vernice said that I knew everyone, but of course that was an exaggeration. To my pleasant surprise, some remembered my mother. Those who did were some of my old childhood friends.

For my mother, this made being there all that more pleasurable. Azel, one of my homeboys from junior high school, was at his customary spot manning the grill. I wasn't sure when he had last seen my mother. He greeted her warmly, obviously surprised to see her. Ma was equally surprised and happy to see him. He made it a priority to make sure Ma got a plate of food. Cyril, a former band member who for years I played music with, knows Ma and warmly greeted her.

Ma was full of smiles as she walked around the park with assistance from her cane and occasional help from Vernice and me. If Ma had had it her way, she would have roamed around the park for hours, something I often did when I lived in Boston and occasionally still do when I visit.

During another visit to Boston, we took Ma to karaoke night at a local Dorchester club. Edmond Gillory, a good friend of mine from my early teen years in the Holy Trinity Drum and Bugle corps wanted me to come and see him perform. He had worked out a musical routine. Ma, Vernice, Evelyn, Paulette, and I went to his show. Ma could hardly contain her excitement. It's fair to say that it had been decades since Ma visited to a nightclub. Ma enjoyed the atmosphere and relished every moment. She was looking around, laughing, talking, and anxiously waiting for Gillory to come on stage.

My old friend put on quite a performance. He wore a black suit and sunglasses. He sang a series of James Brown tunes. His dark sunglasses and swaying movement reminded me of Steve Wonder. His black suit reminded me of John Belushi in the movie, *Blues Brothers*. He sang the tunes flawlessly. He was a big hit. Gillory had done his homework. He could have taken his show on the road. My mother was so impressed. She commented on how good he was and continued clapping after others had stopped. Gill invited us up on stage to sing. Vernice and I both sang a song. Ma got a kick out that. She was having such a good time that it was difficult to get her to leave even though the management was getting ready to close the club. It was a thrill to see how much Ma was enjoying herself. It warmed my heart.

There were times when Vernice, Ma and I went out to eat; Legal Sea foods at the Prudential Center, Doyle's in Jamaica Plain, and Ma's favorite, Victoria Station on Massachusetts Avenue, where Ma had been frequenting for years were all places we dined.

In June of 2015, while visiting Boston I was invited to a jazz performance. Our daughter Bethany, her five month old – baby Autumn, Ma, Paulette, Evelyn and Vernice all went. The gig was held at the home of Curtis Jones. Curtis, Cyril and I were members of the Bacchanalians during the 70's and 80's. One of the floors in Curtis's three family house was devoted to Black Music Inc. BMI was an organization started by the members of the Bacchanalians while I was with them. Curtis and the late Charles Holly continued to keep the organization moving long after the band had disbanded. My props go out to both of them.

The excitement was building as we were waiting for the group to come on stage. Finally they appeared. It was a five piece band; bass, drums, guitar, sax and vibes. For Ma this was particularly enjoyable because she knew Cyril the saxophonist. Curtis played vibes; whom I hadn't seen or heard playing his vibes for decades. It was great seeing him. They did a varied selection of jazz tunes. We stayed for two sets before folks were ready to leave. My mother however, wanted to stay longer. Before we left, Ma gave the band twenty dollars. That was generous of her considering the gig was free. Ma mentioned as we were leaving, that she wanted to get something to eat. It was between twelve and one in the morning, and everything was closed. Ma was full of energy and wanted to continue to celebrate. We went home, prepared food, spent time in conversation, and then retired for the evening.

Jordan Marsh

I remember when I would occasionally visit Ma at the Jordan Marsh Department Store in downtown Boston where she worked; this was in the early sixties. Those were special moments. We were both happy to see each other. It was a joy to see how much Ma enjoyed serving her customers but also how diligent she was with keeping her clothes department organized and visually pleasing. Her co-workers shared with me how patient and kind she was; qualities that I took for granted. Visiting my mother at JM was an opportunity to see her in full bloom; a secret identity I could have easily missed had I not entered into this special setting. These moments were precious.

Ma worked at Jordan Marsh for 15 years from the 70's into the mid-80s. Looking back, I think retirement was probably not the best thing for Ma, particularly when you consider how much she enjoyed the work. Not working left her with too much unstructured time. Idle time and my mother's propensity toward depression, was not a good combination.

I never knew anything about Ma's level of political awareness, and never gave it any thought until 2016. In the course of a conversation, I was told by my sister Paulette that Ma had written to President Kennedy, requesting that her only son not be drafted. The Vietnam War was going on at the time. I had always thought it was curious how relaxed and friendly the recruiter responded to my resistance to the War. I had spoken about this in the section "The Call." I always thought that I had been rejected from the service because of my stance against the war. It became clear that it was probably my mother's intervention that had the most impact on my rejection from military service. Thanks Ma, for your love.

It is easy to see individuals in the light of their frailties and overlook their beauty and strength. To a large extent, I did that. I had let Ma's depression play a central part in my perception of her. I'm glad I finally realized my mistake.

Ma was born on May 20, 1925. She died on April 14, 2017. At the age of ninety-two; her faculties and sense of humor were still intact.

Loving Memory

Mr. & Mrs. Henry and Evelyn Browne

Ms. Paulette Anderson

10 Woodbine Street

Roxbury, Massachusetts 02119

Reverend Elizabeth Thomas presiding

Mr. & Mrs. Evelyn and Henry Browne, Ms. Paulette Anderson

Mr. and Mrs. Sterling and Vernice Anderson

Reverent Elizabeth Thomas Presiding

At the memorial gathering on 10 Woodbine Street shortly after the funeral, many recounted things they remembered about my mother. Uncle Warren, my father's younger brother, had known my mother since childhood; he recalled, "Frances was the kindest person. She was never out of sorts; I always felt her warmth and friendliness." Aunt Barbara, my father's sister who also knew my mother from childhood said, "Frances always remembered people's names." Cyril said, "Mrs. Anderson told me that I should cut my beard because it would make me look younger." Ma could be outspoken at times. As people spoke, I had the opportunity to see my mother from other vantage points. I felt an additional sense of loss and sadness but also wonder because of the things I learned. It was as if a portrait of my mother was being drawn, adding to the fullness of who she was. It was a beautiful time of closeness and reflection.

Whenever Vernice and I are in Boston we always stay at the family home on Woodbine Street. This is always an opportunity to spend time with my sisters Evelyn, Paulette and Evelyn's husband Henry. Paulette, who is ten years younger than me, has shared with me things about my mother that I did not know. She told me of the time Ma blasted out a teacher in front of the whole class because of racially insulting comments the teacher had made. This was a side of Ma's personality that I never had a chance to see.

Chapter Twenty Two

Dad and the Early Years

The Knight

Sterling Ernest Anderson, my dad, was the second oldest of Evelyn's (Nana's) eight children. By all accounts, he was the most helpful and the most responsible. At eight, he began selling newspapers. Instead of keeping what he made, he gave the money to his parents to help with household expenses. His siblings shared stories of my dad helping them through difficult times; his sisters have shared how he would advise and comfort them when they sought his guidance.

During my mid - to - late teen years between 1962 and 1965, my dad's youngest sister's sons Tommy and Kenny, came to stay with us for a while. Their mother my Aunt Janet had six children and needed help from time to time. Tommy Tibbs, her husband, was a professional boxer. He was often away, and my dad was always available to help.

I remember Uncle Tommy being full of life. He would always throw fake punches at me, laughing and having fun whenever I saw him. He was a local boxer trying to work his way up the boxing ladder. If you were not a well-known fighter, the compensation was not adequate for the danger of the profession.

Dad worked at the Eagle Shoe factory in Lynn. This gave him an opportunity to get his younger brother Warren a job there. The factory was a ten-minute walk from our house on Suffolk Street. This was in the early to mid-1950s. The house on Suffolk Street was the first house my Dad bought. He purchased it using the GI Bill after his discharge from the Navy. We lived on the third floor, while my grandmother and five of her adult offspring, Janet, Avon, Audrey, Barbara and Warren lived on the second floor. They had moved from Baldwin Street in Lynn. Arlene, Pearl and Frederick, my father's other siblings, had already married and lived on their own.

The first memory I have of my dad was seeing him as he walked up the street from Eagle Shoe. My sister and I would run to meet him. We must have been four or five.

At the shoe factory my Dad worked on the shoe-lasting machine. The machine connected the bottom of the shoe to the top. It used hot glue to make the connection. The glue would often spatter and attach to my dad's hands. I remember holding and looking at his rough, calloused hands. Even at my young age, I realized they were the hands of a hard-working man. Dad worked a forty-hour week. Sometimes he went in on Saturday if the company did not meet its quota for that week. I went to work on bring your child to work day. Dad showed me the machine he worked on and how it connected the sole of the shoe to the top. To keep pace with the machine one needed to work fast. It required great dexterity, hand eye coordination and intense focus. Dad would stand in one place as the shoes move by. It was a laborious, repetitive eight-hour shift. Dad's pay was determined by the number of cases of shoes he completed in a week. He motivated himself by competing against his co-workers and against the number of cases he did the day before. I remember him proudly telling us how many cases he had completed that day. Nothing could change the fact that his job took a lot out of him. He would regularly fall asleep at the kitchen table.

Dad was the shop steward at the shoe factory. In this position he represented employees in their dealings with management. Taking care of others was a role my father was well suited for.

The Shoe Lasting Machine

The shoe-lasting machine my father operated was invented by Jan Matzeliger. Coincidently Mr. Matzeliger lived in Lynn, Ma. He was born on September 15, 1852 in Dutch Guiana, known today as Surinam, a small country on the northeastern coast of South America. He was the son of a Dutch engineer and an African mother who was born in Surinam. Matzeliger's ability to repair complex machinery was evident at a young age. He was able to make a living doing just that. He made his way to America and worked in the shoe industry. He attended night school to learn English. Soon he could read well enough to understand the technical books that made it possible for him to invent the shoe-lasting machine.[1]

Lynn, Massachusetts was a shoe-manufacturing hub until the early 50's when the industry began shipping manufacturing jobs out of the country. This left a huge void in non-professional jobs. Automation became another contributing factor to continued job losses. These changes in shoe manufacturing influenced my dad's decision to move the family from Lynn to Boston in the mid-fifties.

The Navy

Dad enlisted in the Navy on October 13, 1943; he was twenty one and decommissioned on November 10, 1945. While In the Navy, dad fought against the racial prejudice that was prevalent in the 1940s. As a Seabee, Naval construction worker, he was a part of organized work strikes protesting the Inequality and workplace disparity between Blacks and Whites. One of his sisters told me that he got beat up in some of the protests.

Navy Circular Letter 48-46 February 27, 1946 prohibited all segregation in assignments, ratings, ranks, ships, facilities, and housing. The rest of the armed forces were not completely integrated until 1948.[2] The Navy was the most segregated. It, however became the first integrated service unit. The Port Chicago Disaster, an explosion at the naval munitions depot at Port Chicago California on July 17, 1944 killed 320 men, of whom 202 were Black. This event played a pivotal role in the Navy's progress toward desegregation.[3] I am proud that my Dad, Sterling Ernest Anderson and the bravery of others helped play a role in the Navy's transformation. Of course we know the scourge of racism does not end with the passing of laws and bills; but its acknowledgement is important before future progress can be made.

Dad started courting my mother after his tour in the Navy. Ma said she knew his family; they all lived in close proximity to one another and went to the same schools. My parents married in 1946. My mother lived with the Grandsons' until she married. In those days, it was proper for a young woman to remain home until married.

Haymarket Square

Dad had a special relationship with his mother; one that was different from his siblings. I believe the difference stemmed from his willingness at a young age to help his mother provide for the family both financially and emotionally. These were traits he demonstrated throughout his life. My father's care and generosity toward his mother came from his appreciation of the great effort and sacrifice it took for her to raise eight children after his father died.

Every Saturday the whole family, including my grandmother, would pile into one of my dad's old jalopies and go to Haymarket Square to buy produce for the week. This was a tradition that carried over for three generations from my grandmother, to my father and to my family. Haymarket was a large open-air market in the North End of Boston. Vendors would park large wooden wagons side by side in front of the curbstone that separated the street from the sidewalk.

There was a great variety of fruits and vegetables at bargain prices. There was also a greater chance of get ripped off because you could not choose your own produce. The vendors did that for you. If you didn't check your bags before you left the vendor's cart, you might find more rotten than fresh produce when you got home. You would hear arguments between vendors and customers when customers attempted to direct the vendor towards the produce *they* wanted. Most of the time you could not see what was going into your bag because some produce displays obstructed your view. Most of the real contentious arguments happened when the customer checked his/her bags and demanded the bad produce be replaced. Vendors were rough around the edges. They were real rascals. You learned fast that the buyer had to beware at Haymarket. Too many times we would get home and discover food that had to be discarded.

We usually arrived late in the afternoon and stayed until the market closed, around eight in the evening.

This was when you could get better deals because the vendors were in a hurry to end their day. Nana would often be the last one to return to the car, partially because she was very particular when it came to her produce. This often led to spirited discourse between her and the vendors about the product quality. If Nana was taking too long dad would send me, or we would go together to track her down. While my sister and I may have been impatient to get home, dad was not; at least he showed no signs of it. He was concerned for Nana's safety; not about time.

Some thought Nana was too demanding, particularly when it came to her living arrangements on Woodbine Street, it was understandable. The house was 100 years old. It was built to last forever but it was poorly insulated. Nana's first floor apartment was cold. The ceilings were at least ten to twelve feet high; what heat that was produced went straight up. There were five rooms. Nana was often confined to one or two because the rest of the house was difficult to heat. Dad spent a lot of his time trying to make the house as comfortable as possible. He lowered the ceilings to conserve heat, insulated doors and windows; there was some improvement but even after all that the apartment wasn't comfortable. After Nana's flat was burglarized, security became a concern. Dad installed grates on all the first floor windows. There was a lot of work to do. I helped Dad with the upgrades in Nana's Apartment and never saw him disgruntled; he just did what needed to be done.

Chapter Twenty Three

Family Matters - Religion's Love Claim - Quick Fix and Phony Healers

Family Matters

Out of all the relationships between siblings in my father's family I believe his and Fredrick's were the closest. Fredrick was a year older than my father. Dad would often take my sister and me with him when he went to visit Uncle Freddy at Villa Place in West Lynn. While in the area, we would stop by Cushman's Bakery to get bread and pastries. More than fifty years have passed, and I still remember the name of that store. That's a testimony to how much I enjoyed the treats.

Uncle Freddy lived with his wife, Pearl, and three children, Fredrick Jr., Judy and Steven. It was a short distances from our house on Suffolk Street to Villa Place. We were always excited to see our cousins. We were all around the same age. Aunt Pearl was so sweet; she would always have something good for us to eat.

It was easy to see why my dad spent time with my uncle Freddy. Freddy was friendly, warm, and funny. He was a house painter by trade. Dad would work with him whenever he needed help on a job.

Being able to spend time with our cousins abruptly ended; suddenly we were no longer welcomed. Aunt Pearl had become a Jehovah's Witness and accepted their doctrine of separating themselves from those who were not of their faith. This divided the family. After that, we rarely saw our cousins and they never attended family gatherings.

Religion's Love Claim

Religions claim love as their highest virtue but in my opinion it is not. My aunt's response after her joining the Jehovah's Witness proved to me that love was not, and could not be religions most cherished virtue. The religious love their religion and their leaders consume most of their admiration. I think much of organized religion is a cult of personality. The sheep gravitate towards, and obey, the charismatic entertainers. History has shown there is almost nothing these followers will not do when directed by their religious and / or political leaders. Often the principle concern of religious leaders is the financial gifts that support them.

Religious and political leaders are skilled at manipulating humans' to serve their own needs. This manipulation circumvents common sense. Rational critical thinking and Intuition are smothered while the ideology of the group becomes paramount.

To find comfort with likeminded people is common regardless of the belief system, but just because something feels good does not mean it is good. Whenever you relinquish your ability to think for yourself, you place yourself in the hands and at the mercy of someone else. The world continually proves that when people refuse to think but instead allow others to do their thinking for them, disaster is often the result. I won't bother to give an example because history is replete with them.

Religion attracts those seeking fulfillment and purpose. Houses of worship can provide a community of likeminded people. Regular attendance, prayer meets and tithing are encouraged. These outward demonstrations of obedience do not necessarily mean spiritual growth has occurred. Spiritual growth is a subjective experience that is not necessarily connected to a religion.

Quick Fix and Phony Healers

The superficial actions that are accepted as spiritual growth are evident in the quick fixes and easy solutions to healing; namely the usage of "right" vocabulary and other theatrical displays of so-called spiritual power.

With all the fanfare of healing claims by television evangelists and the like, where is the concrete evidence of these would-be hundreds or even thousands of miraculous healings? Sure there are legitimate healers, but you will probably not see them on television with their fancy religious talk begging for money as they shake down the faithful.

In 1993, Rita Swan founded "Children Health Is a Legal Duty" (CHILD), an organization that lobbies against state laws that protect parents who choose "faith healing" over modern medicine. In 1998 she decided to team up with pediatrician Seth M. Asser to investigate child fatalities associated with faith healing. The two began reviewing the deaths of 172 children whose parents on religious grounds chose not to provide medical care for their children. Their study showed that 140 of these children would have had a 90% likelihood of survival had they received routine medical care. CHILD estimates that since 1976, at least 82 children linked to the church of the First Born have died from lack of medical treatment.[1] The Guardian also did a piece on the deaths of children who did not receive medical care but instead were administered "faith healing."[2]

Many who bought into a religious ideologies preached by con men and frauds have paid the ultimate price. Proper medical information and care increases greatly the likelihood of healing. There are also individuals in the medical field to beware of. The difference between the so-called faith healer and the medical professional is that the medical professional is a licensed healer and regulated by standards. They can be held accountable for their actions. This is not the case with church officials pretending to be healers. In my thirty-plus-year involvement with various churches, I have seen no evidence of anyone being healed from any type of illness. It is irresponsible and dangerous that churches can get away with misrepresenting themselves as spiritual hospitals and not be held accountable for the results. The damage done by these self-professing healers I believe is incalculable. The research of CHILD and the investigation done by The Guardian is a peek into a much larger problem. Consider the millions who are reached by television evangelists and local churches with members who are convinced that their preacher has the ability to heal; some preachers' encourage believers to "step out on faith" and totally disregard medical advice. Hidden under the cloak of religious freedom, individuals peddle their healing fraud along with those who preach divisive ideologies like the one that divided my relatives from my family.

Individuals that preach and groups that support these dangerous and divisive doctrines should be forewarned by authorities that they may be held liable if people seek damages. Legal consequences are the only remedies that will affect change in these rigid institutions. I look forward to the day when individuals are held accountable for their deceptions that leads to damage and death.

Chapter Twenty Four

Stealing Souls

Stealing Souls

The revelation that Catholic clergy have been involved in child sexual abuse is common knowledge in modern times. Whether the same can be said of the Protestant church is more difficult because of the independent nature of congregations. Though some information is available. According to the Associated Press, three insurance companies that insure Protestant churches reported they receive approximately 260 reports a year of child sexual abuse by clergy or others associated with church business.[1] These reported cases are from only three insurance companies. The actual number is probably considerably higher due to the fact this data doesn't include all insurances companies associated with the Protestant Church. We need to also remember that most sexual abuse cases go unreported as well.

It's not hard to figure out that young people are initially groomed by the clergyman and then manipulated into submission. Studies have shown that a segment of abusive clergy use socializing with the victim's family as a grooming tactic. Not only is the child being manipulated in this situation, but the family is being groomed as well.[2] This is one of the techniques of deception used by some claiming to be enlightened. Religion purports itself to be, an angel of light. We are lured by superficial displays of love, which is its greatest appeal. I think that people enamored with, and manipulated by religion and its representatives can be blind to the potential great evil hiding behind the "light."

I have seen that human beings have an affinity towards faith, or at least faith in *something*. They are always trying to find someone or something to follow. This is how we have been trained. We want to follow that which we *believe* is greater than ourselves. We've been trained to accept instructions from others instead of listening to our own council or / inner convictions. Faith has become a method used by some to manipulate individuals into following them. We are convinced that we must follow them and that we will feel lost and guilty if we do not. Those clergy masquerading as men of god use their social and leadership skills to convince others they can lead them to spiritual fulfillment. I think there are great systems of manipulation at play. Liturgical systems have been modified and designed to deceive congregates. If these systems weren't in place, the clergyman and Catholic priests would not have gotten away with child sexual abuse for so long. Unquestioning trust in leaders of faith and leaders in general contributes to our ignorance of evil within the church and within the culture at large. Blind faith gives leaders and others in positions of power the ability to do whatever they choose knowing that they are not accountable to anyone. This blind faith will continue to breed chaos and confusion. *Put faith in yourself first then decide if you want to extend it to others.*

The Deeper Level

On a deeper level those who see it as their responsibility to control humans, have always had the goal of keeping us separated from our true identity, our connection to our spirit; ("the activating or essential principle influencing a person", Merriam Webster Dictionary). Those in power have installed their own version of spirit. A key component of their strategy is the erasing of intuition; ("the ability to understand immediately without the need for conscious reasoning", Oxford Dictionaries). Intuition and free thinking is instead replaced with the controller's information; their rules, regulations, laws, philosophies, religions etc.; things that they themselves often do not adhere to. Their tenets are all designed for one thing; to control their populations. This is all a part of the great system of control. Rulers could care less what you think or believe. Their primary concern is that you stay asleep; unable to disturb their systems of power. Most individuals will stay submerged under the controller's delusions until death. Great spiritual leaders have always been in conflict with societal tenets.

They have attempted to guide humans away from artificial manmade constructions to an independent personal connection to spirit. Few ever listen which is why humans remain under the control of a small elite minority.

Leaders become nervous when people go rogue, when citizens wake up from their pervasive programming, go off script and start interfering with traditional institutions that run the country and control the world. Their breakdown begins when the people understand that *the people* are the power and need not be subservient to corrupt systems of control.

There are certain individuals who are more inclined to deviate from the programmed path of compliant citizen. These include artists, writers, scientists, journalists and thinkers who go beyond the information given to them by the status quo and instead look behind the curtain and discover "inconvenient truths." True spiritual leaders, those not simply sanctioned by cultural leaders also see through the propaganda. When the curtain is pulled back and corruption is exposed the distortion of information by the media becomes turbo charged. For some truth becomes harder and harder to recognize. Free speech is curtailed, the internet is controlled and or shut down. Silencing of independent journalist, defaming and persecutions of political opponents becomes the norm. These are all attempts at maintaining criminal empires.

Systems of obedience and blind faith start to indoctrinate us from the cradle and continue to influence us until death. They permeate every level of society. Today with information at our fingertips these systems of obedience and blind faith are disintegrating. The disintegration of the status quo is a worldwide phenomenon. I don't think the sophisticated weapons of the elite can prevent it; instead they will accelerate it. The globalist manipulation and agenda will crumble but the toll on the peoples will be great.

According to Dr. Bruce H. Lipton, Cell Biologist, Quantum Communications

> "We live in a world today where there is a hierarchy of power. There are very powerful people and there are others people with virtually no power at all. What's very important from a biological understanding is that every human being is equally powerful in their creative ability to shape the planet. Well, then, we {ask} if everybody is equally powerful then how did other people gain so much more power? And here's the joke… they didn't gain any power. The reason they became more powerful is that they took away the power from us."[3]

The Critical Question

The critical question has always been, "what should replace these failed systems of control and power"? People are crying out for an answer. We must first extend kindness, patience and compassion to each other before we can see our away into a peaceful order. We see a glimpse of that new order in our love for our children and those close to us. The underpinning for a transformation has always been in us but I believe intentionally diverted by cultural leaders to serve their selfish desires. The change will not come from the top down. We have been begging them for millenniums, by now it should be obvious, it's not coming. Our spirit power has been taken involuntarily through violence and deception now it is time to take it back; I believe the first step in reclaiming our spiritual identity is to be suspect and or in some cases reject the cultural identity and programming that most have blindly excepted; an identify that is designed to make us completely dependent on the status quo. We need to be careful not to use the same tactics the selfish have used to amass their ill-gotten gains otherwise we will become a mirror image of them. Our methods must be in line with truth not falsehood.

We want system wide change (some have developed plans for that) but the truth is it can't be sustained without individual personal evolution. I must be better. As stated above we already have the blueprint. We have simply been diverted into a blind alley. In chapter twenty nine under the heading non–violent cultures I show how people have managed to bypass deception and violence and live in peace with each other. Many believe that only a heavenly force can bring sanity to the world. Depending on a divine or extraterrestrial superpower to transform ourselves and the world relinquishes the responsibility of humans who made the world what it is.

The following chapter is a direction that has proven helpful for many to liberate themselves from status quo thinking and spiritual bondage.

Chapter Twenty Five

Reprogramming/ Awakening

Reprogramming

Reprogramming is the process of assessing assumptions, traditions and beliefs.

This examination opens one up to a potential paradigm shift in the perception of reality.

Reprogramming enables us to take back the power that Dr. Lipton said was taken from us. To do so one must resist the common inclination of running everything through the cultural grid of ideas and opinions for approval and reassurance. This will require an evolution in free thought and a leap of faith away from the systems and stories that have programmed our thinking and actions. These systems have done precisely what they were designed to do— keep us dependent, controlled, and fearful. Most have accepted the worldview; (religions, values, history, political systems, patriotism, etc.) without question. This new leap of faith is made with our eyes wide open. Now we have become questioners and seekers of truth rather than containers accepting anything the status quo wants to deposit. This is the beginning of an awakening, an internal reprogramming from passivity to an independent, evaluative, self- directed view of the world and our place in it.

Spiritual teachers and positive change agents resisted the societal norms of their times. Buddha, Jesus, Gandhi, Nelson Mandela, Martin Luther King Jr., and many other less familiar names, all experienced intense resistance from the political, religious and cultural leaders of their day; leaders who pretended to serve the people but who only served themselves and those with power and means. King, Jesus, Gandhi and many others were killed for their stances against societal norms.

The Meditation Process

The one person you don't have to worry about having your own best interest at heart is yourself; however when misled even we can work against our own best interest. I believe if one seeks peace by way of the spiritual/spirit and not exclusively through religion or materialism, she/he will be on the right track. Meditation can play a role in loosening the ties and / or perceiving those agendas that are not in our best interest.

Peering inward, using stillness, silence, and observation as a means of personal and spiritual growth has been practiced by cultures for eons in some form or another. There are different types of meditations—mindfulness meditation (the observation of thought without judgment until the mind is clear), spiritual mediation (the reflection on silence or a spiritual idea to connect to being), and mantra meditation (focusing on a sound). These are a few types, but all are geared to create peace, greater awareness, and a connection to higher consciousness. The meditative process at its core opens up states of awareness that are usually inaccessible because of the clutter of daily activity.

The ocean is often used to represent the mind. The waves of the ocean are used to symbolize thoughts that are in constant motion. With practice, meditation silences the business of the mind. I don't mean becoming a slave to a system: most of us have had enough of that in our life. Meditation is freedom. Whatever works comfortably for you, is good for you. Most importantly, just meditate. Meditation enables one to tune into a sense of peace, confidence, awareness, and ease. These experiences are not something you are making an effort to bring about. It happens as a result of meditation. Meditation promotes patience. Patience allows time to bring about events in our favor in a way that is totally unexpected. Serendipity; "the occurrence and development of events by chance in a happy or beneficial way" (Oxford dictionary.com). It is also defined as, "Faculty or phenomenon of finding valuable or agreeable things ***not sought for***" (Merriam Webster. com). You are not asking or expecting anything.

Our dishwasher broke quite some time ago. It was no big deal. I was encouraged to catch a sale or take advantage of someone selling one online. I was tempted on occasion to bite. I didn't.

One day I was called to do a job. A customer wanted a dishwasher removed. As I put it into my truck to bring it to the dump I remembered my need for a dishwasher. It looked in pretty good shape so instead of bringing it to the dump I took it home. It sat in my garage a couple of weeks until I finally had the motivation to install it. I had never installed a dishwasher before, so I knew there was going to be a learning curve. I pulled out the old washer and began to install the "new one" until I hit a snag. I didn't have the correct parts to hook it into the water line. I called a professional. When he came to the house and saw that I had started the installation process he told me that if he completed it he would have to charge me $235.00. Instead, in a relaxed and friendly manner he volunteered to give me the part I needed. He got it from his truck, and then showed me how to install it. He charged me absolutely nothing; not for the part or for a service charge. That was serendipity/the spirit in action; "the phenomenon of finding valuable or agreeable things not sought"

Another experience with serendipity was in the spring of 2021. In 2020 we had an adjuster look at our roof to evaluate our need for replacing the shingles. The adjuster thought the shingles had a few more years left. We stopped thinking about it. In the spring of 2021 a roofer looking for business gave us an estimate of the cost for new shingles. A month or so later a young lady representing another company just happened to be in the neighborhood. She did a close examination of our roof and assured me the roof indeed needed to be replaced due to hail damage. The shingles had not been replaced since the house was built in 2000. It was about time for new ones. She told me that her company works to get the insurance company to pay and not the customer. She instructed me on how to get the process started. I said to myself this looks like serendipity in motion. There were a couple of hurdles that needed to be cleared. A few weeks later we finally got the good news. We were getting the funds for a new roof without the need to even pay the $1000 deductible. We were thankful. It was a welcomed turn of events.

I have come to realize that whenever possible, I need to chill, meditate and allow life to work itself out in its own time and unique fashion. We can become a part of life's flow and enjoy its magic instead of being anxious, frustrated, impatient and at odds with existence. There is a Yogi saying "We are born wise: we are born complete." It is the hustle, bustle and artificiality of culture that distracts us from this reality. Life runs smoothly when I'm meditating.

Overcoming Resistance

Meditation is a simple process by which you need only yourself. Stillness, silence, and observation are the tools of meditation. One common position for meditation is sitting cross-legged with your back straight. In this position, you are less prone to dozing, though you are not immune to it. Any comfortable position will do. Dozing is a common experience when you're new to meditation but it's only temporary.

Meditation is always met with resistance. There will always be something that will take priority. Expectations and demands of everyday life will always command your attention. Find a time that is best for you. In the beginning, sitting still will be a challenge because this is generally not a part of our daily routine. The only way to counter these forces is to *"Just meditate"!!!!*

As you sit to meditate do not be discouraged by physical annoyances; itching, yawning and other physical sensations. Sit patiently. These annoyances are a part of the natural process as you begin the practice of meditation. As distractions arise, focus on the location in the body where the distraction occurs. Observe without emotion or judgment until they dissipate. Mental distractions are just the different side of the same coin. Mental distractions are the most annoying as one "attempts" to clear the mind; simply observe them until they dissipate. Observe without force. Observing the inhaling and exhaling of the breath is a useful technique in clearing the mind. As you continue the practice of meditation, you will discover physical annoyances greatly diminish and mental distractions will be less of a hindrance. Meditate for only a few minutes. Let the desire to meditate longer happen naturally and gradually. *Do not force it.*

After finding success overcoming physical and mental distractions I decided to put meditation to use by attempting to eliminate negative emotional feelings. I had one particular concern that had been irritating me for a while. I located the area in my body where I could feel the negative emotion. I focused on it and to my amazement it vanished. I could really feel a cleansing sensation. Do it until you get results. *Do not use meditation to replace medication without consulting your doctor.*

What are we being distracted from as we prepare to meditate? We are being distracted from the awareness of our higher consciousness that has been high jacked by the ego. Most never become aware of their higher consciousness because modern culture has placed all its emphasis on external and material considerations.

Don't give up because things are not happening according to your expectations. They will not. Giving up is the impatient ego's influence. Free yourself from it. If you feel like quitting, use the same technique you used for physical and mental distractions. Focus on the place in the body where the feeling is. Focused awareness puts a spot light on our uncontrolled half-conscious feelings. Allow the light of awareness to expose these distractions until they disappear. Progress in meditation is often undetectable until the moment you suddenly realize that, something has changed.

There is a difference between you and your mind. You are the one who is separate from your thoughts and from the identification culture has locked us into;

our name, what we do, what we possess, what we have accomplished, plans to achieve and social position. Our thought life and values are all imprinted on us by way of our culture. We have confused the values of our culture and our thoughts that emanate from it, with who we are. Statements like, "I need to find myself" and others relating to self-exploration are an attempt to go beyond the identifications that culture has given us. *A New Earth* by Eckhart Tolle and *Meditation for Fidgety Skeptics* by Dan Harris, are both useful in the understanding and practice of meditation.

Patience

The complaint of many is that the mind is constantly moving from thought to thought. People are easily frustrated because they cannot control its spontaneity. We are not trying to control thoughts but rather simply observing them. It is through observation (awareness) that thoughts and feelings are managed.

We strive for awareness/consciousness. During meditation the mind creates thoughts before we are aware of them. It can be difficult to remember the thoughts. They come and go at lightning speed. Continue observing the mind as these thoughts emerge. Gradually, the real you, the observer, will catch some of them in flight. Observe them until they dissolve. Sometimes the mind gets fixated on a thought or a song. Observe it until it leaves. This is part of the process of awakening.

Enter meditation with humility and not with the worldly expectations of gain. Meditative growth cannot be measured on the same scale as worldly accomplishments. Meditative progress is subtle and often happens without our awareness. As a result of the practice a sense of well-being will increase. For some serendipity becomes a common occurrence. Those events that may seem negative can, work out for the best. Tolle, calls it "being in flow with life." One is learning not to respond negatively to every minor occurrence, and instead accepting the daily rhythm of life as it transpires; an acceptance that comes over time.

The Clearing

In our meditation, the clearing is the place we are working towards. It comes after we pass through the brush of habitual thought and other distractions. It is a place where the mind is quiet: our higher consciousness becomes the gatekeeper of the random flow of the mind/ego/I; the self, created by the over identification with the material realm. Meditation should not be viewed as a one or two time a day event, though this is helpful. The ultimate goal of meditation is to incorporate it throughout the day to ensure the quietness and peace that the higher consciousness represents. The business of the world is constantly drawing our attention outward.

Whenever you can meditate. This breaks the constant chain of thought and the persistent connection with the external for a moment of clarity and peace. Some refer to these moments as an opportunity to get grounded in the present as opposed to being caught up in past or future thoughts which are primary distraction to meditation.

Meditation's Impact on Crime

Meditation is not only beneficial for individuals but has been proven to reduce violent crime in cities. The DC Transcendental Meditation experiment between June 7 and July 30, 1993 reduced violent crime by 23.3% over a two month period, as 1% of a population meditated together.[1]

...A time series analysis was used to evaluate reduction in crime in Merseyside, England. During periods when a meditating group slightly larger than the square root of one percent of the population held sessions the monthly data showed a 13.4 percent drop in crime. This was very significant in contrast to the national crime rate which had actually increased by 45 percent.....Merseyside went from No. 3 ranking in highest crime rates among the eleven largest Metropolitan Areas in England and Wales in 1987 to the lowest crime rate by 1992. The Merseyside Home Office estimated the reduction in crime saved around £1250 million over the five-year period.[2]

Maharishi Mahesh Yogi is the founder of the Transcendental Meditation movement. Meditation being use for crime prevention has been dubbed the "Maharishi effect." Meditation has the potential to change the world but changing the world begins with changing ourselves; our response to situations affects those around us.

What Meditation is and is Not

Meditation is not a religion. Most religions refer to meditation in some form but rarely stress its importance. It is also independent from individuals who demand homage to religious rituals. It is not an attempt to convert you to an ideology or religious belief. Meditation does not instill fear. It does not request a percentage of your income. Meditation does not close your mind and confine you to the beliefs of a particular group. It does not divide. It does not judge you according to your level of participation in a group. Meditation *is not* designed to give you an emotional experience.

Meditation is freedom; freedom from the expectations of man-made rituals and the world's artificial systems of control. It is a means to connect to higher consciousness, peace, the Spirit, the God Consciousness; whatever term you choose to use but without an intermediary; no bells and whistles; just you and the Spirit—the way it was intended. It is not necessary to be involved in external displays of religion to grow spiritually. I was asked what the difference between prayer and meditation is. I gave this a lot of thought and looked at what I do when I meditate. Meditation is simply being with the spirit, and not asking for anything or having any expectation: just being. Prayer is your speaking to God. Meditation is allowing the sprit to speak to you. *Deepak Chopra.*

★★★★★★★★★★★★★★★★★★★★★★★★★★★★

The Control Factor

Cities create an artificial environment that short circuits patience because the pace of city life is not conducive for reflection. Cities are the ultimate system of control. Having everyone in designated locations is the easiest way to control the population and, cities do just that. It may be an evolutionary development, but it is clearly a conscious system of control. Cities are golden cages. They make us dependent on our masters for all our physical needs: housing, food, water, and power (electricity). Luring people into cities was crucial to the provision of the labor force during the Industrial Revolution. People are now at the mercy of their employers. The delusion of freedom and control over our lives becomes clear when, for whatever reason, the provisions stop! This is why we should be prepared to live without assistance from our providers.

Chapter Twenty Six

Science and its Warnings

Science's Giants

Science and those who represent its prominence are lauded as long as they do not come into conflict with the systems of control established by governments and religious leaders. Science is based on asking questions, and it is not unusual for it to be at odds with the establishment. Without asking questions, discovering what is true from what is false is impossible.

Asking questions is the foundation of exploration, the expansion of knowledge, and the understanding of the world. It is through the trial and error nature of the scientific method that we can separate truth from misinformation and confusion. Science is by no means correct in all its pronouncements as it is in essence a never-ending quest for clarification. That is what makes it so valuable. Rigidity and blind faith without asking questions or investigating the truth of words, leaves little room for ethically based growth or advancement.

As Tony Robbins says in his book, *Awaken the Giant Within,* "Questions are the answers."

Tesla and Einstein are two scientists among many who went against the status quo. Nikola Tesla was lauded as a great inventor as long as his inventions and discoveries posed no opposition to the oil barons and others who saw him as a threat to their bottom lines. Einstein was lauded as long as he limited himself to scientific inquiry. Little is known about his fierce anti-capitalistic stance. Einstein stated:

> The crippling of the individual I consider the worst evil of capitalism. Our whole educational system suffers from this evil. An exaggerated competitive attitude is inculcated into the student who is trained to worship acquisitive success as a preparation for his future career. I am convinced there is only one way to eliminate these grave evils, namely through the establishment of a socialist economy, accompanied by an educational system which would be orientated toward social goals.[1]

The Scientific Method

The scientific method can be adapted for questioning that which is true or false in our day to day observations as well as in the field of science. The following is a simple example of how to apply it when discerning truth.

Step 1: Make observations.

Observe phenomenon – anything that manifests itself. Information is constantly coming to us.

Step 2: Propose a Theory/Hypothesis (a supposition (idea) or proposed explanation made on the basis of limited evidence as a starting point for further investigation).

Ask Who, What, When, Where, Why and How. This is the starting point for questioning and / or research. You are seeking to prove the truthfulness/ accuracy of certain information.

Step 3: Design and perform an experiment to test the hypothesis (idea).

Testing for truth means researching information that can confirm or contradict certain assumptions. Be impartial

Step 4: Analyze your data.

After the examination of the data you must determine whether to accept or reject the hypothesis. Does the information support your hypothesis? At this point you need to make a decision.

Co-opted

Scientific knowledge unfortunately can be co-opted by those concerned with their own economic interest and or those who want to maintain cultural stories, myths, and systems of blind faith that have been used to fashion our views. In these situations, analysis is important in order to see through the rhetoric of deception.

Analysis of Global Warming Deniers

Analysis of the global warming story brings certain truths to light. Individuals from independent and governmental agencies, experts in their field, have proven that human activity is a major contributing factor to global warming. Interestingly, those that resist the evidence are the same ones who predicted that the result of burning fossil fuels would cause the heating of the atmosphere, resulting in the heating of the planet. Exxon's senior scientist James Black predicted in July 1977:

> "There is general scientific agreement that the most likely manner in which mankind is influencing the global climate is through carbon dioxide release from the burning of fossil fuels." One year later he warned Exxon that doubling CO_2 gases in the atmosphere would increase average global temperatures by

two or three degrees—a number that is consistent with the scientific consensus today.[2]

Today, politicians, Exxon and others in the industry are actively working to undermine the truth of Exxon's own findings; disregarding evidence gained over the decades that confirms Exxon's prior prediction. If we take the time to analyze the stories we are told, truth is really not that difficult to find.

Environmental Warnings

Devastation hit Florida and Texas in the form of hurricanes in September through October 2017. The destruction was on a scale I don't think has ever been seen before. Puerto Rico and the Virgin Islands, both American territories, were decimated. In October of 2019, the Bahamas was obliterated by a category five hurricane. In addition to this, fires have raged out of control at an unprecedented rate in Northern California. An estimated 5,700 structures were destroyed and the death toll was forty.[3]

Throughout 2018 - 2020 historic blazes have ravaged California, Washington and Oregon. In 2020 wildfires left at least 40 people dead and destroyed 7000 structures, scorching more than five million acres across the three states.[4] One of the most dramatic and freakish demonstrations of climate change occurred in Texas, February 2021. A snowstorm left millions without power or water; dozens died...[5]

There are still those who have political and financial interest in rejecting scientific findings regarding climate change. They persuade large segments of the population to accept their deceptive conclusions. The question should no longer be is climate change real but rather how can we protect ourselves from it.

Carl Sagan 1995

I have a foreboding of an America in my children's or grandchildren's time ... when awesome technological powers are in the hands of a very few, and no one representing the public interest can even grasp the issues; when the people have lost the ability to set their own agendas or knowledgeably question those in authority; when clutching our crystals and nervously consulting our horoscopes, our critical faculties in decline, unable to distinguish between what feels good and what's true, we slide, almost without noticing, back into superstitions and darkness."[6]

Chapter Twenty Seven

Delusion vs. Reality

Delusion vs. Reality

The slogan, "Question Authority" (QA) was popularized in response to the Vietnam War. Daniel Ellsberg led the charge in the questioning of America's actions in Vietnam. Before the Vietnam War, the powers pretty much had their own way; questioning authority could be a cause for discipline. The war, and the opposition to it, woke many people up to the need to question government policies and actions. In 2022 to the present days of 2023, *"woke"* was being mocked by the political right because they would rather you stay asleep.

Asking questions is essential, and is the fundamental tool in the search for truth. It is the spark that ignites exploration, investigation, and is frequently resented by those in authority; particularly politicians, because all too often, they have much to hide. After the real estate crash of 2007–2009, the "too big to fail" rationale was used by politicians to help perpetrators escape prosecution. The idea of "too big to fail" was implicit in the "too big to question" scheme. The 60's Vietnam

War activist cry, "question authority" was urgent and has increased in urgency since. There has been no resolution to the problems the questions represent; war, race, climate change and the huge disparity between the rich and everyone else.

America's strong suit is unfortunately not solving problems but instead pretending to solve them. The problems America has created go to the root of its creation. To solve them requires the root be pulled up and new seed be planted in its place. That does not seem likely.

Questioning authority becomes almost impossible if you get caught in the spin that is meant to hook you on an emotional level. Leaders know that once they get you to "fall in love" with them and their words, they have you. As Donald Trump infamously said during his 2016 presidential campaign, "I could stand in the middle of Fifth Avenue and shoot somebody, and I wouldn't lose any voters." This mindset was again demonstrated by President Trump after his resounding defeat by Joe Biden in the 2020 presidential election; a defeat in the Electoral College and a 5 million vote deficit in the popular vote. President Trump and millions of his supporters refused to acknowledge defeat; echoing unfounded claims of voter fraud. Trump understands the power of what I call the "love delusion." The love of a person, idea or both. According to the American Heritage Dictionary, New College Edition, a delusion is "a false belief held in spite of invalidating evidence. It is held without reservation as a result of self-deception, the imposition of another or mental disorder." Delusions are much more common than one would think. They are easily and quickly succumbed to if we are not mentally and emotionally on guard; as in the case of believing Trump won an election that he had in fact lost. Delusions can have serious and deadly consequences. Five died as a result of the 2021 capital insurrection, by Trump's supporters.

Mind Control Bernays's Style

From the mouth of the master himself, Edward Louis Bernays, referred to as the father of public relations and nephew of Sigmund Freud, Bernays wrote *Propaganda* (1928), "The mechanism by which ideas are disseminated on a large scale is propaganda, in the broad sense of an organized effort to spread a particular belief or doctrine."

"If we understand the mechanism and motives of the group mind, is it not possible to control and regiment the masses according to our will without their knowing about it?"[1]

"The voice of the people expresses the mind of the people, and that mind is made-up for it by the group leaders in whom it believes and by those persons who understand the manipulation of public opinion. It is composed of inherited prejudices, symbols and clichés and verbal formulas supplied to them by their leaders."[2]

"In almost every act of our daily lives, whether in the sphere of politics or business, in our social conduct or ethical thinking we are dominated by a relatively small number of persons ... it is they who pull the wires which control the public mind"[3]

The development of public relations is an extension of advertising. Its primary goal is to bring about the wishes of those in power. Manipulation and deception are tools used often by public relations practitioners. Supreme Court Justice Felix Frankfurter served from 1939 -1962. He described Bernays and his associates as "professional poisoners of the public mind, exploiters of foolishness, fanaticism, and self-interest." The Justice warned President Franklin Roosevelt not to allow Bernays to play a leadership role in World War II. The judge pointed out that Bernays's concerns were not in the public interest but were in Bernays's own self-interests. Bernays's constituency was composed of the powerful. His concern above all was delivering what his constituency wanted. Judge Frankfurter understood that by contaminating the public's mind, Bernays was able to secure victories for his clients.[4]

Government officials and others in power have routinely overtly, and covertly, manipulated and lied to the masses to get what they want. Bernays's contribution was in streamlining and systematizing deception so that it became an art form for the industrial age which used advertising to attract customers.

Strategies of Bernays

Bernays learned about symbolism, the connection between the buyer's desires and the product from his uncle, Sigmund Freud. On television ads, car salesmen place beautiful women standing in front of their automobiles with a luxurious home in the background. This strategy taps into the buyer's conscious and unconscious desire for love and success. The following are three other strategies used by Bernays:

1. The use of authority figures or well-known individuals in the selling of products or ideas.
2. The creation of an atmosphere that puts pressure on individuals to buy; peer pressure.
3. Mass publication via radio, television, internet and newspapers, so as to capture a mental space in the mind of those you want to reach.

Another area in which Bernays's propaganda/advertising was used very effectively was in the manipulation and the changing of people's attitude about thrift. The goal of Bernays's campaign was to inspire a never-ending lust for new things that the manufacturing industries were mass producing.

Bernays used his techniques in the 1930s on behalf of the cigarette industry to encourage women to pick up the habit of smoking. He simultaneously was encouraging his wife to kick the habit; probably because early findings linked cancer to smoking. There nevertheless seemed to be no indication he refrained from promoting smoking or attempted to acknowledge its harm.

Another hallmark of Bernays's propaganda machine was manipulating public opinion in order to support US wars. He was employed by the government to do their bidding. Joseph Goebbels, the propaganda minister of the Third Reich, impressed with Bernays's writings, adopted his system of social control. Today's modern usage of symbolism associating war with love of country (patriotism), bravery, heroism, the spreading of democracy, fighting the communist threat, and other jingoisms come straight from Bernays's playbook. Their effectiveness is undeniable. The jingoism of patriotism and love of country has led men to give their lives for any reason politicians' decree.[5]

Resist the Sales Pitch

Do not get caught up in just any words and pictures. These can be the tools used to draw you in and capture your attention. Beware. Be careful what you accept as truth. Do your own research, and don't be afraid to ask questions. If you are thinking about buying something because it claims to fix a problem you have, or believing in an idea for the same reason, stop, and say, "Let me investigate these claims." Take the time to look at similar products, check the veracity of statements by checking reviews online or asking your peers. Be careful sometimes online reviews are not reputable. *Ponder before you make a decision.* These steps will help prevent you from being hooked into a scam. Do not allow yourself to be manipulated into making immediate decisions. Pressure is a part of the sales pitch. **Above all be patient.** Rarely is there a need to make an immediate decision unless pressured into doing so. Stay objective. Do not get drawn in by slick presentations designed to create and emotional attachment to a thing, idea or presenter.

Remember, a sales pitch is all about selling something. **Truth can be irrelevant.** It is all about getting you invested. Be an emotionally detached observer. Simply say, "Not interested," or "I'm not ready to make to decision", "I need time to think about it." This will give you time to contemplate before you make a decision; there is no hurry, except for the pressure created by the sales person.

Those being persuaded are usually unaware that they are being guided through a manipulative process using subliminal, repetitive and or overt and covert messaging as pointed out in Bernays's strategies.

In the realm of ideas one must want to know the truth if one is to escape the delusions and manipulation that are often cast by influencers. *Do you*? Or is it more important to simply be led by your emotions, believing what feels good? Never questioning what you believe is a key stumbling into error.

While attempting to discern truth from misinformation and downright lies: Beware. Do not ignore contradictions. If things do not appear to make sense, it's probably because they do not. Pay attention to what others are saying, even though you may disagree with them. Pay attention to your stomach/gut; focus in on the message your senses are trying to convey before accepting what others are trying to convince you to believe. **Often we ignore our internal warning systems to our detriment.**

History and present events, for the most part, are simply reflections of each other and are indicators even predictors of future events. If you want to know the truth about a person or a story, take the time to check out the history. When you hear individuals telling you what they think you want to hear, examine who they are. If they are politicians take note of their voting records, and compare it against what they say they're about. That information will help give you, an indication of their ideological persuasion and also strip away fantasy and the dream state they may be trying to lull you into. Do your homework. **The truth is often not what it appears to be.**

Decision Time

At some points you will make decisions about your life and the individual things that will influence it. You will draw your own conclusions about the world. This will be difficult for many depending on what they were taught during childhood. As a child there was little need to think. Others did most of that for us. Many ideas that are acquired during childhood are carried over into adulthood. One could be confronted with questions about their assumptions for the first time. Wading through years of nonfactual information might make one feel lost, and foundationless. I know this from personal experience; believing things to be true that turn out not to be. I have found that real freedom is when you come to conclusions for yourself, and when you're not always being spoon-fed what to think, what to believe, and how to exist.

While teaching a high school history class I was asked, "How do you know what is true?" I responded, "You don't. It is your responsibility to seek truth, not to blindly accept what you have been told." I was almost fired for encouraging students to think; to question what they are being taught.

The most potent barrier to seeking truth is the assumption that one already knows the truth, and therefore have no need for additional insight. If one is able to get past assumptions and begin to ask questions, they will often be faced with inconsistencies and contradictions, and realize they have believed some downright lies: stories constructed by those in positions of authority designed to help themselves instead of those they say they serve.

Many forfeit the right to examine what they have been taught and are left to the mercy of the status quo and to those who are in the business as Bernays puts it, "engineering your consent."

Chapter Twenty Eight

Profit vs. Spirit

Profit vs. Spirit

Einstein stated, "Anyone who becomes seriously involved in the pursuit of science becomes convinced there is a spirit (a consciousness) manifested in the laws of the universe, a spirit vastly superior than that of man."[1]

For eons, indigenous cultures have been aware of this spirit or universal consciousness. They believe it animates and connects all. As these cultures reassert themselves in resisting the destruction of what little land they have left, they once again come into bitter conflict with those who have given themselves the right to take what they want. They are the same forces that the indigenous people of the earth have always fought; individuals and governments who value above all, man-made things and money. For them the natural world, including its people are expendable.

It is doubtful those who control the capitalist systems can refrain from their rampage of destruction. It is nevertheless our responsibility as the citizenry to come together and resist their destructive urges.

At the People's Expense

Systems of power that currently exist keeps the common person from exploring their true nature, or getting to know their true identity which I believe is rooted in peace. Individuals filled with greed, and lust for power have always made it their business to suppress the true knowledge of humans replacing it with falsehoods in order to gain and maintain power.

Human beings are pliable and can be manipulated by those who are in control. These elites exercise power over freedom, ruthlessness over compassion, and deception over truth. They have manipulated and violently forced humans into following their vision of the world where the few control the many.

This system of top down control is an ancient one and has its foundation in religion. Religion in general uses fear, obedience, a twisted form of love and unquestioning loyalty as a means by which to gain and maintain your service. Without questioning, one is left to follow blindly, at the mercy of their leaders. Belief systems that question and or run contrary to religious, cultural, and the political order are relentlessly attacked. Those in power fear that the brainwashed minds of the mass populations will awaken. Who would fight their concocted wars if the populace found out that war increases the elites' power and wealth at the people's expense?

Chapter Twenty Nine

Alternative Reality

Religion or Spirituality

When I was a child I attended the Catholic Church with my family. It was a traditional large stone structure within walking distance from our house on Suffolk Street in Lynn. I don't remember much about the church or those associated with it. I do remember however the larger than life statues that circled the inside perimeter of the church and also how uncomfortable it was to kneel on the padded wooden planks called kneelers. Kneelers are usually padded pieces of furniture attached to pews or in front of alters for kneeling during prayer. If you are or were Catholic, you know what I am talking about.

My mother was raised Catholic, and she continued the tradition. In her days, attending church was just something you did. It was simply a part of the routine of life; at least that is how it appeared to me. For some, I think it may have given them a spiritual high and peace of mind regarding their ultimate destination. The motivation of the participants and those who performed the Mass was perplexing to me. The Mass was said in Latin, a language I assume was foreign to most of the congregation. Historically the Mass had been performed in Latin since the sixteenth century. Despite the language barrier the Catholic Church grew all over America. It was not until the 1960s that Mass started being performed in the language of the people.

In America, among the indigenous and early slave population's growth of the church was a result of brutality and domination. Once cultural beliefs were supplanted by the new religious framework, future generations simply accepted what was handed to them.

From my observation the proclamations of religious conservatism / fundamentalism is skilled in keeping people in a daydream and in a world of emotional fanfare. They proclaim exclusivity on truth and an insistence that their way is the only way to God. Religious leaders and others in positions of power are keenly aware that it is primarily emotion, not truth, knowledge or understanding that moves people to take action, be it for "good" or for "evil." The coffers of leaders swelled while poor, indigenous and slave populations remained destitute.

Organized religion has always proclaimed itself as the moral standard-bearer. In this day of unprecedented access to information, religion has come under scrutiny and is often held accountable for its claims. The revelation of errant priests and preachers do not engender confidence in religion for the general population. Many have sought out alternatives to organized religion.

Some have checked out of religion altogether. There is consequently a sample group of non-religious people that can be compared against those who claim religious and moral superiority.

"Research linking religion to prejudice suggests that highly religious individuals, and religious fundamentalists specifically, may be especially susceptible to expressing prejudice toward dissimilar others, whereas people who are less religious and some fundamentalist do not show the same effect."[1]

"In a survey of six religions in six nations, regular attendance at religious services positively predicted a combination of willing martyrdom and out-support hostility, but regular prayer did not."[2] Those who spent time in prayer opposed to structured religious services were less likely to be hostile to those outside of their group. The potential violence that results from regular attendance at religious services is not a given; it would clearly depend on what is being taught, who the leaders are and the vulnerability of those listening.

Fundamentalists not only are more likely to exhibit prejudice toward outgroups but are also pro-social toward people they agree with or are close to. Fundamentalist submission to religious authority varied according to the religious text they were exposed to.[3]

On the positive pole of the continuum, one can find open-minded religious and spiritual dimensions. This is the case with spirituality which Piedmont (2007) has framed in terms of connectedness (a sense of connection and commitment to others and humanity as a whole) and universalism (a belief in the unity and purpose of life), be it within or outside a context of a specific religious tradition.[4]

These observations should not be surprising to anyone who is an honest observer of how the world operates. For centuries religious Fundamentalism / fanaticism has run rampant on the planet. It has been a source of control for a few and by no means a spring of enlightenment for those who follow the leaders; instead of enlightenment often the delusion of superiority masquerades in its place only to create division and conflict. When individuals go beyond the rote programming served up by regular attendance at dogmatic worship services and instead spend time in prayer and or meditation, they are severed from the tether of hierarchical domination and the delusions of in-group superiority. In true spirituality one does not follow blindly. Instead one receives peace and insight in one's quiet personal time, meditation and / or prayer and personal study.

.

.... In the end, it would seem that it is not religion per se, but rather the way in which individuals hold their religious beliefs, which are associated with prejudice.[5]

In the United States, during the 60's, many turned to Eastern philosophy which emphasizes personal quiet time in meditation. This new philosophy was an alternative to traditional western religion. Free thinkers were drawn to this way of connecting with the spirit. It continues to be popular.

Sinful by Nature?

The "sinful by nature" concept is predicated on the story of the fall of Adam and Eve in the Garden of Eden as told in the Bible; their disobedient act of eating the forbidden fruit being the Original Sin. According to this story, this is how sin was introduced into mankind and as a result humans need a savior (i.e. God, or Christ).

It is clear, even with all the religious doctrines floating around; humans still display a streak of evil. A veneer of so-called civilization only masks inhumanity. War is common; but to be more accurate these wars are constructed by the politicians and others in power. The wars are mindlessly carried out by those they have programmed to fight them. The primary objective of some government's is the acquisition of resources at any cost. The only lives at stake are civilians and the government's enlisted forces. The powers that be don't risk their own lives to fight the battles to acquire the resources.

The powerful steal from and slaughter those who do not have adequate weaponry to fend them off. It is interesting to note how the ongoing war between Ukraine and Russia is handled. America and European powers were cautious not to antagonize Russia into greater acts of violence that may lead to a nuclear confrontation. Bullies respect each other; either of which have been able to win a war against the most meager opponents. The superpowers live in a delusional world believing their weaponized technology will enable them to win wars, but over and over again these things have been unable to overcome the will of the human spirit. Since these powers have not been able to win a ground war against their opponents, if someone or something does not stop theses psychopaths, I fear we will eventually enter into a nuclear confrontation.

I think the story of Original Sin is simply an excuse for some people to do evil. The commonly used phrase, "I am only human" is evoked by many to excuse immoral deeds. It is no wonder evil has run rampant in the world; it has been given a cover story.

Is the story of Original Sin true or is it just another fabrication among the long list of deceptions told by those in power? It appears to me, the story of Original Sin ultimately advantages the select few; the religious profiteers who have used it for profit. They reap the material benefits now while promising their followers benefits in the afterlife. There are concrete instances that put into question the doctrine of Original Sin. They will be explored in the next section, non-violent cultures.

There are those who have theorized that humans come into the world with no preconceived notions of good or evil. There was data shared in chapter eighteen that points to love as our primary instinct. I don't think humans are evil by nature or because of a single event in the distant, ancestral past; but instead as many social scientist agree become what they have been consistently exposed to. Humans adapt to their environment. I believe love is at the core of human existence but is distorted by environmental factors.

Living in peace without lawlessness and violence may be a dream for the so-called civilized world, but some have learned to turn that dream into reality. They are a contradiction to the sin laden philosophy of Original Sin and those who profiteer from it.

Non-Violent Cultures

There are peaceful cultures where murder and war are not present and neither are the prerequisites that spawn these perversions. Negative emotions that modern society have accepted as part of "human nature" are an aberration in some cultures. The following represent four different cultures that exemplify what I am talking about:

Chewong Society

One such peaceful culture is the Chewong, an indigenous people living in the protected environment of the Malaysian game preserve. They are a small group of a few hundred whose numbers are dwindling as civilization encroaches. The Chewong, see themselves as part of nature. They view all life as sacred. There are no leaders. Competition is non-existent; everything is shared. The Chewong have no violence in their mythology and cannot conceive of murder. The killing of another individual has never been recorded in their oral or written history. In 1982 Norwegian Social Anthropologist, Signe Howell lived with the Chewong for nearly two years. During that time she witnessed nearly no quarrels or anger except for children's temper tantrums. In the Chewong culture, Howell did not learn of any crime. An accusation by a jealous wife of her husband committing adultery proved not to be true. The breaking of a blowpipe was the only untoward act Howell observed while there. This was a highly unusual act that upset the community. Chewong's concept of human nature is, ***"To be angry is not to be human, but to be fearful is."***[6]

Ifaluk Society

Historian Edwin Burrows and anthropologist Catherine Lutz lived a year and a half with the Ifaluk people on the Ifaluk Island in the South Pacific. The population was about six hundred. Burrows reports he never saw any expression of anger even when some may have had too much alcohol. Lutz noted, "They are as kindly and non-aggressive as they think they are." Lutz reported the year she spent with the Ifaluk, the most serious act of aggression committed was one man touching the shoulder of another, which resulted in a fine.[7]

Hutterites Society

Some religious groups have learned to live out the true meaning of their faith. One such group is a five-hundred-year-old Christian collective called the Hutterites. There has not been a murder in the 500 year history of the group. They live in the upper part of Great Plains of the United States and Canada. They comprise a population of about fifty thousand; living in colonies of about a hundred. Originally from Switzerland, Austria and Germany, between 1874 -1879 they migrated to America. They patterned their lifestyle after the New Testament Christians. Hutterites reject state sanctioned, organized religion. They are pacifists and refuse to serve in the military. Hutterites live a communal life, separate from modern society. Over the centuries they have endured severe persecution for their stances. Resistance to the Selective Service Act of 1917 resulted in retaliation. Some were …"beaten and tortured to death for their pacifist stance", prompting moves to Canada.[8]

Nubians Society

The Nubians are another peaceful society. Their civilization stretches back beyond 2000 BC. Their present-day population is about 100,000. They are predominately Muslims, who live along the Nile in Southern Egypt.[9] He reports that when he lived with them, no form of violence existed. In the 60s, the

Egyptian government resettled the Nubians in order to build the Aswan Dam. In 2002, Fernea reported he had visited the Nubians several times after the dam was built and observed the continuation of their peaceful culture. It's not eating forbidden fruit or other such stories that create chaos and violence but instead chaos and violence is caused by what is taught and what is observed.

Popular culture has often portrayed Native American culture as savage but Benjamin Franklin, a newspaper journalist by trade, diverged from negative propaganda in the essay Remarks Concerning the Savages of North America. "...all their government (referring to the Iroquois Confederacy) is by the Council or advice of the sages; there is no force, there are no prisons, no officers to compel obedience or inflict punishment."[10]

Throughout Franklin's article he highlights the civility, politeness, kindness, hospitality and organization of the indigenous people. John Locke referred to Indians as being in a state of "perfect freedom" and argued that power should not derive from a monarch but from the people, an idea obtained from the Iroquois.[11] These accounts of peacefulness and intelligence are consistent with European explores who encountered indigenous nations in North America. English explorer Arthur Barlowe, in his July 13th through Mid-August of 1584 chronology recalls: "We were entertained with all love and kindness and with as much bounty, after their manner, as they could possibly devise. We found the people most gentle, loving and faithful, void of all guile, and treason, and such as lived after the manner of the golden age".[12]

The peaceful cultures of the Chewong, Ifaluk, Hutterites and Nubians are among others that represent a contradiction to what modern cultures have come to represent; violence and immorality are a part of so-called civilized cultures of today. Cultures have managed to construct civilizations where violence, war and its prerequisites do not exist. What have peaceful societies learned that most of the "civilized religious world" has not? Earth is not for humans to plunder, nor for a few to hoard resources in order to gain riches and power at the expense of the majority of the human family. Theses fundamental distortions of humanity's relationship to the earth and one another has spun our planet and its inhabitants into chaos and destruction.

The present order that is characterized by religiosity, secrecy and deception is losing its grip on power. The internet has made this system of control increasingly difficult to maintain. Be prepared for increased regulations, laws, and state violence as governments struggle to maintain control. Violence is how governments have gained power and this is how they'll try to keep it. They know no other way.

John Lennon's song *Imagine* speaks to the fact that we must imagine a world of peace, free from the boundaries of the status quo. Lennon sings, "You may say I'm a dreamer but I'm not the only one." That is the beginning of the shift.

Chapter Thirty

"The Good Old Days"

Tied Up

As a youngster, 3 or 4 years old, I remember being tied with a rope around my waist, and the other end tied around a tree. This was to prevent me from running out of the backyard; my mother's way of keeping tabs on me while she was hanging clothes. One day I managed to escape. I ran out of the yard, hit the sidewalk and kept running; giggling in flight. There was no fence separating the yard from the sidewalk, which made for an easy path to freedom. Fortunately, my mother caught me before I reached Main Street.

Excitement and Fear

Dad began to teach me how to ride a bike when I was around five or six. I would practice in a nearby lot. Dad would push me from behind, holding the seat as I peddled. My uncle Warren initiated my first solo flight. He put me on his red and white Columbia bike and pushed me down Suffolk Street. He ran behind me, holding the seat while giving me instructions to push down on the pedals in order to stop. After a few seconds of silence, I realized that my uncle was no longer behind me. I was terrified. The bike gathered speed cruising toward Main Street. I could hear my uncle yelling in the background, "Put the brakes on!" With my mind racing, I finally gathered my wits and pushed down on the pedals to slow the bike, bringing it to a crash landing just before I got to Main Street. This was the first time, that I had experienced a rush of *excitement and fear.*

Suffolk Street

I lived on Suffolk Street in Lynn, Massachusetts until I was 8 years old. It was a quiet location. In my imagination I can still see the street and feel the stillness of the area. We were among the very few people of color living in the neighborhood. I remember seeing another Black child who lived on a court off Suffolk Street. It was a short walk from where I lived. I wanted to get to know him. It turned out that his family were Jehovah's Witnesses. They have a reputation of being antisocial to those outside of their group. We never met.

Clams

The location where we lived in Lynn was within walking distance to Lynn Beach. I remember Dad taking my sister Evelyn and I clam digging. We would walk along the beach, watching for squirts of water coming up through tiny holes in the sand. That would tell us where to dig. By the time we were finished digging, we would have a bucketful of clams. My Dad and Ma were both seafood lovers. When we got home, Ma would prepare the clams to be cooked; washing the sand and any other material off the shells. She would then steam them. Minutes later we would open the shells, add butter and salt, and have our own delicious homemade clambake. Just thinking about it makes my mouth water. Dad would occasionally take us fishing. We fished off a local pier. I never caught a fish but I do remember pulling up an old boot and a crab.

Baseball Cards

While in Lynn, one of my favorite pastimes was collecting baseball cards. I had hundreds. One way of obtaining them, other than buying them, was to win them by playing a game called Leaners. Players would lean cards against a wall, back up about six or seven feet, then "shoot" at them by flinging cards, holding the card between the tips of our first two fingers supported by our thumb. With a quick flick of the wrist, we would shoot at the cards leaning against the wall until the last card was knocked down. The person who knocked down the last card would win all the cards on the ground; that could be a significant amount. It was exhilarating to win, but it was a real letdown losing what could be a substantial portion of your card collection. I won more than I lost. That was how I built my collection. Word would get around about who owned a card collection. Boys would go from street to street, challenging one another to a game of Leaners. There were always those who were poor sports. They would argue in an attempt to keep the cards they had lost. I understood how they felt because I had also lost cards playing Leaners. We all knew the rules. We had to be prepared to win as well as lose. Those who would not abide by the rules of the game were ostracized from the card-playing community.

Swimming

Dad was an excellent swimmer. It was a requirement of the Navy, the branch of the military in which he served. During the summer months, we would go to Lynn Beach. I would watch him swim so far out that I could barely see him. Sometimes I would ride on his back as he swam far out into the ocean. I don't remember being afraid. I didn't questioned my dad's ability. It was just fun.

Dad also gave me my first swimming lessons. I, unlike my dad never developed into much of a swimmer. In fact, I almost drowned trying to swim across Houghton's Pond in Milton, Massachusetts. My teenage friends and I would ride our bikes up through the Blue Hills to the pond. I remember looking across the pond thinking I could swim the distance across. Oh, the foolishness of youth. What looked possible soon became impossible. Barely halfway across the pond, I began to lose steam. I knew I was not going to make it. I had not yet begun to sink but I was anticipating that death was near. It is embarrassing to admit, but I felt more uncomfortable panicking and hollering for help than meeting my maker. I wanted to die "cool". My ego was in control and I was concerned about appearances. Wow! Fortunately, like a vision appearing from nowhere, a lifeguard rowed up beside me and helped me into *her* boat. Since then, any serious swimming has been confined to swimming pools. Though I have tried, I have not yet arrived at the point where I feel proficient at swimming. I am nowhere near the swimmer my father was. It's sure not in the genes.

Transition

In Roxbury there was a large track of woodland behind our house on Intervale Street. It stretched the entire length of our city block, close to a quarter mile. It was called the quarry. After school with my homework completed, I would make my way to the quarry to play Blacksmith, my favorite game. The object of the game was simple. Everyone would run into the woods and a player who had been chosen through the process of elimination would chase us down. When he caught his first person, he would hold him and say, "Blacksmith,

blacksmith, you're my man, caught by me one, two, three." These two would form a team and chase down the other players. When others were caught they would repeat the phrase and they would join the team chasing the rest until all were caught. You were never sure if the player approaching had been caught. He would pretend he hadn't been in the hope of catching you before you ran. There could be five to ten boys playing. Ronnie Keith and Billy Duffin had the most endurance. They would run you down until you dropped. You didn't want either one of them on your tail. Every day I looked forward to playing, but things eventually changed. I would run into the quarry, looking for the guys but no one was there. Where did everyone go? I soon found out the guys had found a new pastime, girls. To my disappointment, Blacksmith had become a thing of the past.

I soon joined my peers in their new interest. I missed Blacksmith, but I learned to enjoy our new form of recreation. As I think about the transition, I recall it was as if a switch had been flipped. It seemed so abrupt; one day we were running in the quarries, and the next day we weren't.

Off Limits

Carson Beach is located in South Boston. It was a few minutes from the Black community by car. One did not enter that part of the city (South Boston) because of the intense hatred displayed toward Negros; that's what we were called in those days. Instead of going to Carson Beach we would go to Salem Willows, Revere, or Nantasket Beach. These beaches were a significant distance from our homes, but they felt safe.

It is not easy to understand the loathing that some whites harbored against Blacks and other people of color. I have come to believe these negative feelings are learned, and are mindlessly passed down from generation to generation by those whom the masses follow. What are the origins of this hatred? Blacks have always wanted one thing from the white predominantly "Christian" majority, that is, to be treat the same way they would like to be treated. If for some that's not possible, then just leave us alone. Even in today's America both of these request seem to be off limits for some.

Blue Laws

From America's early history, Sunday was respected as a holy day. It took on a unique character. Businesses closed and the hustle and bustle of daily life ceased. This contributed to Sunday's special quality—a quality that has been lost since the death of the Blue Laws. In the United States, "Blue Laws," were called such because of the blue paper on which Puritan leaders printed the Sunday trade restrictions. This law dates back to at least the 18th century. Many forms of commerce were regulated or restricted so that workers could spend time in church and or with their families.[1] Today there are hardly any stores closed on Sunday. I miss the stillness that Sunday brought.

Chapter Thirty One

The Move

From Lynn to Boston

My father's work in the shoe industry prompted our move to Boston. Shoe factories in Lynn were closing. The closest factories that were still open were in Boston or its nearby towns. There were those in the extended family who thought the move to Boston had been a mistake because the location we had moved to was not as prosperous as the one we had left. They were only looking at the decision from a single perspective.

In 1955, we moved from Lynn, Massachusetts, to Roxbury, which was a part of Boston. I was eight years of age, and my sister, Evelyn, was seven. I had always thought until recently that the move was solely because of the availability of work. According to Evelyn, that was not the only reason, and it may not have been the primary one. Sis explained we also moved because of the racism the family was experiencing in the predominantly White community. I don't remember my parents specifically stating that as a reason. Parents don't usually explain the reasoning for the decisions they make to their children. In the case of racism, I believe the sooner one understands the reality of prejudice, those who are discriminated against won't blame themselves for the dysfunction of others.

I was horrified and angry when Evelyn told me of an incident when she was lured into a house by two dangerous white youngsters who lived across the street. The deranged older brother of the girl who lured my sister threatened to kill Evelyn. He held a fork to my sister's neck and forced her to kneel down backward, with her neck hanging out the window. The girl yelled to her brother, "don't kill her, you don't want to go to jail for killing a "nigger." How many other incidents did our family experience? I remember my dad occasionally speaking of racism he had experienced at the shoe factory where he worked. Sadly, my father's move to escape racism, if that was the case, it is a consistent story in the saga of Blacks in America. The Great Migration is a perfect example.

The Closings

Factories in Lynn were closing, but the truth was that factories all over the country were closing. The owners had decided to ship the shoe industry overseas where they could increase their profits. Moving industry overseas was the beginning of the elimination of manufacturing jobs in the United States.

Since the beginning of wage jobs, the workforce have been at the mercy of the corporate elites, whose mentality was not much different from the slave masters of the South. The primary difference was that slaves were owned like property. These factory workers nevertheless, had to work under similar degrading conditions that were unsanitary and unsafe. Child labor was rampant. There was no recourse to counter injustices in the workplace. Workdays often lasted from sun up to sundown. Meager wages kept most in a state of poverty and perpetual debt.

After decades of struggle, pain and death, working conditions and job security improved. Unions have been essential in this advancement. In the last few decades, with unions declining, computerization, automation and the exporting of jobs, job security is no longer an expectation. Robots have also shrunk job availability in manufacturing. In 2016 robots began performing basic surgery which was once the sole domain of human surgeons. There seems to be no limit to what robots can do. In 2013 Dr. Carl Frey, an Oxford researcher, predicted that automation would put 47 percent of the US work force at risk. The sweep of self-checkout machines in all the big box stores since 2013 - 2022 is a clear indication of the impact that automation is having on jobs.[1]

The closing of the Lynn and Everett shoe factories permanently ended my father's employment in the shoe industry.

Chapter Thirty Two

A New Beginning

A New Beginning

I would often ask my dad when were we going back home, which was code for returning to Lynn. Evelyn (Sis) told me she was asking Dad the same question. I am reminded of the old saying "The devil you know is better than the one you don't." I think it rings true hear. Lynn was quiet and peaceful, which was starkly different from our congested, noisy location in Boston. Lynn wasn't all peaches and cream, but it felt like it was, when compared to where we were now.

The move gave my parents the opportunity to separate themselves from my father's immediate family. They could build a new life for themselves without the emotional strings that so closely connected my dad to his mother, brothers, and sisters. This move was a new beginning. Moving from a white suburban town to the inner city was a culture shock for the whole family. Maybe that wasn't the case for my dad. His experience in the Navy exposed him to a wide range of people.

Even in the face of the difficulties of adjusting, it was still a positive experience. We needed to be amongst other families like our own in order to relate realistically to ourselves and others like us. Being raised in Roxbury was, as they say, "keeping it real." It's difficult to be who you are when growing up in a community where simply being who you are alienates you. I am so glad we never moved into a white suburban town.

My dad wanted to live in the nicest place he could afford. I could not blame him for that. Sometimes the desire for better obscures what is best. I don't think growing up in an all-white town and attending an all-white school would have been in my best interest. We might have moved into one of those towns, but redlining prevented that. Good.

My dad did look at some of those suburban towns, though. The real estate agent was happy to show them to him, when he was by himself. That all changed when my dad brought my sister and me with him. You see, my dad could easily pass for Italian or some other Mediterranean ethnic group, but my sister and I could not. After the real estate agent saw us the suburban fantasy ended. We began to only be shown houses in the predominantly Black locations of Boston.

As a result of redlining the population of Roxbury and parts of Dorchester and Mattapan were predominately Black. Redlining, is the term used when services (like obtaining a loan) are denied to potential customers who live in areas deemed hazardous for investment. In practice this process affects significant numbers of racial and ethnic minorities which attributes to discrimination. This process resulted in the Jewish population which had dominated Roxbury to move. The common terminology used at the time for White relocation was called "White Flight." By the time we moved to Roxbury in the mid to late 1950s, the White owned businesses had not totally moved out. They could make money no matter what the color of the population. After the uprising in the sixties resulting from the assassination of Martin Luther King Jr. on April 4, 1968 white store owners largely left the Black neighborhoods. Though the intent of redlining was restrictive and meant to segregate the Black population, it worked out just fine for me. History has shown that when Black people are left alone without racist policies and physical intrusion into our communities we can do just fine.

Dudley Street

Fifty three Dudley Street in Roxbury was our first address after moving to Boston. It was a three bedroom brownstone apartment connected to three or four other apartment buildings. It was a three-story building that stood at the top of a steep hill which led down to Dudley Station to the east, which was the local bus and train station. Fifty three Dudley Street was a place to lay our heads until my dad bought a house.

The Bacon School was the first inner-city public school I attended. It was in walking distance from my Dudley Street home. I was in the third grade. It was quite a culture shock from what I was accustomed to in Lynn. Chaos and confusion reigned every day in my class. The poor teacher was always at her wits end. How she could deal with it day after day was beyond me. I simply kept my head down and ducked for cover. Despite the craziness, I don't recall having any difficulty with the kids. In fact, I hit it off pretty well with my classmates. A couple of girls took a liking to me. I think they viewed me as an oddity since I didn't participate in any of the hooliganism.

My sister Evelyn went to an all-girls school named the Dillaway; it was also in walking distance from our house. This was before the days of desegregation. Evelyn's experience at the Dillaway was difficult. Girls bullied her and the classroom teacher ignored the bullying. Thankfully, for both of us we only spent a short time on Dudley Street before my dad bought a house and we both changed schools.

Fight or Flight and the First Kiss

From Dudley Street we moved to Quincy Street; this was the first house my parents bought after moving to Boston. My sister and I attended the same public school, the Quincy E. Dickerman Elementary School. The atmosphere in Dickerman was much more comfortable than either the Bacon or the Dillaway. It was at the Quincy E. Dickerman Elementary School that I received my first kiss. I found a note in my lunch box that said, "Kiss me," and it was signed N.R. I nervously met her in the coatroom. I was nine years old at the time. We puckered up and kissed. She appeared more relaxed than me. This was probably not the first time she had dropped a note in a boy's lunch box.

By the time we entered middle school my parents found a new house that was more to their liking. It was a three family house on Intervale Street in Roxbury, a few blocks from Quincy Street. I found adjusting to this *new* neighborhood more anxiety provoking than the others neighborhoods we had lived in. Dudley and Quincy Street did not have a neighborhood feeling. Once I was home from school, I didn't usually see kids out and about on Dudley or Quincy Street. On Intervale Street kids were *everywhere*. You could not help but run into someone; many times it was just the person I didn't want to see. I, being the new kid on the block, always anticipated being challenged to a fight. Walking down the street to the local store was like walking through a gauntlet. It wasn't my imagination. One day, on the way home from the store, I found myself surrounded by a crowd of neighborhood kids. Someone in the crowd stepped out, or perhaps another kid pushed him out to fight me. It was fight or flight. I was surrounded. Flight was not an option. Thanks to my father's boxing lessons I was able to quickly dispatch my opponent. One of my punches landed on his nose, and blood started flowing. He ran home crying. I walked home victorious. I never encountered much trouble from the neighborhood kids after that.

Chapter Thirty Three

The School Experience

The School Experience

After graduating from the Quincy E. Dickerman Elementary School, my sister and I attended the Patrick T. Campbell Junior High School. It's now known as the Martin Luther King School on Lawrence Avenue in Roxbury. The junior high school teachers stand out amongst all my public school teachers; because of their colorful personalities.

I was usually left feeling invisible in most public school classrooms. Middle/junior high school was the exception. There was one particular teacher who took an interest in me. He was determined to make sure that I did well in his class. From my perspective the majority of teachers weren't there to teach, but to talk. The only ones they were talking to were those who understood what they were talking about. I often did not. That's part of what made me feel invisible. I saw, during my time in Public School, how some kids acted out. You were pretty much ignored unless you were strong academically or were artistically or athletically talented. Misbehaving was the only way for some to get acknowledged.

It was a relief to finally have a teacher take an interest in me. In my experience most teachers only seemed interested in helping those who picked up the material quickly. It does not take much skill to teach those students.

The Teachers

While in middle school five teachers stood out: four because of their own particular weirdness. The fifth, Mr. Cummings was my favorite, who I will speak about after the other four.

Throughout public school Mr. Jo and Mr. Je, were my only African American teachers. Mr. Jo, taught math. He was an impeccable dresser; Mr. Je, the history teacher was just the opposite. Mr. Je's dark reddish brown suit was slightly oversized. I recall that detail because that was the only suit he wore. Mr. Je had a subdued personality; a little nervous and high-strung, but a decent guy who really wanted to teach history. He was hampered by his difficulty in controlling the class. This kept him defensive and on edge. I remember trying to approach him in a friendly manner. He was aloof, probably anticipating an ulterior motive. All I wanted to do was befriend him. I could feel his discomfort. My empathy has gotten me into real danger on a couple of occasions. Mr. Je was prone to outbursts when he was under pressure. He would pace up and down the classroom to vent his anger. The kids loved to antagonize him. He would call the students, "sweethearts." I simply saw it as a term of endearment, but the boys spread rumors about him being homosexual. The term "gay" wasn't used in the 60s. I never got that impression; but it was a reasonable assumption. Calling girls sweethearts was one thing, but referring to boys that way was not cool, particularly with some of those ruffians. I remember the time that Mr. Je attempted to discipline a student. He broke out his bamboo switch, better known as the "rattan." The rattan was about four feet long, round, narrow and flexible. It was used to strike the fingertips. When done correctly, it was quite painful but Mr. Je had not mastered the art. The one time I remember him using it, it shattered into pieces when he hit the student's fingers. The class burst into laughter. The Rattan needed to be kept in vinegar to maintain its strength and flexibility; something, Mr. Je had neglected to do.

Mr. Je may have done well in a suburban school. He was not suited to handle inner-city youth. Those kids need a personable and caring touch along with tempered discipline. I have found my years of working with youth this prescription is a winning combination. Inappropriate, over-the-top discipline only escalates minor problems. Mr. Je's high-strung, anxious personality made it difficult for him to find the right mix for dealing with high per active or poorly disciplined students.

Mr. Jo was my homeroom and Algebra teacher in the all-male ninth grade class. He was the polar opposite of Mr. Je. Mr. Jo stood about 6'5 the tallest teacher on staff. His outgoing personality and booming deep voice dominated the landscape. He was clearly in control of his environment and stood out from among his colleagues. He was always impeccably dressed, adorned in high-fashion silk suits; he wore a different color suit for every day of the week.

Mr. Jo talked about cultural and individual pride and gave the impression he had our best interest at heart. With all he seemed to have going for himself, his pompous air of self-importance and unnecessary use of corporal punishment detracted from this claim. I believe he *thought* he had our best interest at heart, but actions *do* speak louder than words. He prided himself in the use of "the board of education," which was a name for the paddle he used for discipline. He administered a whack across the fanny whenever he needed to enforce his will. This happened far too often and for minor infractions. I was paddled for turning my head around while seating. It appeared to me he enjoyed disciplining by the way he dramatized the process; chattering incessantly before whacking you. Being paddled for turning around was the last straw for me. I told my Dad about the incident, something I had never done because that was just the way it was in those days. Physical punishment was accepted. I did not want to look like a wimp but I felt Mr. Jo had crossed a line that I felt was unacceptable. I knew he would think I'd betrayed him, but that was something with which we both had to come to grips with. My dad was cool. He set Mr. Jo straight in a respectful way. Those in authority who may have thought they were important didn't intimidate my dad or me. I recently talked to David an old friend. We were in the Holy Trinity Drum and Bugle Corp and ran track together in high school. David ran good enough to get a track scholarship from high school to college. He was also in Mr. Jo's eighth grade class and unbeknown to me he and other boys in the classroom heard the conversation between Mr. Jo and my dad; they silently cheered, and were impressed that my dad stood up for me.

Mr. Jo was the first Black teacher I had and the first to encourage us to be proud of ourselves and our heritage. When he saw me display my pride as I walked proudly through the corridors, he yelled out, "Who do you think you are, Mr. Anderson, strutting?" I wasn't aware I was "strutting." I was just walking. This comment came from a man who took pride in his perfect upright posture. Since middle school I have never seen an individual stand as straight as Mr. Jo. He was literally as straight as an arrow. Yet when I displayed the pride that he had encouraged, I was publicly called out. Despite what I perceived as Mr. Jo's flaws, after a conversation with David I have come to agree with him that Mr. Jo did have our best interest at heart.

Mr. La. was the Dean of Discipline. I'm not sure what that meant because other teachers would discipline as they saw fit. He had black hair, a suave complexion, a thick build and always wore herringbone suit jackets. It is often the case that the person least suited for the job is the one who has it. This was the case with Mr. La. He was known to dish out harsh punishment. To my dismay, I once experienced his brutality.

I was told there was a rule that prohibited a teacher from raising their hand above their shoulders when disciplining with the rattan. If there was such a rule, Mr. La clearly disregarded it. He wound up and brought the switch all the way down to the floor. He would swing with all his might as the switch came crashing down on your fingertips; as I write about it, I can feel the pain.

Mr. La and Mr. Jo were both much too zealous as disciplinarians. From Mr. Jo you did not get the impression that he was trying to destroy you, but with Mr. La you did. In those days if a teacher didn't like you, they could potentially find any excuse to punish you. I was told a witness needed to be present when corporal punishment was administered. I assume for the interest of the child. There was two or three present when Mr. La used the rattan it appeared to me to be a source of entertainment for them rather than concern for the student. When Mr. Jo used the paddle he never had a witness. If there was such a rule, it was not taken seriously.

Mr. L my English teacher was incapable of controlling the class. He kept a bottle of whiskey in his desk draw to get through the day; a sad situation.

Physical Punishment a Roadblock to Growth

The "legitimacy" of corporal punishment I believe is rooted in Proverbs 23:13–14, which indicates that one should not "spare the rod." I suspect that for many this verse has been used as a justification to simply vent their anger against those who do not measure up to their expectations. Those who have worked with youth know that violence is not the way to produce positive change. It has been my observation after teaching in public school that much of the misbehavior in the classroom is age appropriate silliness. Taking negative behavior personally and overreacting is like throwing gasoline on a fire.

Staying calm, particularly under pressure is the key to gaining respect as well as maintaining order in the classroom. Refraining from anger is a positive example for students. Teachers will be forced to resist reactionary behavior if they expect to be affective in the classroom. They should exemplify what they expect of students. "Do as I say, not as I do" is not an effective strategy.

Many schools have banned corporal punishment to ensure student safety. They have adopted less aggressive means of discipline. Today, teachers have to learn effective alternatives to corporal punishment. Some have received specific training in de-escalation of adverse behaviors or have learned techniques on their own through classroom experience. A win- win for all.

Teachers (continued)

The fifth teacher on my list is my middle school math teacher Mr. Cummings. He was my favorite teacher. He was not prone to outbursts, and did not engage in any type of physical punishments. He took the time to help me succeed in math, a subject in which I had little success. Other teachers would simply go through their teaching routine, and seem to be satisfied to focus on students who were quick learners. If you didn't catch on quickly, then too bad. Mr. Cummings was different. He was willing to take the time to help me and other students work through our difficulties. He assured me that I would do great in his class, and I did. For the first time, I received an "A" in math. I remember him coming to my desk and showing me the steps in addition, subtraction and multiplication of fractions. We would meet after school if I needed extra help. Mr. Cummings had a serious demeanor. He rarely smiled. His warmth nevertheless was unmistakable. It showed in his desire to see you succeed.

After being exposed to a caring educator, students like myself unfortunately had to return to teachers who didn't seem to care. Students who needed the most attention, most often got the least.

Students, who appear to show very little interest in learning, are often those same students who have been neglected for years in the educational setting. They are hampered by their inability to catch on as quickly as others. It is easy to blame parents for not working with their children as the reason for student failure. Many parents work two jobs to make ends meet and may not have the time, patience, or energy at the end of the day to make sure that their child had learned what had been taught: some may not understand the subject matter well enough to be able to help their children. It is not unreasonable to expect a child to learn the basic skills of reading, writing, and arithmetic in school. This is where they spend eight hours a day five days a week for the majority of the year? If for whatever reason the goals can't be achieved in 8 months, then by all means provide teaching assists, tutors and educational specialists to help students succeed. For a student to graduate from high school lacking basic skills is inexcusable.

High School

After graduating from the Patrick T. Campbell Junior High School, I attended Dorchester High, a predominately white school in Dorchester's Codman Square area. Roland Fonseca, David Roderick, Langford Reynolds, Livingston Blackmen, Joel Smith and Albert Jones were some of the neighborhood guys who attended Dorchester High. Each of these young men had their own special stories; my associations with each had its own unique flavor; some with whom I sang with, ran track with and hung out with.

Back in the late 50's and 60's racial prejudice was blatant. It was a way of life in America. To some degree, we were insulated from it because we lived in a Black neighborhood amongst our own. At Dorchester High we were all in store for a lesson in a type of racism that was associated with the South, for which we were quite unprepared. We experienced blatant prejudice in stores where we shopped. White storeowners would watch us or even follow us as we tried to shop. Police officers would stop us for no apparent reason. It was frustrating and demeaning, but you didn't necessarily feel like your life was in immediate danger.

A weeks or so after starting Dorchester High, there was a scuffle between a Black and a White student. That incident caused a huge backlash for Black students. After we were dismissed from school, we were confronted by a multitude of angry White men, not boys. It sent chills up my spine. It looked like there were hundreds. We did the only thing we could do; run for our lives. They threw things at us as we ran toward the bus stop, which was at least a quarter mile from the school. The crowd soon dissipated and we made it to the bus stop. As far as I can remember no one got hurt.

The area where the school was located was not exclusively white. I went to Codman Square to shop and never had a problem. I suspect that the organization of that mob was instigated by individuals from a part of the city known to be dangerous for Blacks; South Boston. Blacks only went into South Boston if they absolutely had to. There were hard-core racists in that part of the city. I was told that other racial incidents occurred where gangs met Black students after school, and they were not there to play a friendly game of baseball. Track practice spared me from becoming involved in those incidents.

Attitudes began to slowly change toward the early to mid-1980s. This transition began because of the integration of schools and public housing.

Racism is institutionalized in America and is designed to be quietly carried out. You may be able to hide the process of racism but you cannot disguise the affect. Lack of job opportunities, disproportionately low wages, housing and home buying discrimination, poor or no access to health care, limited educational opportunities and unequal treatment by the justice system are some of the manifestations of modern American racism. Some may have become desensitized to its subtleness even though it stared us right in the face.

In the three years I had attended Dorchester High the only member of the staff who I can recall showing an interest in me was Mrs. Groves. She was the librarian, and as far as I know the only Black professional in the school. My friend Roland and I would show her the poetry we had written. She would read our poetry and encouraged us to keep writing. I find it amazing that in the twelve years of public school education I can recall very few words of encouragement.

For the most part Blacks and Whites stayed to themselves at Dorchester High, although there were some exceptions. I developed an association with a redhead name Robert B. He was full of tales about his life's unique experiences. Some of the stories I doubted due to the fact he was only in high school. The stories, true or not were entertaining. He had a style of speaking that reminded me of President Kennedy. He seemed out of place in high school. He wore tweed suit jackets which were reminiscent of a professor on a college campus. He would surely have fit in there. He was interesting and friendly, and had an air of mystery. During my three years at Dorchester High he was the only white peer with whom I associated.

Decision despite Uncertainty

After graduating from high school I was not sure of what to do next. I had no marketable skills, only a diploma. Some students went to college; others had received academic, athletic or art scholarships. Others had certain skills obtained in high school shop classes or other interests that enabled them to make a living straight from school or build on what they had learned from school or at a job. I unfortunately fell into none of these categories. My father suggested that I consider looking into becoming an electrician's apprentice. Now *that* was a plan! I would not only be getting paid but would also be learning a great skill. Electricians were always in demand and they were well paid. I followed through on my father's suggestion.

Too often young people reject the advice of parents or other adults only to sometimes regret it. You can spend a lifetime of uncertainty, not committed to anything, remaining in a perpetual state of confusion if you have no marketable skills or talents. Support and encouragement is particularly important for these individuals.

Electricians, Max Showstack and his partner Jerry took me under their wing. They had a shop in the Beacon Hill area of Boston. I worked with them. To become a licensed electrician you needed to learn the theory behind the practical work. I enrolled at Wentworth Institute, a technical school. For me to be successful there I needed encouragement and individual help, none of which was to be found there. I finally concluded that electrical work wasn't the best fit for me; not only because of the school environment but my interest had always been in the field of Social Service. After three years of working with Max I thanked him and went on my way. At that time I had no idea how to transfer my Social Service desire into a way to make a living. I had shared my decision with my dad. He told me that he was happy that I had given the apprenticeship an honest effort and he had no problem with my decision.

Dad was aware of the pitfalls of allowing uncertainly to prevent you from making a firm decision. He knew a trade would give me focus and a skill I could depend on to make a living. Throughout my life I've been able to put into practice the skills I learned as an electrician's helper. It became particularly useful in 1972 when I started my handyman business.

After I left my job as an apprentice, I still needed to work in order to pay my rent and provide for my daily needs. I was 21 at the time. In those days wages and living expenses were on par. You did not need to work two or three jobs to survive as many need to do today. There were affordable rooms available in the nicest parts of Boston. I lived at 103 Beacon Street across the street from the Charles River and the Boston Public Gardens; a beautiful location. Every time I went outside I was inspired. Outside of work, running, practicing yoga, and playing my trombone were my primary pastimes.

Shortly after I left my job as an electrician's helper I landed a job working at the Main Post Office in Boston. It was a couple of miles from my room but for me within walking distance. Many of the people working at the post office felt they were set for life. They had landed a federal job. I knew this was only temporary for me. While working at the post office my life took a dramatic turn toward the direction I wanted it to go.

Post Office to University

At the post office I met James M. We had many political and intellectual conversations. He was attending the University of Massachusetts (U. Mass). He encouraged me to attend college explaining that the University was offering scholarships to Black students who had graduated from high school. The opportunity James shared was a game changer; but it took me a while to recognize it. Some of the guys I had grown up with went to college straight from high school, mostly on athletic scholarships. When I saw them at parties, they seemed so full of themselves, wrapped up in their fraternity rituals; it was impossible to communicate with them. I saw college through the image they projected, and it turned me off. James's persistence helped change my mind. He gave me an application to the University of Massachusetts and told me to get it in as soon as possible; I did. James turned out to be just the person I needed to point me in the right direction. I was excited and looking forward to the college experience; as a result I was able to fulfill my desire to work in the social service field.

To me college had always seemed to be the domain of Caucasians; another door I think the cultural elite made sure was kept closed to people of color, particularly African Americans. Lack of finances, inequality of education and lack of encouragement by teachers in inner-city schools made sure these doors stayed shut, unless you had skills that impressed high school teachers. Those who possessed such skills and were fortunate to have someone take interest in them were guided down the path that made college at least a possibility.

Many African American parents had not finished high school never mind college; college was foreign to them. My father asked me an honest question "how will college help you to get a job?" I was not sure at the time and was unable to explain it to him. Dad nevertheless, did not discourage me.

I knew my talents were rooted in the area of the social services – the helping professions. I often encouraged my mother when she was depressed and advised friends and acquaintances regarding life issues. Sometimes circumstances would arise where strangers would ask for my opinion or advice. Could going to college help me use my natural talents to make a living? I was thrilled at the possibilities.

College was exhilarating. The professor in my creative writing class complemented my writing and the insights drawn from stories by John Steinbeck. Decades later this positive reinforcement has remained an inspiration for my writing.

College was a struggle. I dropped out for a year but returned after encouragement from a close friend. I contacted my favorite teacher, Criminology Professor Jerry Garrett. I had taken classes with him and done an internship under his guidance. He made it a point to really get to know his students. Jerry was an excellent teacher, and had written his own text book on the subject of criminology. He was an especially caring person. This is what truly made him special. He made it possible for me to re-enroll into the university. I graduated from the University of Massachusetts in May of 1976. Till this day I am thankful beyond measure for Jerry's interest in seeing me succeed.

Teaching at South Boston High and Desegregation

The East and North End of Boston were primarily Italian; South Boston was predominantly populated by those of Irish decent. African Americans were redlined into Roxbury, and parts of Dorchester and Mattapan. These rigid demarcations began to change when court ordered desegregation of public schools and public housing began in 1974–1988. South Boston was ground zero for the desegregation of public schools and public housing. If desegregation could work in Boston's most hostile neighborhood, it could work anywhere.

After graduating from the U. Mass I taught for a few years at South Boston High School as a Special Education Teacher in training. I worked with students who had educational deficits which prevented them from being main streamed into regular classes. Most deficits were academic, although behavioral issue also affected their performance. Remedial assistance raised academic performance. Extra help and concern eased or eliminated behavioral problems.

There was tension among some of the teaching staff at S. Boston High and occasional fights between black and white students. Staff, for the most part worked together professionally and students managed to coexist despite the tension. The teachers I worked with could not have been more professional and congenial. I would remain at South Boston High from 1976 to 1978.

The Student

There are students that stand out in my memory. Isiah was one of those. The first day I met him he walked into my Special Ed. classroom full of anger, hollering curse words. I introduced myself and asked him why he was so angry. He shouted about an incident he had with a teacher which led to a suspension from that classroom. The teacher Isiah had experience a problem with eventually sent down the social studies materials he needed to work on. After blowing off steam he sat quietly but refused to work; no surprise. He showed up the next day irritable but with his materials; that told me he was willing to do some work. With some coaxing we began reading. As we read it became clear that he was functionally illiterate. I had to help him sound out almost every word. For the short time we worked together Isiah put forth a sincere effort to learn the mechanics of reading and was making progress. Every day I looked forward to seeing him. One day I was told he was thrown out of school for having another incident with a teacher. What a disappointment, and what a tragedy for Isiah. At this late date Isiah was still invested in learning how to read. How did the system fail him? How could it be that a young man in high school could not read? I assumed it was due to some level of neglect; perhaps Isiah did not pick up information quickly or at least as quickly as he was expected to. Without individual help or assistance in a small group, chances for success were negligible for students like Isiah and they often become behavior problems. These students are chalked up as failures and passed from grade to grade until they graduate or drop out.

I believe Isiah's rage was rooted in not knowing how to read (though he may not have been aware that was the source) and in the system that failed him yet blamed him. I think that was a darn good reason to be enraged.

The National Institute of Literacy estimates 32 million Americans adults cannot read. This impediment severely affected their quality of life. In 2019 the population of the U.S. was approximately 329 million that means an estimated 10% of Americans can't read. Why? There are many extraneous reasons; poverty, attention deficit issues and lack of parent involvement are often cited as the reasons for poor reading, but in the final analysis they are excuses used by the educational establishment to excuse their own incompetence. It has been known for decades that Phonics, the mechanics of associating letters and words with their sounds, is how people learn how to read. Phonics is the only method that has been scientifically proven to produce readers. The continued use of other methods, whole language, balanced literacy etc. will only contribute to a widening gap in American's ability to read. I thought Isiah was an exception; unfortunately his reading predicament is shared by far too many students who are being taught by reading methods that do not work.[1]

Social Work and Desegregation

After three years at S. B. High, I decided to go into the line of work I felt drawn to, Social Work. For approximately fifteen years I worked in a variety of capacities in the field of social worker; child abuse and neglect at the Department of Social Services, individual, couples, and group counseling under the supervision of a psychologist, program developer, social work supervisor and eventually program director. A major part of social work is obviously helping those in need. Paradoxically, sometimes encouraging and persuading individuals to receive help is also a considerable part of the job.

After working in the social work field and a few years in the teaching profession I unexpectedly started a handy man business in 1995. My wife and I moved from Boston to North Carolina in 2005. It is now 2023 and I'm still in business. We have been in NC for 18 years and to our pleasant surprise we personally have not experienced even a hint of racism in our daily comings and goings. It's been up north where the racism was prevalent. When I tell people who are native to the state about northern racism, they are surprised. Many have the mistaken impression that racism only exists below the Mason–Dixon line. That is another delusion debunked.

While visiting Boston In 2007, Vernice and I were invited to a friend's house who lived in South Boston. We were apprehensive. We had not been in South Boston since my teaching at South Boston High in 1978. To our surprise the atmosphere was totally transformed. African Americans walked the main streets visiting stores without fear of insult or bodily injury. The old days of in your face racism were gone. It appeared that the neighborhood had finally come to grips with the reality that racial antagonism was no longer *openly* acceptable.

There are different points of views as to whether or not Boston's desegregation efforts were successful. I can walk through the streets of South Boston today without the fear of being threatened. From that perspective, I feel that desegregation was a success.

Chapter Thirty Four

Dad Was Always Growing

Dad was Always Growing

On Woodbine Street, my dad was always busy doing something around the house to make our living situation better. I would often help. We painted and did repairs. I maintained the grounds by keeping the bushes trimmed and cutting the grass. I was responsible for the overall upkeep of the yard; something I took pride in. My dad discouraged me from working after school. He said, "Tommy (my nickname) there is no need to start working now, you'll be working soon enough. Once you start, you'll be working for the rest of your life." That attitude and advice gave me the opportunity to be a part of the Holy Trinity Drum and Bugle Corps. If I had worked after school, I would not have been able to participate in drum corps, learn how to play the trombone or may not have developed my interest in music.

I don't think my dad had envisioned working in a shoe factory all his life. For the time being it had enabled him to provide for the family. His various interests indicated to me that he had envisioned possibilities beyond the shoe factory. He was always reading something geared toward personal growth. Napoleon Hill's book, *Think and Grow Rich* was one of the books he shared with me; "Whatever the mind can conceive and believe it can achieve." This is somewhat true, but by no means a golden rule. Approaching challenges with this attitude is a definite source of motivation.

Dad's wide range of interests often fell outside traditional boundaries; this was also the case with his mother. Like his mother, in religious matters he found scant acceptance among religious family members. It has been my experience that the religious worldview is very narrow and rarely goes beyond religious parameters.

Handwriting analysis was one of those activities that the religious found questionable. Some without understanding associated it with the occult; a code word for evil. Dad worked diligently at developing this skill, regardless of the views of others. He created a system that could help him to analyze an individual's script quickly and accurately. His work, without question, was of a professional quality. Those whose handwriting he analyzed testified to his expertise.

I was attending middle school during the time my dad was studying and doing handwriting analysis. I would bring home handwriting samples of my friends and classmates. My dad could easily cross check some of his findings because I knew these individuals. His accuracy was truly amazing. Analyzing the handwriting from a variety of individuals was one way he could test out the accuracy of his system. What stands out for me was his ability to target the temperament of an individual. It was as if he were looking through a window into their lives. He would tell me, "Tommy, certain information I won't share with your friends because it's too personal. It's not in their best interest because they are young, still developing and changing."

Personality and temperament can be revealed in the slant of letters, the cross of the T, the dot of the i, the opening or closing of the O's or other letters can indicate follow through or the lack there of. My dad shared with individuals the positive aspects of his findings. When he did allude to negative aspects, he would do it to encourage growth in those areas. He encouraged me to close my O's and other letters because doing so represents completion and following through on tasks. To this day when I write, I remember to follow my dad's instructions. When I gave my friends the results of their analysis they were flabbergasted. They could not believe that someone could find out so much about them through their handwriting.

Dad offered his services to the police department as he explored ways to convert his skill into financial opportunity. He worked on a couple of cases. The information he uncovered was useful, but they wanted him to have some sort of credential, certification, or degree in the field. Dad continued to do it on the side.

Dad invented an adaptation for storm windows that enabled them to be installed from the inside. He designed and produced a prototype and submitted a patent application. I remember my Dad trying to find ways to mass produce the window. That proved to be a major stumbling block.

My earliest memories of my dad's entrepreneurial efforts were when I was in elementary school. Dad was making Plaster of Paris Asian ornamental figurines. They were about five inches tall, male and female, seated and dressed in traditional Asian attire. After meticulously preparing the mixture, he would pour the plaster into a rubber mold. They would set for a day or two. When they were hard enough, he would carefully open the mold take them out and prepare them to be painted; highlighting their fancy ceremonial dress. Sis and I would help in the painting. To our disappointment some of the figurines would crack or break as we attempted to take them from the mold. These were discarded. If they could have been recycled they would have been because at that time thrift was valued.

I was impressed by the care and attention to detail dad would approach all his work, but especially how much time and effort he took to complete his handwriting analysis system. Years later I tried on a couple occasions to track down dad's handwriting material. I was not able to recover it. I feel sad that his work was not preserved considering all the time and effort he had put into it.

Dad enjoyed science fiction and thus sparked my own interest. *The Mind is the Simplest Thing* by

Clifford D. Simak was one of those great stories. It was a fascinating tale about people telepathically reaching out into the universe and contacting beings from other worlds. Dad believed in the existence of extraterrestrial life. He did not need others to tell him what to think or believe and no longer do I.

I was always involved at some level in my dad's ventures, even if it was only to encourage him but a significant contribution was getting the handwriting samples from my friends.

In the mid-sixties dad trained to be a television repair technician. He opened his own television repair shop on Blue Hill in Roxbury, and operated it during the late sixties through the seventies. He also taught TV repair and assisted in carpentry and plumbing classes at Madison Park Public High School. These activities grounded to a halt once dad became sick with cancer.

I believe I inherited my dad's spirit; one that finds no room for boredom. I find it odd when individuals speak about how bored they are or how they have nothing to do. There is so much to develop within and equally to explore without. People should resist allowing themselves to be limited by restrictive boundaries or artificial limits. These walls are erected by societies; self-doubt, traditions and prejudices are common obstacles that limit our reality. I say allow yourself to be open to new and varied possibilities; those that come your way and those you create for yourself.

Dad was always growing, and although I believe he didn't receive the acknowledgment or recognition he deserved, the joy of doing, gave him the positive strokes he needed. I could see it in his excitement while working on his projects. Dad drew on a special energy that was independent of the admiration and acceptance of others. He was very much like his mother, independent of agendas set by others. Having an independent, questioning and inquisitive spirit can cause one to feel some degree of detachment from others because often others are lacking these qualities. I believe some degree detachment is part of the territory when one has an independent mind. Dad, I love you. Thank you for your hard work in making a life for our family and instilling in me the desire to work hard and also the ability to enjoy it.

A Special Energy

That special energy mentioned above is available to everyone. It is locked inside waiting to be released. One must break the bonds of the ordinary to encounter it.

My son told me about a decision he had made to start his own business. He was excited. It was an excitement and energy I was familiar with after having starting a few businesses over the years. His excitement got me to thinking about this phenomenon of energy and the feeling of freedom it gives rise to.

Once these creative juices get flowing, the excitement they create can make it irritating for one to be at the whims of others for their own sustainability. The desire for liberation is felt long before the acquisition of financial gain. This thrill is independent of the monetary systems that cultures have created. It is a spirit, a Special Energy that is often at odds with cultural precepts and expectations. This energy can open us up to roads "less traveled" or to even follow a path previously unknown. Be open to the energy and enjoy the ride.

Availability

Dad was a chip off the old block, and like his mother, reserved. Emotions were kept in check as was the case with many of his generation. They were more apt to evaluate a person by their deeds, not by their rhetoric or emotive exhibitions; a yardstick that I have come to find extremely useful. Dad provided leadership for the family. He provided stability, and part of that stability was to make sure he owned his own house. His intense work ethic always made it possible for us to feel secure. We never wanted for *necessities*. I don't remember many rolling conversations between Dad and myself, though he was always available if I needed him. Dad's teaching me how to box after we moved from Lynn to Boston was a skill I needed in the community we move to. Proving I could defend myself lifted my self-esteem and my stature among my peers. After high school his guidance regarding a career path was very helpful; it was advice that I followed. Dad encouraged me to give myself a little more time before I made the move to go out on my own. I was eighteen or nineteen at the time. He may have thought I was not ready to be on my own. I think the bottom line was that dad knew he was going to miss me.

At His Bedside

Sterling Ernest Anderson was born on December 26, 1921. He died in November 1974. I was twenty-seven and working my way through the University of Massachusetts when Dad died. I was with him at his bedside in the hospital when he passed. It was as if I was meant to be there. Some of my relatives had left the room shortly before I came. I was alone with Dad. He was not able to talk but I assumed he could hear as I was whispering into his ear telling him I loved him and appreciated all he did as my father. Only now as a father, do I have an experiential understanding and a greater appreciation of the love, effort, dedication, and sacrifice it took to raise us particularly during a time when racism was unhinged, and unashamedly displayed. In some quarters there is still no shame.

Chapter Thirty Five

Forward in the Face of Roadblocks

Complainers and Haters

Elementary and secondary schools in predominantly Black areas were generally inferior to the education in predominantly white schools. On July 2, 1964 Affirmative Action was signed into law by President Lyndon B. Johnson. Affirmation Action redresses the disadvantages associated with past and present discrimination against Black Americans. There are those who complain that Blacks and others of color were getting special treatment regarding the race-based opportunity to enter college. It is important to note that since color was the metric by which people of color were being rejected it's only fair that it became part of the process by which Black students were accepted. Without this added consideration Blacks would continue to be rejected by mainstream colleges; Affirmative Action was the only way Blacks, for the most part could get into White colleges. Racially discriminatory practices restricted Blacks from receiving higher education.

These practices are tantamount to a higher learning institutional apartheid. What was once policy that had been in place for hundreds of years and accepted by the White majority was still seen in discriminatory practice by the wide margin of Black applicant rejected. Today, some have the nerve to cry "reverse racism." It is my belief that those who whine about reverse racism are simply exposing their own hypocrisy. In 2019, thanks to *Operation Varsity Blues*, we found out that at least 53 rich White families were paying bribes to school administrators to get their kids into the colleges of their choice. Some were granted athletic scholarships despite not playing sports.[1] I'm am sure this is only the tip of the iceberg.

The rightful opportunities and remunerations Blacks have acquired (though thankful) were not given from the kindness of the US governments heart but born through persistent and unweaving struggle of many in the Black community. In the process many Black lives were lost; but there was also some courageous whites who paid the ultimate price. Any compensations will never offset the centuries of degradation, destruction of communities, endless murders and abuse inflicted on black and brown people indigenous to America and those decedents from Africa. Injustices that have not ceased until this day. Attempts by government to redress these grave injustices through Affirmative Action and other government "solution" will never rectify past and present day wrongs. Efforts to address them at least reveals a spirit of acknowledgement, a prerequisite to any ongoing *meaningful* change.

Unfortunately there are efforts to get rid of Affirmation Action and other efforts are presently being made by the GOP to keep Black people "In their place." Republicans have introduced 361 bills that disproportionately restricts the right to vote for people of color and those of low income.[2]

HBUCs

The Civil Rights Movement led by Martin Luther King Jr. made it possible for the Civil Rights Act of 1964 to become law. It prohibited racial segregation in schools and made it possible for Blacks to enter schools of higher education. For a brief period some of the prerequisites to get into college were waived. It was a gesture by the government and some colleges to address one of the multitudes of injustices against people of color in America. The problem was, so few could take advantage of this opportunity because many were not prepared for higher education in high school. Those who were admitted into schools of higher education often found the expectations and social pressures difficult to overcome.

African Americans (AA), fortunately, had not been sitting around waiting for politicians to do what was right by them. AA, often with some help from progressive Whites had been working toward developing their own communities, schools, and colleges before the Emancipation Proclamation of 1863. Historic Black Colleges and Universities (HBCUs) are a crowning achievement in the effort of AA taking authority over their own educational destiny. HBCUs gave African Americans the opportunity to attend college when excluded from white institutions; they provided the care and remedial help that was often needed for Blacks to be successful. In 1965 the doors of white colleges and universities may have been open to Black students but the supports systems provided in Black institutions were nonexistent in White institutions of learning. Alienation was an ever-present problem. In 1966 Jerry Varnado and James Garrett started the first Black Student Unions (BSU) at San Francisco State University; a support system that became institutionalized across the country. It helped Black students to traverse the educational and social barriers of college life.

For more than a hundred years HBCUs have served Black student's higher educational needs. HBCUs do not have the deep pockets of their counterparts, yet are serving a population financially and educationally deprived. Despite these factors HBCUs have managed to produce an impressive record. "Though HBCUs make up only three percent of the country's colleges and universities, they enroll 10% of all African American Students and produce 20% of all African American graduates."[3]

HBCUs have been a major contributing factor in the rise of Black professionals and the Black middle-class. Langston Hughes, Thrugood Marshall, Michael Strahan,

Spike Lee, Martin Luther King Jr., Dr. LaSalle D. Leffall Jr. (surgeon, oncologist and medical educator), Barbara Jordan (lawyer, politician and educator), Barrington Irving (youngest person to pilot a plane around the world) and Kamala Harris, current Vice President of the United States, these are just a few of the many who have been educated at HBCUs.

Daniel Payne

Daniel Payne was a pioneer pushing for the education of African Americans. He was born in 1811 in Charleston, South Carolina to Black and Native American parents. Payne was a fierce believer in education. He was educated at the Charleston School, which was established by free Blacks.

In 1826, after joining the African Episcopal Church (AME), Payne opened a school for African American children. The school was forced to close in 1834 because of laws passed by the South Carolina legislature that banned the education of African Americans. Payne went on to become the sixth bishop in the African Methodist Episcopal Church (AME Church). He was a proponent of an educated ministerial staff. In 1856 Payne was one of the founders of Wilberforce University of Ohio. In 1863 The AME Church acquired ownership of the University from the white owned Methodist Episcopal Church. In that same year Payne became the first Black president of the university.[4]

Chapter Thirty Six

Encouragement - Spiritual Quest

Encouragement

In 2014 I started substitute teaching. As a substitute I subbed primarily in middle and high school settings. On this particular day I was subbing in a sixth-grade gym class. The sub plan explained that the students should run or walk three times around an outside track. It was a challenge to run around once at a brisk pace, let alone three times. Most students walked. Some dared to run the three laps. Of the students who ran, three were talented runners. I had never seen students with such skill, considering they were only sixth graders. These three ran as if they had prior training though only one was able to briskly complete the three laps. He was exceptional but all three were gifted runners and could easily have a future in the sport.

I acknowledge their athletic ability and encouraged the three of them to continue to develop their running skills. I ran track throughout high school. I knew talented runners when I saw them. Whether students ran, walked or chose not to participate, I encouraged all of them. Among the students there was surprise and a thankfulness to be acknowledge. It's natural to encourage the talented. Those without readily identifiable skills may get ignored. They are the ones that may need encouragement the most. Without it, some may become discouraged and unmotivated. This lack of acknowledgment may plant the seeds for misbehavior in a misguided attempt to be recognized.

Encouragement has the power to deactivate negative feelings. Along with support, it can reenergize individuals and give them hope for positive outcomes. I think you should shower all students with encouragement. Do not reserve it for a special few. Most of us do not get enough. A word of encouragement can have the power to change the course of a person's life. You never know its impact so loosen up, and let it flow.

All seeds have different rates of growth. They flower at different times. We as individuals are no different. Water people with encouragement, add some patience and kindness then individuals will have the opportunity to flower in *their* season. Encouragement is always in order. Look for opportunities to dispense it and if you cannot find one, create one.

Mr. Cummings, my middle school math teacher and Ms. Groves the high school librarian, were among my encouragers during my public school years. Ms. Groves encouraged those of us who enjoyed writing poetry to keep writing and Mr. Cummings encouraged struggling math students and worked with them to assure success. These individuals were encouragers in an atmosphere of indifference.

I had not enrolled in the college course in high school. Writing was not a major part of my curriculum. I mentioned earlier it was not until I attended college, 10 years after I had I graduated from high school that I was once again encouraged to write by my creative writing Professor. Those words of encouragement reverberated for decades. They were the driving force in my first literary endeavor. In November of 2006, I began publishing "The Americans" a politically conservative newspaper. It was distributed in the Wilmington North Carolina area. When I shared the paper with others who I thought were fellow conservative thinkers, I quickly realized that Black conservative thinkers regardless of what they brought to the table were not valued at least among this particular group of conservatives. I quickly disassociated myself from this crowed and eventually completely from the Republican Party.

The egregious stimulus packages given by George Bush and Barack Obama to bail out banks and other corrupt financial institutions thus saving them from financial insolvency set me on the path to becoming independent of status quo ideologies. No longer was I going to believe *anything* on face value!

In 2010 as a result of my new found liberation, nomorefairytales.net was created. It was an online newspaper; a collaboration between me and my son Uriel. He did an extraordinary job laying out the paper. Its goal was to expose fabrications widely excepted as truth. The seeds of encouragement planted decades ago gave me the confidence to write for a mass audience. I have since decided to put my thoughts into book form. "*Escaping the Delusions of Culture*" is a result of that endeavor. Thank you, encouragers.

★★★★★★★★★★★★★★★★★★★★★★★

Spiritual Quest

I was about six years of age when I had an unusual experience. While balancing as I walked along the curb outside of my house I suddenly felt a sensation of weightlessness. It felt like I was outside of my body. I never mentioned this to anyone. It was during the writing of this book that the memory resurfaced. I suspect that this might have been the seed that sparked my interest in the spiritual.

I was raised Catholic as a child. When I was old enough I made my own decision regarding faith and truth. I was twelve or thirteen when I made the decision to join the Nation of Islam. The Nation was founded in the 1930's by Elijah Muhammad. It was a religious movement based in the Islamic tradition but focused on the needs of the "so-called American Negros" in North America. By uplifting Black people the Nation gave me a sense of pride. They taught a set of beliefs that glorified Black existence as opposed to practitioners of western religion and ideologies who viewed, and some continue to view Black people as objects to be exploited.

I believe the Spirit intervened once again in my mid-teens while Evelyn and I were on vacation at my Aunt Ann and Uncle Bill's house in Pittsfield, Massachusetts. My aunt and I went into a bookstore. I was drawn to a book titled *Yoga* on the bottom shelf in the self-help section. After browsing through it, I bought it and began practicing the postures that same day. This was in the early sixties before Yoga had become popular and commercialized. Yoga, like the Nation of Islam, gave me a perspective separate from white supremacist propaganda that had been fed to people of color for centuries. After a year of practice I decided to look for a Yoga teacher. I found an East Indian teacher at the Integral Yoga Institute on Beacon Street in Boston. Evelyn and I attended the yoga classes together. The Institute was established by Prudence Farrow a devotee of the Maharishi Mahesh Yogi.

As progressive as my father was, he found my decision to join the Nation of Islam interesting and my study of Yoga disconcerting. He tried to prevent me from selling the newspaper the Nation published and was concerned with the amount of time I was spending in my room practicing Yoga exercises. I can understand my Dad's concern. The Nation was profoundly controversial and Yoga was pretty much an unknown quantity in the West. These decisions never negatively affected the relationship between me and my dad.

In the late sixties after I had graduated from high school in 1965 I moved from my parent's home. I found a room on Beacon Street not far from the Yoga school that I had attended. Over fifty years later I continue to practice Yoga and have long since incorporated meditation into my practice. I mark Yoga and the Nation as significant contributors to my good health and my personal and spiritual growth.

.

Approximately a decade later, life threw me a curve. I had gradually drifted away from the organized structure of the Nation of Islam; and free from its expectations. I continued to do Yoga, practice my trombone and run. These activities kept me at peace. Between 19 and 29 years of age, I had no organized religious affiliation, and that was just the way I wanted it, but life's curve was coming. I got married in July of 1978 and this triggered the change in direction I've referred to. I joined the African Methodist Episcopal (AME) Church a year or so after marriage. I definitely didn't see that coming! My wife attended church regularly, and she would invite me, but I wasn't interested. My interest was piqued when I heard Alan Watts, a Buddhist teacher who I would listen to on the radio occasionally. I thought to myself, the next time Vernice asks me to go to church, I'll go with her. I went the next Sunday. After the preaching was over I answered the call to accept Jesus as my savior. I cried uncontrollably feeling release/ cleansing, joy and freedom. I was without question impacted by the preaching, the call to "salvation" and the powerful emotional impact created by the music. This was the beginning of my religious and very politically opinionated journey; influenced not by spirituality but by "doctrine." It is easy to mistake religious talk, its emotional appeal and the ambience created in a church environment for spirituality. This is a mistake most unwittingly make. Religions by their nature create competition and division; each religious ideology claiming their doctrine's superiority over others; creating stories and interpretations to legitimize their points of view. True spirituality prioritizes co-existence, tolerance and love. Its essence is to connect people at an unspoken spiritual, intuitive level that is beyond the words of doctrine.

Spirit and spiritual crying is independent of religious doctrine. Religions claim the work of the spirit unto its particular brand of religiosity; Catholic vs. Protestant and the list goes on. The Spirit can independently reveal itself in any context and in any culture it is not bound by a religious framework. Spiritual crying and the cleansing, joy, freedom and peace experienced from it are a human phenomenon not bound to any one religion or culture. Religions, often hijack the Spirit (God) by claiming their particular group has a lock on it.

Spiritual Crying, a wave of peace, happiness, a presence of the divine can also be experienced during meditation and or by individuals having no religious affiliation.[1] StreamMeditation.com./ *crying-during-meditation-the-ten-reasons-why/.*

From my personal observation I have seen how religion keeps one bound to leaders and to the leader's religious ideas. Often leading to psychological and emotional dependence. After dependency is established a person's ability to think independently or rationally is impaired. The world is seen through the lens of whoever they are following. The ability to receive intuitive or spiritual insight is short-circuited. All is subjected to the demands of their spiritual and or political leaders.

After thirty years in religion, I find myself pretty much back to where I started; viewing life from a spiritual perspective instead of from the exclusivity of a leader centered religion.

Chapter Thirty Seven

The Meeting, Life Together, and Musicians

The Meeting

Dances and house parties were what my friends and I looked forward to on the weekends. I might have continued that life style "God forbid" if I was not pleasantly interrupted. At a neighborhood dance, in the fall of 1975 I met my future wife. I guess when you think about it the whole point of the party scene is to find a mate either for a temporary fling, maybe for a long term relationship, but marriage, **NO WAY**!; but life *is* full of surprises. On the last song of the night I was asked to dance. That was a first. I was flattered. How could I have imagined that this beautiful young woman was going to be my future wife?

At the age of 29 I met Vernice. She was 25, and a nurse working at Boston City Hospital. I was working my way through the University of Massachusetts to complete my Bachelors of Arts Degree, concentrating in Sociology. While attending U. Mass I was working part-time as a cashier at Star Market on Boylston Street in Boston. It was during this time I began dating Vernice. I graduated from the University in the summer of 1976. The spring before graduation, an internship in Ghana was being arranged. I was excited, but to my disappointment the funding for the trip never materialized. I instead substituted it for a trip to San Francisco. This meant saying goodbye to Vernice, at least temporally. I found a one bedroom apartment in the Height Ashbury area, and ran the steep hills leading to Golden Gate Park. After some weeks of getting to know the area, I realized home was where I wanted to be and Vernice was who I wanted to be with. I anxiously caught a bus back to Boston with the aim of asking Vernice to marry me. My fear was that she might have found someone else. That thought haunted me on my long bus ride back.

I made arrangements to see Vernice as soon as I arrived. Vernice was reserved. She gave me the impression that her feelings had changed. She had never been in favor of my going to San Francisco but never made a fuss. I wondered if our relationship could get back on track. I knew if I rushed her it would probably make things worse. This turn of events made me realize how much Vernice really meant to me. I was determined to gain her acceptance; it was all that was on my mind.

Later she told me that her mother had encouraged her to start dating. The question was, had she? It turned out she hadn't.

On July 22, 1978, amidst family and friends we were married in the rose filled garden at the family home on 10 Woodbine Street.

There are decisions, experiences and people that propel one into becoming a more complete person. Reaching goals and accomplishments are a part of that development, but making the decision to marry, now *that* was truly life altering. It challenged me to develop in areas of my personality that were underdeveloped and not clearly visible to me before marriage. One such area was acceptance – allowing Vernice to be who she was without attempting to redesign her to suit my wishes.

Marriage is a major shift in perspective from self-focus to us focus. This is where so many get tripped up; in the inability to understand the need or the unwillingness to exert the effort needed to make the transition from me to us. Without this willingness to change, marriage becomes a solo voyage of two individuals living two separate lives Instead of two individual living their lives together. This does not mean that one ignores his or her own individuality but instead, incorporates it into a broader framework.

I quickly learned that it was easy to "fall in love" but it was going to take some effort to grow love. "Falling in love" is one thing but maturing in love, well that is a whole different story; which is something

I found out. We have been led to believe that euphoric, and pleasurable feelings are the essence of love. They are not. These are in my opinion precursor to a deeper experience where individuals are on a continuum of learning to love through the good and the not so good times. Too often people forfeit that deeper experience thinking euphoric love is all there is, not realizing that part of love is working to overcome personal and cultural hang-ups. These things we must work to overcome in order to say we truly love. It is probably more accurate to say we are in the process of learning how to love. The way we are, is not good enough, and the sooner we realize it the better off our relationship will be. The attitude of, "This is just the way I am" is for children, not adults. The truth, as quiet as it may be kept is that; no one really wants you the way you are. They may tolerate or even accept you, but with the underlying hope that a more mature version of you will begin to emerge. These thoughts are rarely spoken; if they were spoken relationships would be based in reality. I don't know about you, but I still have a lot to learn in the love department. 1st Corinthian's 13's definition of true love heightens our awareness and inspires us to make the effort to grow in loving by making the effort to eliminating habits and actions that counter love. Sincerely apologizing and / or seeking forgiveness for our shortcomings are demonstrations of one's willingness to work at loving.

Life Together

A few months after our marriage, Vernice and I moved to the third floor apartment in the family home on Woodbine Street. There, we began our family. Malachi, the twins Uriel and Oshea, Bethany and Sterling Jr. were all born on Woodbine Street. I worked at the Department of Social Services in Cambridge Mass. Vernice worked weekends on the night shift at the Jewish Memorial Hospital. This made it possible for one of us to always be home with the children. Raising five children was demanding but also fun. Family trips to Franklin Park, weekly trips to Market Basket, attending church, birthday parties, family camps, Suzuki violin classes and other activities made family life busy, hectic, and sometimes frustrating, but rewarding.

We lived on Woodbine Street for ten years. During this time we were able to save enough money to put twenty percent down on a home. The low rent my mother charged us made this possible. Without her help, home ownership would have been pretty much a pipe dream or taken a lot longer than ten years. Woodbine Street had been a safe, supportive environment for raising of our children, but we needed more space. We bought a newly built condominium on Terrace Street across the street for Roxbury Crossing subway station. We were excited to be in our new home. We literally danced with joy. It was perfect for our family with enough room for everyone's comfort. Living there however ended up being bitter sweet. Three months after moving into our new home, Malachi our oldest at the age of ten succumbed to a congenital heart condition. Our home that had been filled with joy was now consumed with grief. Family, friends, faith and bereavement counseling helped us during this difficult time.

After a few peaceful years at Terrace Street the environment became toxic. The neighborhood adolescents were out of control and their parents unable to set limits. Attempts to address the situation only made things worse. After verbal threats, home invasion and the torching our car, moving was our best alternative. On December 23rd, 1993 we bought a single family home on Cohasset Street in Roslindale Massachusetts. It was our Christmas present. We thanked God and the whole family danced with joy. Roslindale was a family centered community. We grew to know most of the families on the street. We worked together to organize sidewalk sales and block parties that were loads of fun. We lived on Cohasset Street for 12 years.

Having lived in Massachusetts all my life, I had a desire to step outside my comfort zone. I occasionally talked to Vernice about moving out of state, but had not seriously considered it because of the need for Vernice to be near her mother and grandmother both of whom she was very close too. In the early 2000's both Vernice's mother, Corliss Upchurch and grandmother, Vernice Younger passed away. What I remember most about Vernice's mother was her laughing; it was infectious and made those around her want to laugh. Vernice said her mother loved to dance which might explain Vernice's love for dancing. Whenever we go out dancing we stay on the dance floor and are usually the last to leave.

Vernice's grandmother was the most industrious person. We would visit her often. She would start cooking or already had prepared something for us to eat whenever we visited. More often than not, we would leave with a container of great tasting homemade fudge. At 100 years old Vernice's grandmother was president of the shopping club at the assisted living facility where she lived. She got a key to the city given to her by Mayor Menino on her 100th birthday.

My father had passed years ago and my mother was still living at the time of our move to North Carolina. Ma lived in the family home on Woodbine Street with my sisters. I knew she would be in good hands if and when we moved from Massachusetts. Even with that knowledge, the thought of leaving loved ones, particularly my mother, was unsettling. Vernice was leaving familiar surroundings with which she had become attached – our house and neighborhood. I did not realize the extent of her attachment until we made the move to North Carolina. It took her quite some time to make the adjustment.

Four or five years before our move to NC, we started buying real estate. Our first major purchase was a three family house in Providence, Rhode Island. Investing in Real Estate was a decision that led us to the purchase of our home in Leland, NC.

While living in Boston, a home building company contacted us. They were selling lots and building houses in Port Saint Lucie, Florida. The company paid for transportation and lodging. There was no obligation to buy. At that time we were looking for a place to move. We were open to the offer. We took the opportunity. We thought it would be a nice trip, even if we did not purchase. It was a great experience. We liked the location; the housing models were beautiful. The people representing the company were professional and pleasant. We went back to the hotel and struggled with a decision. We decided to buy. After the house was built, Vernice thought that Florida was too far and too hot of a place to live. We rented the house out, and began a new search.

I was now fifty eight and ready to venture forth into the unknown, freeing myself from familiar surroundings to develop a new life. The children were grown and pretty much on their own. If I was going to fulfill my dream, I needed to get started. Vernice on the other hand was somewhat leery, but game. Moving to a new state was my way of stepping out of my comfort zone and putting faith into action.

My cousin Deborah and her husband Charles had moved to North Carolina. They invited us down to look at houses. Charles had found one he thought we might like. After looking around we settled on the house Charles had chosen. The rest was history. The house was beautiful; something that would have been probably two times the price in Massachusetts.

I felt reassured that Evelyn and Paulette would hold the fort down by caring for Ma while Vernice and I explored new horizons. For this reason I felt that my sisters were also connected to my exploration. Thank you, sisters.

I am the adventurous one of the two of us, although Vernice is always up for the challenge. The move to NC was not without its difficulties - at least for a couple years. We had bought some income properties in addition to our primary residence. We were put in a precarious financial situation with the collapse of the real estate market. My desire to be a real estate tycoon nearly brought us to financial ruin. I should have listened to Vernice when she suggested using our profits to pay off our primary residence. Vernice's work as a registered nurse prevented us from going over the financial cliff. In my 15 or so years of doing business as a handyman and real estate Vernice kept the books and was always willing to pitch in if I needed help on handyman projects. Vernice also helped with the editing of this book. In 2022 after my coronary by-pass surgery Vernice was the life-saving part of my recovery. Five months later Vernice, along with the skillful support and collaboration of her sister Renee, who is also a nurse, pulled me through Covid. To say I love Vernice is an understatement. Vernices's qualities of self-worth, trustworthiness, goodness, humility and authenticity are only a few of the adjectives to describe the woman I love. In our 44 years of marriage Vernice's, grace, love, and hard work has always shined; even in the most difficult of circumstances.

We have been living in Leland, North Carolina for 18 years. Moving to N.C has turned out to be one of our best decisions. It took Vernice a considerable amount of time to overcome her nostalgia for our Roslindale neighborhood. Now whenever Vernice speaks of N.C she describes it fondly as "quiet, green and clean." After a week's visit to Boston Vernice can't wait to leave the congestion of the city and return to the wide open spaces of N.C. We didn't move to escape the cold in Boston; but the short cold season in N.C. is a welcome relief from the six months of cold and the heating bills in Boston. The air conditioning bills of North Carolina in no way compares to the heating bills in Boston.

We have found the people in NC to be polite and friendly. The racism that is commonly associated with the south is something, we fortunately have not experienced; at least not personally. We hope that continues to be the case; but with the increased level of craziness going on in America, which I think has been accelerate as a result of Donald Trump's entering into politics. Black people should increase their level of vigilance.

Our adventurism in the move to Leland N.C prompted my daughter Oshea and her husband Sebastian to move from expensive and congested Lynn, Massachusetts to N.C. They repeatedly tell us how thankful they are to be here. They live a short distance from us. It is wonderful having them close.

Musicians

Before I refer to the musicians I have had the pleasure of playing with, I want to return to the roots of my musical interest, the Holy Trinity Drum and Bugle Corp. This group was the major contributor to my musical interest and development. In the late 50's and 60s while in middle school and high school, I sang with the guys in my neighborhood. We liked music, but more importantly, we all had an ear for harmony; Phil Harris from Laredo Street, Langford Reynolds and Lloyd Horton (Tim). Willie Brown was another talent that would occasionally sit in. Tim Horton's ability as a tenor made it possible for him to do solo gigs. Keeping him in a singing group was difficult. Making music with these guys was a thrill.

While in high school in the mid–sixties, Robert Mincey, Stephen Moss, Howard Badget, and I formed a group we called the Young Realities. We made our first public appearance, at a talent show at the Boston Technical High School auditorium in Roxbury Mass. We sang acapella. Robert Mincey with his smooth, silky voice sang lead on "My Girl," and I sang lead on "Danny Boy." We choreographed steps to go along with our music. Our practicing paid off. The crowd was electrified. They were screaming before and after we finished our songs. We were flabbergasted at the response. Joel Smith, Livingston Blackman, and Don Jermont were members of a competing group; all homeboys who lived in the area. They were good, but we were sure we won the contest by the crowd's response to our performance. It seemed to us a no-brainer. To our disappointment, we were told we were too professional to perform in a community talent show. We thought the idea was to be as good as possible. After all the work put into rehearsing, we felt that being told we were "too good" was not fair. What a disappointment.

I would now like to acknowledge the many Jazz musicians with whom over the years I've had the privilege of performing with. I was able to compile this list of musicians with the help of Cyril Chapman, a fellow musician whom I've played with for approximately two decades. These people were talented musicians and were enjoyable to be around.

In February 1968 and into the early nineties, I played with the Bacchanalians Afro Jazz Group. For a brief time I departed from my Jazz roots and played with trumpet player Stanton Davis and saxophonist Bobby Eldridge, backing up a consummate rhythm and blues singer and band leader Ralph Graham.

Bertram Alleyne, founded the Bacchanalians. He gave us novice musicians a chance to strut our stuff. Bertram played Conga Drum rest of the group consisted of its rhythm section, Charles Holly on bongos and various rhythmic instruments, Ralph Kimball (aka Tuffy) on trap drums, Hassan Requib, (formerly known as James Hogg) on bass, Curtis Jones on vibes, Gregory Obyant on tenor sax, Cyril Chapman on alto sax, and yours truly on slide trombone. Over the course of the Bacchanalians time together trumpet players David Roderick and Stan (the man) Cleveland, both contributed their music making genius. We performed at colleges in the Boston area; Boston University, Lesley College, Wellesley College, Wheelock College and others. We also performed at neighborhood festivals, political events, dances and private parties. Our driving African Rhythms and melodic tones were in demand.

Others who shared their talents with the Bacchanalians over the years were the following:

Trap drummers – Ronnie Ruff, Robert Houltmen, Eddie Ross, Steve Ambush, Chauncey Hutchinson, Lewis Robinson, Dorian Magee, Milton Duvo, Art Gore, Ray Lampkin, Lenny Payne, Curtis Warner and Mickey Starks.

Conga Drums – Juma Santoes.

Bass guitar – Richie Harris, Jim Diamond, Jeff Jones and Rollins Ross.

Upright Bass – Jamil John Jones, Harkim Jamin, Calvin Hill, Larry Roland (bass and spoken word).

Guitar – Anthony Adderson, Phil Stine, and Jose Alicia, who cannot only be mentioned as a musician but also the force who made it possible for me to receive my master's degree in education. Thanks Jose.

Piano - Ali Yusif, Neil Rolnick, Sid Simmons, and Greg Allison.

Trumpet - Stan (the man) Cleveland, Dwight Sutton, Milton Ward and David Roderick, we have been friends since childhood and started out our musical journey together in the Holy Trinity Troubadours, while we were in junior high school.

Slide Trombone - Darryl Robinson, and Sterling Anderson.

Tenor sax - Billy Thompson, Bill Peirce, Gary Hammond.

Dancers - Andrea Sanders and Linda Eubanks also contributed their talents to the Bacchanalians.

Singers - Barbara Wedgworth, Tanya Hart, and Richard Short (aka Dick).

Poets - Virgil Logan, and Robert Ruff who also played Cello.

Poet and Announcer - Bob Warthol.

Phil Gregory - silk screen professional was also part of the gang.

For a brief time during the mid-1970s, Cyril Chapman organized a "smoking" jazz group called

Kilimanjaro. The music was a step above in complexity from the music we played in the Bacchanalians. This gave us the opportunity to stretch out our music making capabilities. A particularly memorable performance was at the now defunct Western Front Jazz club in Cambridge, Massachusetts. The group consisted of Marlik Farced on drums, Yusef Harlim on bass, with Mawlemo Beamon, Elliot Slaughter, and Greg Allison all who played piano at different times during the life of the group. Cyril Chapman played alto sax and yours truly Sterling Anderson on slide trombone. Drummer Steve Ambush also briefly contributed his talent.

Years after the Bacchanalians and Kilimanjaro had disbanded, some of the old members of both groups attempted to put together another group called Beyond the Bacchanal. This was in the mid-1990s. Curtis Warner was on drums, Jose Alicia on guitar, Cyril Chapman on alto sax, with myself Sterling Anderson on slide trombone we were all a part of that effort. We did a couple of gigs; but disbanded because we could not find a consistent rhythm section.

After our move to North Carolina in 2005 and years of not playing the trombone I began to get my chops up after being recruited to be a members of a startup band we named the Love Connection. From 2007 to 2014 we played jazz standards and rock tunes. Personnel consisted of Wayne Webster on sax and band leader. Tracy Love on piano and Sterling Anderson on trombone and vocals. Lead singer and MC Janci Hartley. Our bass and drums were electronic until we found Jennet and Marty Evans. Jennet played bass, and her husband played drums. What an improvement over the electronic bass and drums. Jennet and Marty were a perfect musical fit. Both were eager to learn our repertoire. Their musical talents enhanced our sound. They could not have been more congenial. We disbanded because folks relocated.

Conclusion

During our lifetime we are absorbing information, much of which I contend is irrelevant; not serving the purpose for positive personal growth. The intuitive/ spiritual part of our being is in constant struggle to assert itself against the mundane. It is here in the unseen realm where real growth takes place. It is my hope that "Escaping the Delusions of Cultural" inspires one to be open to the difficult task of ideological, personal self-examination and growth. Seek truth. Dare to ask who, what, when, where and why. Putting to work the quiet tools of meditation, and or prayer can be helpful in this process.

Some may view this book as controversial, challenging and even offensive because it rubs counter to the grain of established beliefs. Uncomfortableness is usually a part of the requirement for growth. Feel it. Push on. Growth will follow.

The End

Contact Information

becomings02@yahoo.com

Edited by starvingwritersguild.com

and Vernice Anderson

Endnotes

Chapter One - Race Relations – A Predatory System

1   Shin, Laura, *The Racial Wealth Gap: Why a Typical White Family has 16 times the Wealth of a Black one,* March 26, 2015, forbes.com.

2   Palmer, Vernon V., *The Customs of Slavery: The War Without Arms,* 2006.

3   *Black Codes,* history.com editors, January 21. 2021.

4   en.wikipedia.org/wiki/*Black Codes, United States.*

5   Forehand, *Striking Resemblance,* 1996.

6   Fraser and Freeman, *Creating a Prison Corporate Complex,* 4/19/ 2012.

7   Vermont population 2021 worldpopulationreview.com/ Vermont-population.

8   Adriana, Rezal, *The Racial Makeup of American's Prisons,* U.S. News and World Report, 9/2021.

9   *Los Angeles Times, Harvey Weinstein Sentencing,* March 11, 2020.

Chapter Two – Hidden from View

1   Lee, William Poy, Esq., *China's "Never Again" vs America's Full Spectrum Dominance,* Oct,2021.

2   Fifield, Anna, *Contractors Reaped 138B from Iraq war,* cnn. com/2013/03/19/business.

3   Ibid.

4   Reuters Staff, *Leaked U.S. Video Shows Deaths of Reuters' Iraqi Staffers*, reuters.com, April 5, 2010).

5   Snowden, Edward, National Whistleblower Center (NWC), whistleblower.org.

6   Hosenball, Mark *NSA Collected American's Phone Records Despite Law Change*, Reuters, May 2, 2017.

7   Harding, Luke, *What are the Panama Papers? A Guide to History's Biggest Data Leak*, The Guardian, April 2016.

8   *Paradise Papers: Biggest Ever Leak of Offshore Data Exposes Financial Secrets of Rich and Powerful*, The Guardian.com, October 3, 2021.

9   Trager, Rebecca, Senior US correspondent, Chemistry World), *EPA's Chemical Evaluation Process 'high – risk'*, January 29, 2009, chemicalworld.com.

10 The Canadian Medical Association Journal, *Artificial Sweeteners Linked to Risk of Weight Gain, Heart Disease and other Health Issues*, www.sciencedaily.com/releases/2017/07/170717091043.htm.

11 Aspartame controversy, en.m.wikipedia.org.

Chapter Three – Family History

1   Anderson, Sterling Thomas – www. Ancestry.com/dna/origin.

2   Ramsey, John "Facts" Ancestry,com, undocumented data.

3   Ramsey, John – move to S.C. – Charleston, South Carolina; Year: Page Number: 24. U.S. and Canada, Passenger and Immigration Lists Index, 1500s-1900s, Ancestry.com, Ancestry.com Operations, Inc., 2010 Provo, UT, USA.

4   "Public Member Trees," database, Ancestry.com. Last accesses date 1/27/20, Meekins Family tree by LaToia Meekins – John Ramsey married Jane Hervey. Undocumented data also found in other member trees.

5   "Public Member Trees," database, Ancestry.com. Last accesses date 1/28/20, Meekins Family tree by LaToia Meekins.

Alexander E. Ramsey married Mary Eggar. Undocumented data also found in other member trees.

6   Alexander Edgar Ramsey Sr. - *U.S., Find a Grave Index, 1600s-Current* (database on-line). Lehi, UT, USA: Ancestry. com Operations, Inc., 2012. www.findagrave.com/ memorial/10490836/alexander-edgar-ramsay.

7   Ramsey, Alexander A., and Ramsey, Martha - *U.S., Find a Grave Index, 1600s-Current* (database on-line).Lehi, UT, USA: Ancestry.com Operations, Inc., 2012. www.findagrave.com/ cgi-bin/fg.cgi.

8   "Public Member Trees," database, Ancestry.com. Last accesses date 1/28/2022. Meekins Family tree by LaToia Meekins. Alexander E. Ramsey Jr. married Sarah Hartgrove.

9   Ramsey, Alexander Edgar Jr. and Hartgrove, Sarah – Year 1850; Census Place: *Eastern Divison, Pickens, South Carolina;* Roll: 857; Page 524B.

10 "Public Member Trees," database, Ancestry.com last accesses date 1/24/22, Meekins Family tree by LaToia Meekins for Evelina – slave. Undocumented data.

11 Ramsey, Albert P. 1880; Census Place: Beaufort, Beaufort, South Carolina; Roll: 1221; Family History Film: 1255221; 71A; Enumeration District: 043. Ancestry.com.

12 Ramsey, Albert P. New England Hisorical Genealogical Society; Boston, *Massachusetts; Massachusetts Vital Records, 1840-1911.*

13 Ramsey, Evelina 1880; Census Place: Beaufort, Beaufort, South Carolina; Roll: 1221; Family History Film: 1255221; 71A; Enumeration District: 043. Ancestry.com.

14 Crowder, Evalina Year; Census Place: *Lynn Ward 6, Essex, Massachusetts;* Roll: *T624-585;* Page: 19A; Enumeration District: 0401; FHL microfilm: *1374598.*

15 Anderson, Evelena, Massachusetts, U.S., Death Index 1970 – 2003, Ancestry.com.

16 Brown, Pearl – daughter of Evelyn Crowder Anderson – Interview by author (2006) in the home of Pearl Brown

in Lynn Ma., "biological father of Evelyn C. Anderson". Undocumented data.

17 Public Member Family Tree – Evelyn Anderson – Granddaughter daughter Evelyn Crowder Anderson – Facts - "Evelina was the daughter of Aurthur Reed". Ancestry.com. Undocumented data.

18 Ibid.

19 Reed, A.W. Michigan Department of Community Health Statistics; Lansing Michigan; Death Records, Ancestry.com.

20 A.W. Reed Day, Race Mourns Founder of Atlas Power, Detroit Diurnal Newspaper, July 2, 1945.

21 Ibid.

22 Ibid.

23 Reed, A.W. The U.S. Commissioner of Patents, Internal Combustion Engine Fuel System and Cooling Means, March 28, 1950.

24 A.W. Reed Day, Race Mourns Founder of Atlas Power, Detroit Diurnal Newspaper, July 2, 1945.

25 Picture of Internal Combustion Engine Fuel System and Cooling Means.

26 The U.S. Commissioner of Patents, Patent Office, Patent for Internal Combustion Engine Fuel System and Cooling Means, March 28, 1950.

27 Detroit Diurinal, July 1945, "Leader of the Common Man". Author unknown.

28 Reed, A.W. Detroit Diurinal, July 1945, Memorial Column.

29 Browne, Evelyn – Granddaughter of Evelina Ramsey Crowder – Oral family history – telephone interview by author (n.d.), "Ford Car Manufactoring Co."

30 Detroit Diurinal, July 1945, "Leader of the Common Man". Author unknown.

31 Browne, Evelyn – Granddaughter of Evelina Ramsey Crowder – Oral family history – telephone interview by author (n.d.), "Reed tries to contact Nana".

32 Crowder, Everett Massachusetts, U.S. Marriage Records, 1840 – 1915 for Evelina L. Ramsey, Ancestry.com.

33 Crowder, Everett – U.S., City Directories, 1822-1995 Lynn, Massachusetts- City Directory 1937.

34 Crowder, Everett E. – Cherry Street - Swampscott, Massachusetts, City Directory 1908, U.S., *City Directory*1822 – 1995 (database – line). Lehi, UT, USA: Ancestry.com Operations, Inc., 2011.

35 Browne, Evelyn – Granddaughter of Evelina Ramsey Crowder – Family oral history – telephone interview by author 2019, "Albert P Ramsey bought house for Evelina".

36 Picture of Evelina Ramsey Crowder – provided by descendants of Crowder family. (n.d.).

37 Browne, Evelyn – Granddaughter of Evelina Ramsey Crowder - Family oral history – telephone interview by author (n.d.), "Nigger".

38 Ibid.

39 Crowder, Everett E. - Swampscott, Massachusetts, City Directory 1908, U.S., *City Directory*1822 – 1995 (database – line). Lehi, UT, USA: Ancestry.com Operations, Inc., 2011.

40 Crowder, Evelina – Charles Street - Year: 1910; Census Place: *Lynn Ward 6, Essex, Massachusetts*; Roll t621 – 585; Page: 19A Enumeration District: 0401; FHL Microfilm: 1374598, Ancestry.com.

41 Crowder, Evelina – Villa Place Year 1930; Census Place; *Lynn, Essex, Massachusetts*; Page: 10B; Enumeration District: 0172; FHL Microfilm: 2340635, Ancestry.com.

42 Carter, Arlene –Family oral history – telephone interview by author (n.d.), "Visiting Granddad Ramsey".

43 Arkord, Jacqueline – Family oral history – telephone interview by author (2020), "Albert P. Ramsey was a veterinarian".

44 Ibid.

45 Browne, Evelyn – sister of author - Family oral history – telephone interview by author (2019), "Crosses burned on the lawn".

46 Browne, Evelyn – sister of author – Family oral history - telephone interview by author (n.d.), "Ernest Anderson was born on an Indian reservation".

47 Browne, Evelyn – sister of author – Family oral history – telephone interview by author (n.d.), Whites treated Indians even worse".

48 Anderson, Sterling Thomas – www. Ancestry.com/dna/origin.

49 Gates, Henry Louis Jr.: The myth of African and Indian ancestry 4/21/14.

50 Picture of Ernest and Evelyn Anderson – date unknown - provided by Crowder/Anderson descendan

Chapter Four – Great – Grandfather James Anderson

1 Anderson, James, Year: 1900; Census Place: East Granby, Hartford Connecticut Page 2; Enumeration District: 0126; FHL microfilm 1240135. Ancestry.com.

2 Cooper, Augustus – Massachusetts, U.S., *Marriage Records, 1840- 1915* (database on-line). Provo, UT, USA: Ancestry. com Operations, Inc., 2013.Massachusetts Vital Records, 1840-1911. New England Historic Genealogical Society, Boston, Massachusetts Vital Records, 1911-1915.

3 Vermont 1777: Early Steps against Slavery – https:// nmaahc. si.edu> stories >Vermont.

4 The 14th State – Vermont – www.vermontexplorer.org.

5 Browne, Evelyn – Great-granddaughter of James Anderson - Family oral history – telephone interview by author (n.d.), "The tribe of James Anderson…was extinct".

6 Connecticuthistory.org/topics-page/native-americans.

7 Anderson, Ernest – Year: *1900*; Census Place: *East Granbury, Hartford, Connecticut;* Page: 2; Enumeration District: *0126;* FHL microfilm: *1240135.*

8 Crowder, Evelyn - Massachusetts, U.S., Marriage Index, 1901- 1955 and1966 – 1970 (database on-line). Provo, UT, USA: Ancestry.com Operations, Inc., 2013.

9   Carter, Arlene – daughter of Ernest Anderson - Family oral history telephone interview by author (n.d.), "devoted and hardworking".

10   Browne, Evelyn – granddaughter of Ernest Anderson - Family oral history – telephone interview by author (n.d.), "nursed Ernest back to health".

11   Anderson, Ernest – Year: 1920; Census Place: *Lynn Ward 6, Essex, Massachusetts;* Roll: T625-695; Page: 9B; Enumeration Disrtict: 183 Ancestry.com.

12   Anderson, Ernest – Year: *1900*; Census Place: *East Granbury, Hartford, Connecticut;* Page: 2; Enumeration District: *0126;* FHL microfilm: *1240135.*

13   Anderson, Ernest – Massachusetts, U.S. Death Index, 1901-1980 {database on-line}. Provo. UT, USA: Ancestry. com. Operations, Inc., 2013. Department of Public Health Registry of Vital Records and Statistics. Massachusetts Vital Records Index to Deaths {1916 -1970}. Volumes 66-145.

14   Carter, Arlene – daughter of Ernest Anderson - Family oral history – telephone interview by author (n.d.), "death devastated the family."

Chapter Five – Struggle for Equality

1   Muhammad, Elijah - Encyclopedia.com.

1a   Augustyn, Adam, *Marcus Garvey,* Britannica.com, updated 4/05/2023

2   Barid, Keith E. Dr., *On Common Ground News*, ocgnews.com, 11/18/2021.

3   *World Military Spending Rises Almost $2 Trillion in 2020,* sipri. org, April 26, 2021. (Stockholm International Peace Research Institute)

4   Whitlock and Woodward, *Pentagon Buries Evidence of $125 Billion in Bureaucratic Waist, Washington Post,* 12/5/2016.

5   Sirgany*, Aleen, The War on Waste,* cbsnews.com, 01/29/2002.

6   Kotlikoff, Laurence, *Has Our Government Spent $21 Trillion of Our Money Without Telling Us?,* Forbes December 8, 2017.

Chapter Six – "African Americans" Who We Are – A Secret, Not A Mystery

1   Friedmann, George P., The End of the Jewish Nation, (Paris: Gallimard, 1957) publisher Anchor/Doubleday, January 1, 1967, Wikipedia.org

1a   Hendawi, Hamza, AP *Prominent Nubian Activist Died in Detention in Egypt*, 11/5/2017.

2   *de Volney, Constantine M., Travels through Syria and Egypt in the Years of 1783, 1784 and 1785*, London, 1787 p.80-83.

3   *Mysterious Black Russians ancestors of the Kemetians*, Sopdet, destee.com, 05/2003 - *Ancient Wisdom –Kemet State*, Aziz_ Ali_Aki, kemetexperience.com, 03/2019.

4   Barton, Paul, *The Black Washitaw Nation of America*, africaresource.com 5/12/2010 - Rastalivewire.com.

5   Bey, Shabazz, Umar Dr., *We are the Washitaw*, hotep.org, May, 2006 Page 40.

6   Culotta and Gibbons, *Aborigines and Eurasians rode one migration wave*, Science.org, Sep, 2016).

7   (Lipson, M., et al. (2020) Ancient West African foragers in the context of African population history, January 22, 2020).

8   Ghosh, Pallab Science correspondent (*'First of our kind' found in Morocco*, BBC News, Paris, 06/7/2017, Prof. Hublin, Jean Jacques, Prof. of the Max Planck Institute work is published in the Journal Nature.

9   Webstersdictionary1828.com.

10   Penrice, Ronda Racha, *Black Explores We Should Celebrate Instead of Columbus*, thegrio.com/2015.

11   Morgan, Edmond S., *Columbus's Confusion about the New World*, smithsonianmagazine.org, October 2009.

12   Ibid.

13   Ibid.

14   Wikipedia.org/wiki/*Black Indians in the United States*.E

15   www.history.com.>news>trail-of-tears-conditions >, *How Native Americans Struggled to Survive on the trail of Tears*.

16 Doctrine of Discovery, 1455 Pope Nicholas V. doctrineofdiscovery.org>-dum-Diveras.

17 Fell, Barry Dr., *America B.C. Ancient Settlers in the New World*, pocket book, 1976, NY, chapter 17 The Egyptian Presence pages 253-276).

18 Barton, Paul, *The Olmecs: An African Presence in Early America*, theperspective.org/Olmec, 2/28/2001 also in Encyclopedia Britannica.

19 Chengu, Garikai, *Before Columbus: How Africans Brought Civilization to America, 2014.*

19a ibid

20 Heyerdahl, Thor, *Journey from Morocco to Barbados*, History.com 2/9/2010 updated 2/28/2019.

21 Bailey, Diane Blackmon, *The History of Queen Califia and the California Blacks*, eurweb.com/history, 04/2015).

22 Britannica.com. *The founding Fathers and Slavery.*

23 M, Katie, *What is A Superiority Complex, And What Does It Affect*, wengood.com. March 8, 2022.

24 Gupta, Sanjana, *What is a Superiority Complex*, verywellmind.com, January 18, 2023.

25 Gates, Henry Louis Jr., *How many slaves landed in the US*, theroots.com, 06/2014.

26 El Bey Turner Goston, Verdiacee *Return of the Ancient Ones*, Washitaw Pub. Co, 01/01/1993.

27 wampumchronicles.com/benfranklin.

28 Giovanni Verrazano's Letter to King Francis the First of France, July 8, 1524) also in (Encyclopedia.com/giovanni-da-verrazano.

29 (me.me/i/jonnieaborigine-*the-negro-type-is-seen-in-the-most-ancient*-10491112) (17 Aug 1935, page 6 – The New Age at Newspaper.com *Carlos Cuervo Marquez –Early African inhabitants in America*) Kurimeo Mediations part 1 & *America is a Negro Continent* – YouTube sites.

30 Zadik, Daniel, Postdoctoral researcher in genetics, University of Leicester, *Albert and Adam Rewrite the Story of Human Origins,* TheConversation.com July 22, 2013.

31 Lucy…Say Hello to Lucia2012.caliwali.com/lucia.

32 Resendez, Andres, *"The Other Slavery"*, 2016.

33 Ibid.

34 Keegan, William F., *Destruction of the Taino*, in Archaeology. January/February 1992, pp 51-56.

35 Anderson, Sterling Thomas – www.Ancestry.com/dna/origin.

36 Gates, Henry Louis Jr.: *The Myth of African and Indian Ancestry* 4/21/14.

37 Haines, Elijah M., *The American Indian (uh-nich-in-na-ba)* Chicago.. mas.sin-na-gan, 1888, pp 232-237.

38 Sailors Narratives of Voyages along the New England Coast, 1524-1624. Boston: Houghton, Mifflin, 1905, p. 35.

39 Finkebine, Roy E., *"The Native Americans Who Assisted the Underground Railroad,* Sept.15, 2019.

40 Julianne, Jennings, anthropologist, *The Tragic History of African Slaves and Indians,* ICT NEWS, original Sep 12, 2018 original update Sep 29, 2013.

41 Katz, William, *Black Indians: A Hidden* Heritage, 06/1986.

42 Krauthamer, *Black Slaves Indian Masters,* (2013) Ch.1, p. 17-45.

43 Black settlements in Oklahoma, justiceforgreenwood.org.

44 Holland, Kathryn E. Braund, *"The Creek Indians, Blacks, and Slavery"* (1991). The Journal of Southern History.

45 Keels, Larry, *Slavery and Native Americans in British North America and the United States,* 01/2007.

46 Joy, Natalie, *Cherokee Slaveholders and Radical Abolitionists,* 07/2010.

47 Smithers, Gregory professor of American History at Virginia Commonwealth University.

48 Roos, Dave, *How Many People Died on the Trail of Tears,* 05/30/2019.

49 Miles, Tiya, *Pain of 'Trail of Tears' Shared by Blacks as well as Native Americans,* tiyamiles.com, Feb 28, 2012.

50 Hirst, Kris K., *How Black Seminoles Found Freedom from Enslavement in Florida,* thoughtco.com, 11/18/2020.

51 Bird, J.B., *The Largest Slave Rebellion in U.S. history*, Revision 10/26/2012.

52 Hirst, Kris K., *How Black Seminoles Found Freedom from Enslavement in Florida*, thoughtco.com, November 18, 2020.

53 *Black Indian United Legal Defense and Education Fund*, 1866 Treaties-Ethnic (Black) Indians and freedmen, blackindians5tribesembassy.org /1866-treaties- freedmen.

54 White, Taryn, nationalgeographic.com, 06/21.

55 Roberson, Ph.D., Ray Von, *A Pan-Africanist Analysis of Black Seminole...*, rvrobertson@my.lamar.edu, 09/2011.

56 Clark, Juliana, *Black Seminoles Were Left Behind in COVID-19 Tribal Relief*, Prismreports.org, 03/2021.

57 *African American Settle in Fort Mose*, fcit.usf.edu/florida.

58 *Seminole History*, Florida Department of State, dos. myfloridahistory.com/Seminole-history.

59 Stannard, David E., *American Holocaust: and the Conquest of the New World*, New Oxford: University Press, Nov. 1993.

60 Manley, Benjamin, *An American Genocide: The United States and the California Indian Catastrophe, 1846-1873*, Yale University Press, 05/24/2016.

61 *Washington's Letter, May 31, 1779,* Founders.archives.gov.

62 Stannard, David E., *American Holocaust*, New York: Oxford University Press, 1992. pp. 118-121.

63 Harless, Richard, *"Native America Policy"*, George Mason University, mountvernon.org.

64 Amadas and Barlowe, Fort Raleigh National Historical Site North Carolina, nps.gov/amadas-and-barlowe.

Chapter Seven – The Big Lie from Black to White

1 Mgeti, Faoud, Professor, *The Story of Africa,* Alexandria University, bbc.co.uk, 03/2001, ancientegyptonline.co.uk/ankh.

2 Tesfu, Julianna, *Axum,* blackpast.org, 6/29/2008.

3   Fayez, Armia, Christianity in Nubia, coptic-wiki.org.

4   *Cesare Borgia: The False Image of Jesus Christ,* YouTube, Part 1.

5   Malcioln, Jose V., *How the Hebrew became Jews*, U.B. productions, 01/1978, page 8.

6   Windsor, Rudolph, R., From Babylon to Timbuktu, Windsor Golden Series publication, 1988, page 16

7   Arkell, A. J., *Cush (Kush), History of Sudan,* jewishvirtuallibrary. org<cush-kush.

8   Linsley, Alice C., *Just Genesis: Abraham's Kushite Ancestors,* 2010.

9   (Britannica.com/Tigris-Euphrates- river-system).

10   worldatlas.com/articles/ *What-Was-The-Original- Name -of-Africa.*

11   blacksinthebible.net/phut, *(Unger's Bible Dictionary 3rd edition p. 863 and 904).*

12   *Unger's Bible Dictionary 3rd edition p. 170-172).*

13   Windsor, Rudolph R., *From Babylon to Timbuktu: A History of Ancient Black Races Including the Black Hebrews,* Windsor golden Series Publications 1988 p. 16).

14   Wooten, Shante, *Scientists Reveal the First European Faces Were Not "White,* Politicalblindspot.com.

15   Marrs, Texe, *Conspiracy of the Six Pointed Star,* 2011.

16   *Study Sheds Light on the Origin of the European Jewish Population,* sciencedaily.com, 1/16/2013.

17   *Nasser, Abdel Gamal, 2nd President of Egypt, abovetopsecret.com.*

17a Sultan, Ahmed, Abu, History of Palestine: Canaan Before it was Israel, arabamerica.com, 5/24/2021

18   Morales, Robert, *Debunking the Doctrine of Discovery: Colonial Excuse for the Seizure of Lands and Oppression of Peoples,* 1/20/2013.

19   Morales, Robert, *The Great Land Grab in Hul'qumi'num Territory,* 2014.

20   Misachi, John, (Berber/Ethnipedia/Fadom), *Who Are the Berber People,* worldatlas.com, 08/01/2017).

21   Ochone, Moses Dr., of Vanderbilt University, *No.900: Arabs Race Denial,* laits.utexas.edu>africa

22 Ntreh, Nii, *Do You Know What North Africans Looked Like before Islam and the Arabs Invaded,* face2faceafrica.com 09/26/20190).

23 Ntreh, Nii, *How Libya Came to Have Its Name,* face2faceafrica. com, January17, 2021.

24 Marniche, Dana - Reynolds, Anthropologist, *The Indigenous Berbers of Africa – by Natural Mystics,* africaresourse.com July 12, 2013.

25 Brett, Michael, *Berber,* Britannica, June 23, 2014.

26 Pruitt, Sarah, History.com/*Where did the Word Barbarian Come From,* August 29, 2018

27 Amazigh – Wiktionary

28 Ungar-Sargon, Batya, *The Mystery Stone,* tabletmag.com, February, 27, 2013.

29 *Bat Creek Stone,* josephsmithfoundation.org> bat-creek-stone.

30 Miller, Mark, *The Mound Builders: North America's Little Known Native Architects,* Ancient Origins, June, 2017

Chapter Eight – System of Suppression

1 Unionfacts.com/article/crime-and-corruption/discrimination-by-unions.

2 laborunionreport.com/2011/04/10/*Union-Racism-an-Age-Old-Institutional-Problem-Continues-Unabated*).

3 Bernstein, David E, Professor, *The Racism Behind Prevailing Wage,* New York Daily News January, 25, 2016.

4 Mishel, Lawrence *New York Union* Economic Policy Institute in March 2017.

5 Bucknor, Cherrie, *Black Workers, Unions, and Inequality,* Center for Economic and Policy Research, CEPR 2016.

6 Saharra Griffin and Malkie Wall, *President Trump's Anti-Worker,* Agenda Center for American Progress Action Fund, 08/28/2019).

7 LaVeist, Thomas, PhD., *Liquor Stores in Black Communities,* John Hopkins School of Public Health, 8/15/ 2000.

8   Hart, Carl L., *How the Myth of the 'Negro Cocaine Fiend' Helped Shape American Drug Policy*, associate professor of psychology at Columbia University, 01/29/2014, www.thenation.com.

9   Mohl, Raymond A., *The Interstates and the Cities: Highways, Housing and the Freeway Revolt*, 1/1/2002.

10   Halsey, Ashley lll, *A Crusade to Defeat the Legacy of Highways Rammed through Poor Neighborhoods,* the Washington Post, 03/29/2016.

11   Badger, Emily and Cameron, Darla, *How Railroads, Highways and other Man-made Lines Racially Divide America's Cities*, the Washington Post, July 16, 2015.

12   Badger, Emily, *Why Highways Have Become the Center of Civil Rights Protest*, the Washington Post, July 13, 2016.

13   Wilmingtonraceriots.org.

14   https://www.History.Com/ topics/black-history/*Chicago-Race-Riot-of-1919.*

15   https://www.history.com/topic/roing-twenties/*Tulsa- Race Massacre.*

16   Woodruff, Nan Elizabeth, Dr., *The Forgotten History of America's Worst Racial Massacre*, New York Times, Sept 30, 2019.

17   *State of the Dream Report, 2008*, The National Association of Real Estate Brokers and the Pew Research Center.

17a Badger, Emily, *The Dramatic Racial Bias of Subprime Lending During the Housing Boom*, Bloomberg.com, 08/16/2013

18   Mosbergen, Dominique, *Neo-Nazi Site Daily Stormer Praises Trump's Charlottesville Reaction: "He Loves Us All"* HuffPost, 8/13/2017).

19   Wilson, Jason, *White Nationalist Hate Groups Have Grown 55% in the Trump era,* the Guardians, March 18, 2020.

20   Wilson, Jason, Southern Poverty Law, *Center Year in Hate and Extremism 2019.*

Chapter Nine – Killing the Leaders and Destroying Alkebulan (African) Civilization

1   Diop, Cheikh Anah, *The Ancient Name of Africa was Alkebulan*, theafricanhistory.com, July 3, 2020.

2   Brittain, Victoria, *Africa is a Continent Drenched in the Blood of Revolutionary Heroes,* the Guardian, 1/17/2011.

3   Sekou, Toure, Britannica.com.

4   Lome, Koffide Opinion: *Sylvanus Olympio's Assassination Two Days before He Withdrew Togo from the CFA Franc Zone,* Face2Face, Jan 21, 2019.

5   http:Africa-facts.org *Thomas Sankara in Burkina.*

6   Nzongola-Ntalaja, Lumumba, the Guardian, January 17, 2011).

7   Chiwanza, Takudzwa Hillary, *Africa enjoys Unlimited Telecommunication Service Thanks to Gaddafi/* africanexponent. com, October 7, 2019.

8   Wintour, Patrick, *"MPs Deliver Damning Verdict on Cameron's Libya Intervention."* The Guardian, September 14, 2016.

9   Sahiounie, Steve, *The Reason for Qaddafi's Overthrow,* journalist and political commentator /July 27, 2020, mideastdiscourse.com.

10 Wikipedia.org. *List of Assassinations in Africa*

11 GlobalBlackHistory.com *How France Continues Slavery and Colonialism in the 21st Century,* 12/14/2015.

12 www.diplomatie.gouv.fr/IMG/pdf/24_Lombart.pdf.

12a Mbamalu, Socrates, *Italy's Deputy Prime Minister says France Creates Poverty in Africa,* 12/22/2019, thisisafrica.me

13 Agence France-Presse (AFP), *France Warned it is Missing the Boat on Africa Growth,* hearld.co.zw, 12/05/2013.

14 Norton, Ben, *The 5 US Colonies,* March 13, 2015.

15 Papenfuss, Mary, *60 Top Corporations Paid Zero Federal Taxes Under Trump Tax Law,* Huff Post 4/12/2019).

16 https://founders.archives.gov/documents/Jefferson/ 03-01-02-0118.

17 abarim-publicaions.com/ashan.

18 Bowdich, Edward T., *Mission from Cape Coast Castle to Ashantee*, London: John Murry, 1886.

19 Doctrineofdiscovery.org

20 Miller, Robert J. Prof. *The Doctrine of Discovery*: *The International Law of Colonialism* (DoD), 2006-Doctrine of Discovery.org.

Chapter Eleven – Bacon's Rebellion, Infant Mortalty, Stoking the Fire, Hope

1 Zinn, Howard, *A People's History of the United States*, Harper Perennial Modern classics, 1999, chapter 3.

2 Fredrickson, George, racepowerofanillusion.org / *Historical Origins and Development of Racism*, 2/2016.

3 Roediger, David R., nmaahc.si.edu/*The Historic Foundation of Race*

4 americahealthranking.org/learn/reports/2021-annual-report/international-comparison.

5 Hogan, Ekemini, Okorie, Obasi and Effiong, Utibe, MPH' 14, *Infant Mortality among Black Babies*, October 29, 2020, sph.umich.edu.

6 Durant, Ariel, *A Great Nation is not Conquered…*,brainyquotes.com

Chapter Twelve – The Political Billionaire's System

1 Cato Institute study, *54. Special – Interest Spending and Corporate Welfare*, 2017.

2 Institute for Tax and Economic Policy, itep.org/*60-Fortune 500-Companies-Avoided-All-Federal-Income–Taxes-in-2018*.

3 Ingraham, Christopher, *Dozens of American's Biggest Businesses Paid No Federal Income Tax-Again*, The Washington Post, April 2021.

4 marketwatch.com/investing/stock/MCD/financials.

5 expatistan.com/cost-of-living/country/united states.

6 *Trump's FY 2020 Budget Exposes His False Promises and Misplaced Priorities,* americanprogress.org, News March 11, 2019.

6a *Insurance PACs contributions to candidates, 2017-2018,* opensecrets.org

7 *2020 Trump Budget: A Disturbing Vision,* Center on Budget and Policy Priorities, March 11, 2019.

8 Ritchie, Hannah and Roser, Max, ourworldindata.org/emission by sectors.

9 *What's in North Carolina Drinking Water* today.duke.edu, February 7, 2020.

10 Moss, Laura, *The 14 Largest Oil Spills in History*, treehugger.com, updated 1/2/ 2022.

11 Rappeport, Alan and Tankersley, Jim, *Trump Administration Mulls a Unilateral Tax Cut for the Rich*, New York Times July 30, 2018.

12 Gillin, Joshua, *Income Tax Rates Were 90 Percent Under Eisenhower, Sanders Says,* Politifact.com, November 15, 2015).

13 *The 35% Corporate Tax Myth*, Institute of Taxation and Economic Policy (itep.org), March 2017.

14 Gaza, *Killed for Protesting: 6 Things to Know about the Great March of Return,* jewishvoiceforpeace.org, 03/27/2019.

15 Haddad, Mohammed *Nakba: What Happened in Palestine in 1948? Aljazeera.com>news>2022/5/15.*

16 *Israel - Closes – Gaza- border - Crossing –Again*, Aljazeera.com>news > /05/18/ 2021.

Chapter Fourteen – Free Will?, Unjust Laws and the UFO/UAP

1 Einstein, Albert, Living Philosophies (pp. 3-7), New York: Simon Schuster, 1931.

2 Wills, Matthew, *The Evolution of the Microscope,* daily.jstor.org, March 27, 2018.

3 *How did Galileo Die*, reference.com, April 4, 2020.

4   Martinez, Alberto, A., *Was Giordado Bruno Burned at the Stake for Believing in Exoplanets*, Scientific American.com, March 19, 2018.

5   Petruzzello, Melissa, *Michael Servetus,* britannica.com, April 29, 2022.

6   Janos, Adam, *Why Have There Been So Many UFO Sightings near Nuclear Facilities?* June 23, 2019.

7   wikipedia.org/*Roswell incident.*

8   *wikipedia.org /wiki/ufo government studies.*

9   Elliot, Josh K., *Leaked Video Appears to show UFO Plunging Under Water off California, Global News May 18, 2021.*

10 Forti, Kathy Dr. J., *African Dogon Tribe Reveals Man's True Origins,* June 7, 2017.

11 Clarke, Ardy, Sixkiller, *Sky People*, 2015.

Chapter Fifteen – Berta Caceres, The Generals and Manifest Destiny

1   Watts, Jonathan, *Berta Caceres, Honduran Human Rights and Environment Activist, murdered,* The Guardian, 3/04/2016.

2   Gallon, Natalie, *Environmentalist's Murder a Criminal Plot, New Report Says* / CNN, November 7, 2017.

3   Chekuru, Kavitha, *Berta Caceres Murder Trial to Begin Despite Family's Doubts,* Aljazeera.com, September 17, 2018.

4   Mackey, Danielle, Eisne, Chiara R., *Inside the Plot to Murder Honduran Activist Berta Caceres,* the interecept.com 12/21/2019.

5   Lakhan, Nina, *Berta Caceres Assassination: Ex-head of Dam Company Found Guilty,* the guardian.com, July 5, 2021.

6   *Biden Announces End to US Support for Saudi-Led Offensive in Yemen,* The Guardian, Feb 4, 2021.

7   Butler, Smedley D., *War is a Racket,* 1935. Radical.org/ratville/cah/warisaracket.htlm.

8   *15 Major Corporations You Never Knew Profited from Slavery,* Atlanta Black Star.com, 8/26/2013.

9   Brockell, Gillian, *Wealthy Bankers and Businessmen Plotted to Overthrow FDR. A Retired General Foiled It,* The Washington Post, January 13, 2021.

10 Stone and Kuznick, *The Untold History of the United States* p.522-523, 2013.

11 Ibid.

12 Stone and Kuznick, *Untold History of the United States* p. 522.

Chapter Sixteen - The Call, Breaking Through, the Eyes

1   Weiser, Kathy, *Villages of the Salem Witch Trials"* updated September 2020. Legendsofamerica.com/ma-witchtrialtowns.

Chapter Seventeen - Holy Trinity, Music, Introvert or Extrovert, Family and Religion, Commitment

1   Cherry, Kendra, *How You Can Tell You're an Introvert,* 10/18 /2019: medically reviewed by Steven Gans, MD, verywellmind.com, 5/11/2017).

2   Tarico, Valerie, *Atheist Marriages May Last Longer than Christian Ones,* November 1, 2013.

Chapter Eighteen - Civilized Humans?

1   Tenenbaum, David J., *whyfiles.org./Animal-Love,*2011.

2   du Plessis, Susan, *edubloxtutor.com/Amala-kamala/*2021.

3   Sinicki, Adam, *healthguidance.org/Modern-Cases-of-Feral-Children,* 03/04/2020.

4   Mihai, Andrei, *zmescience.com/Feral-Children,* 01,29,2021.

5   Bekoff, Mark, *Animals are Conscious and should be Treated as Such,* New Scientist, Sep 19, 2012.

6   Galpayage, Hiruni Samadi Dona and Lars Chittka, *Charles H Turner, Pioneer in Animal Cognition,* Science, Oct 30, 2020.

Chapter Nineteen – Ma's Parents and Her Caretakers

1   Uboat.net/allies/merchantscrews/person, *Crew List of Ships Hit by U-Boats.*

Chapter Twenty – Ongoing Injustice

1   Tamir, Christine, *The Growing Diversity of Black America*, pewresearch.org, *2021/03/25.*

2   Levin, Sam, *'It Never Stops': Killings by US Police Reach Record High in 2022,* the Guardian, Jan, 2023.

3   *Race Police and the US – in Numbers,* bbc.com/news/ December 5, 2014.

4   (Swaine, Laughland, Lartey, and McCarthy, *Young Black Men Killed by US Police at Highest Rate in Year of 1,134 Deaths,* the Guardian 2015).

5   Cooper, Alexia and Smith, Erica L., Bureau of Justice (BJS) Statisticians, *Homicide Trends in the US, 1980-2008,* US Department of Justice, Nov. 2011, p.13.

6   Gaille, Louise, *26 Poverty and Crime Statistics,* Ittans.org, January 3, 2017.

7   The United States Department of Justice, *2020 FBI Hate Crime Statistics.*

8   Goodwin, Sheppard and Sloan, *Police Brutality Bonds,* The Action Center on Race and Economy, 2018. P.17).

9   Gilpin, Lyndsey, *Native American Women Still have the Highest Rates of Rape and Assault,* High County News, June 2016.

10 Rosay, Andre B., *Violence against American Indians and Alaska Native Woman and Men.* 06/01/2016.

11 Hansen, Elise, *The Forgotten Minority in Police Shootings,* CNN November 13, 2017.

Chapter Twenty Two – Dad and the Early Years

1   blackpast.com /*Jan Matzeliger.*
2   history.navy.mil, put in search box, *African Americans in the Navy after World War II Through the Korean War.*
3   Smith, Michael, Stolp, *Port Chicago Munity (1944)*, blackpast.org, March 27, 2011.

Chapter Twenty Three – Family Matters, Religion's Love Claim, Phony Healers

1   Weisman, Carrie, alternet.org/belief/*shocking -Numbers-of Children-die -in -America-When-Their-Parents-Turn-To-Faith-Based-Healing,* November 28, 2014.
2   Wilson, Jason, *Letting Them Die: Parents Refuse Medical Help for Children in the Name of Christ,* The Guardian, April 13, 2016.

Chapter Twenty Four – Stealing Souls

1   The Associated Press, *Tallying Sexual Abuse by Protestant Clergy*, New York Times, 6/15/2007).
2   Analyzing Paraphilic Activity, Specialization and Generalization in Priests Who Sexually Abuse Minors, Talon and Terry, May 2008.
3   Lipton, Bruce, H. Dr., Cell Biologist, Quantum Communication).

Chapter Twenty Five – Reprogramming/ Awakening

1   Worldpeacegroup.org/*washingtoncrime_study.*
2   Mudd, Mimi, *Research Shows Group Meditation Can Reduce Crime Rates*, guardianlv.com, April I, 2014).

Chapter Twenty Six – Science and its Warnings

1   Einstein, Albert, *Ideas and Opinions*, Wings Books p.151-158 Why Socialism? Originally in the Monthly Review, New York, May, 1949).

2   Hall, Shannon, *Exxon Knew About Climate Change 40 Years Ago*, Scientific America, October 26, 2015.

3   Taylor, Alan, *Deadly Wildfires Continue Across Northern California,* The Atlantic, October 15, 2017).

4   *Fire Map: California, Oregon,* the New York Times, October 1, 2020.

5   Sparber, Sami, *At Least 57 People Died in the Texas Winter Storm Mostly of Hypothermia,* on line edition of Texas Tribune, March 15, 2021.

6   Sagan, Carl. 1995 Print Novel. *The Demon-Haunted World: Science as a Cradle in the Darkness.*

Chapter Twenty Seven – Delusion vs. Reality

1   Bernays, Edward, *Propaganda*, 1928, p. 47.

2   Bernays, Edward, *Propaganda*, 1928, p. 92.

3   Bernays, Edward, *Propaganda*, 1928.

4   Gunderman, Richard, *The Manipulation of the American Mind: Edward Bernays and the Birth of Public Relations*, theconservation. com, July 9, 2015).

5   Ibid.

Chapter Twenty Eight – Profit vs. Spirit

1   (UQAE) 2010, *The Ultimate Quotable Einstein*, Edited by Alice Calaprice, Section: On or to Children, page 80, Princeton University Press, Princeton, New Jersey. (Verified on paper)

Chapter Twenty Nine – Alternative Realities

1   Brandt, Mark J. and Tongeren, Daryl Van R., *People Both High and Low on Religious Fundamentalism are Prejudiced Toward Dissimilar Groups,* Journal of Personality and Social Psychology, November 2015.

2   Ginges, Hansen, & Norenzayan, *Religion and Support for Suicide Attacks*, Psychological Science, 2009.

3   Blogowska, Joanna and Saroglou, Vassilis, *For Better or Worse: Fundamentalists' Attitudes Toward Outgroups as a Function of Exposure to Authoritative Religious Text*, semanticscholar.org, March 2018.

4   Barmola, Kailash Dr., *Religion/Spirituality as Related to Wellbeing and Productivity*, Researchgate.net, November 2013.

5   Hunsberger, Bruce, *Religion and Prejudice the Role of Religious Fundamentalism, Quest and Right* – Wing. Authoritarianism, Journal of Social Issues Volume 51, issue 2, summer 1995, pages 113-129.

6   Howell, Signe, *Chewong of Peninsular Malaysia*, Society and Cosmos 1984.

7   (*Ifaluk/Peaceful Societies*). Burrows and Lutz's Experience Living with the Ifaluk is summarized under the heading "But how much Violence do they Really Experience".

8   Hostetler, John A., *Hutterites Society*, Baltimore, MD: the John Hopkins University Press 1997.

9   Fernea, Robert, *Nubians in Egypt: Peaceful People, 1973.*

10 founders.archives.gov, *Remarks Concerning the Savages of North America*, 1782-1783.

11 Gilio-Whitaker, Dina "*Native American Influence on the Founding of the US*" 8/22/2019.

12 Amadas and Barlowe – Fort Raleigh National Historic site NC, chronology and text of direct quotations by Lebame Houston and Wynne Dough, April, 14, 2015.

Chapter Thirty – "The Good Old Days"

1   Stone, Lyman, *Blue Laws*, Vox.com, October 2, 2018.

Chapter Thirty One – The Move

1   Hamacher, Adriana, *The Unpopular Rise of Self-Checkouts (and how to fix them)*, Future May 9th 2017, BBC.com.

Chapter Thirty Three – The School Experience

1   Hanford, Emily, *Kids Struggle to Read When Schools Leave Phonics Out*, 9/11/2018.

Chapter Thirty Five – Forward in the face of Roadblocks

1   Kates, Graham (march 12, 2019). "Lori Loughlin and Felicity Huffman among Dozens in College Bribery Scheme." CBS News. Archived from the original on March 12, 2019.

2   *Republicans Lawmakers Have Introduce Hundreds of Bills to Restrict Voting Rights Nationwide*, Grossman, Sarah – Ruiz, Huffington Post, April 2, 2021.

3   Bridges, Brian, *African American and College Education by the Numbers,* 2020, uncf.org.

4   Facing History and Ourselves, "South Carolina Freed People Demand Education, Last updated May 12, 2020.

Chapter Thirty Six – Encouragement and the Spiritual Quest

1   StreamMeditation.com/*crying-during-meditation-the-ten-reasons-why.*